Richard Youens

ITS ALWAYS FRIDAY

Autobiography of a film insurance troubleshooter

Richard Youens

ITS ALWAYS FRIDAY

Autobiography of a film insurance troubleshooter

MEREO
Cirencester

Mereo Books

1A The Wool Market Dyer Street Cirencester Gloucestershire GL7 2PR
An imprint of Memoirs Publishing www.mereobooks.com

It's Always Friday: 978-1-86151-560-5

First published in Great Britain in 2015
by Mereo Books, an imprint of Memoirs Publishing

Copyright ©2016

Richard Youens has asserted his under the Copyright Designs and Patents Act 1988 to be identified as the author of this work.

A CIP catalogue record for this book is available from the British Library.

This book is sold subject to the condition that it shall not by way of trade or otherwise be lent, resold, hired out or otherwise circulated without the publisher's prior consent in any form of binding or cover, other than that in which it is published and without a similar condition, including this condition being imposed on the subsequent purchaser.

The address for Memoirs Publishing Group Limited can be found at
www.memoirspublishing.com

The Memoirs Publishing Group Ltd Reg. No. 7834348

The Memoirs Publishing Group supports both The Forest Stewardship Council® (FSC®) and the PEFC® leading international forest-certification organisations. Our books carrying both the FSC label and the PEFC® and are printed on FSC®-certified paper. FSC® is the only forest-certification scheme supported by the leading environmental organisations including Greenpeace. Our paper procurement policy can be found at www.memoirspublishing.com/environment

Typeset in 10/15pt Century Schoolbook
by Wiltshire Associates Publisher Services Ltd. Printed and bound in
Great Britain by Printondemand-Worldwide, Peterborough PE2 6XD

Contents

Dedication

Chapter 1	A little family history	P. 1
Chapter 1	A post-war childhood	P. 19
Chapter 1	Prep school	P. 29
Chapter 4	Sherborne	P. 45
Chapter 5	Switzerland	P. 78
Chapter 6	Looking for a career	P. 91
Chapter 7	The apprentice loss adjuster	P. 106
Chapter 8	The film business	P. 132
Chapter 9	A man of property	P. 147
Chapter 10	Settling claims	P. 154
Chapter 11	Settling down	P. 168
Chapter 12	Georgina	P. 180
Chapter 13	Hot spots and hotshots	P. 186
Chapter 14	Globetrotting	P. 198
Chapter 15	Singapore	P. 209
Chapter 16	Third parties, fire and theft	P. 248
Chapter 17	Another tragedy	P. 271
Chapter 18	New York, new friends	P. 276
Chapter 19	Back to the Far East	P. 306
Chapter 20	Settling down in the UK	P. 325
Chapter 21	Tale's End	P. 381
	Index	P. 392

Dedication

It may be an urban myth, but the Duke of Edinburgh is said to have advised Prince Charles, as a bit of self-discipline when he was a boy, to try and remember last thing at night everything he had done during that day. Certainly I've tried it myself many times and it's not a bad way of getting off to sleep.

In this narrative I have tried to remember everything of interest, to me at least, that I have done during my life as a kind of longer-term discipline and in the earnest hope that it might be of interest to my grandchildren Thomas, Oliver, Flora, Livia and Elisa, to whom the story is dedicated with more love than I've been any good at showing them in the flesh. I live in hope that it might be of some interest to my two children Christian and Arabella, even my darling bride of forty-four summers and counting, Annabelle, so it's for them too and in memory of our two other children Olivia and Adam, who are no more. Our long line of Shih Tzus surely deserve a mention too: Sam Sam, Zoo Loo, Kato, Mango, Chutney and Tiffin.

Richard Youens
Rushall, Wiltshire
2016

CHAPTER 1

A little family history

Our character and mental approach to life are formed, like it or not, not only by our own upbringing but by the lives and experiences of our more immediate ancestors so, to set my story in context, I'll kick off with what I know of mine.

Grandparents

My paternal grandfather, Fearnley Algernon Cyril Youens and married to Dorothy Mary (née Ross), was the local priest in Buxton, Derbyshire in the early 1920s. Fearnley's family originally came from High Wycombe in Buckinghamshire, where they made furniture. They must have been quite successful: there is a Youens Road in the town to this day. Fearnley was 33 when he married Dorothy at the tender age of 17, just before the Great War, and my father, John, was born a year later in 1914.

Dorothy's father was a successful businessman and one of the founders of Brunner Mond, a chemical manufacturer, which became the (one time) blue chip Imperial Chemical Industries but is now no more. He retired at the very youthful age of 40 and devoted some of his time to the affairs of the Public Trustee. This was a government-sponsored organisation, which managed the investment of private trust funds.

My mother's family were in business. Her grandfather, Lincoln Adam Chandler, worked for Vickers Armstrong, where he was responsible for supervising the construction of the first tanks, which were eventually to be used in the Great War. It was his job also to sell the idea of tank warfare to the generals at the War Office. However, whilst he was convinced that in theatre tanks had to be supported by ground troops, the generals were not persuaded and many brave soldiers were killed before Great-Grandpa's tactics were adopted. After the war he was offered a seat in the House of Lords in recognition of his services, but his conscience would not allow him to accept in the light of so many, in his view unnecessary, deaths.

His son, my grandfather Alfred, was also with Vickers Armstrong early in his career. However after service in the Royal Artillery during the Great War, when he was awarded the Military Cross, he was gassed at the Battle of the Somme and invalided out of the army. By this time he had married Esmé Black, whose family were the publishers A&C Black. Their main claim to fame was *Who's Who,* that lexicon of the great and the good. Her great-grandfather Adam had been Provost of Edinburgh and a Member of Parliament as well as founding the publishing business on the back of his best client, the novelist Walter Scott of *Ivanhoe* fame.

After Alfred Chandler's health recovered he joined Glovers Cables in Manchester, by then owned by Vickers Armstrong, which manufactured all the cabling for the London Underground as well as making trans-ocean telephone cables. During the Second World War Glovers, where by now Alfred was Managing Director, built a pipeline intended to transfer fuel from Portsmouth to Normandy after the D-Day landings in support of the advance into France. The project, known as 'Pluto' (pipeline under the ocean), was very hush-hush and for days at a time the Manchester Ship Canal had to be closed so that the prototypes could be tested, albeit in benign conditions.

It would not be unreasonable to suppose that with all these antecedents I should have been born with a silver spoon firmly between my teeth, but this was not entirely the case, although my grandfather Alfred left a trust fund, which provided for my sister's and my education, and for which I am truly grateful.

History does not relate what happened to Fearnley Youens' inheritance, if any. He was an avid follower of the flat and was on the telephone to his bookie in Doncaster every morning having studied the odds in *The Sporting Pink*, a newspaper dedicated to horse racing and so named because it was printed, like the *Financial Times*, on pink paper. However, when he died there was less than £5 in his account.

He also used to go off on his own on holiday, allegedly cycling in Europe every summer, so the casinos in France may well have also relieved him of his funds. When Dorothy died in 1973 her estate, which was believed to have been quite substantial when she inherited it in trust, was worth less than £20,000, thanks to the complete incompetence of the Public Trustee. Their investment record was abysmal, in addition to which they milked the fund for fees.

Lincoln Chandler (Great Grandpa) disinherited my mother when she married Dad because he disliked her father-in-law Fearnley Youens intensely, the reasons for which have been lost in the mist. He also disinherited her brother, known as Mike but christened Lincoln Adam (the Chandlers alternated these two names with the eldest boy of each generation, but they were rarely so called). Mike did not go into business as expected by his grandfather but chose farming instead. As a result the inheritance of Lincoln Adam's other grandchildren increased and the sums involved must have been not insignificant. When Lincoln Adam's youngest granddaughter, Joyce, died aged close to 100 a few years ago her Trust fund was worth well in excess of a million pounds. LA Chandler lived in Angmering, Sussex, with his housekeeper, who was known only as Penstemmon. By all accounts she would have given Mrs Danvers a good run for her money. The old man would offer his guests half a glass of champagne, then put the cork back in the bottle. No suggestion of the other half being offered. No doubt he drank the rest of the bottle after his guests had left. However he was reputed only to drink champagne at eleven in the morning, so at least he got that right. Champagne is best taken before lunch.

My father and his family

My father, John Ross Youens, was born in Buxton, Derbyshire, in 1914, the eldest of six children, and educated at Buxton College until he was sixteen, when he was sent to Kelham Theological College near Newark to become a priest. Dad wanted to go on the stage, but his father, Fearnley, did not give him any choice. He was the eldest son and he was off to the church - like it or lump it.

The original building of Kelham was a private house, which was destroyed by fire in 1857 and rebuilt to the design of George Gilbert-Scott, the architect of St Pancras Station in London. The Society of the Sacred Mission purchased the house in 1903 for use as a theological training college as well as their Mother House. Just before my father arrived the monks added a chapel with a huge Byzantine dome which would not look out of place in Istanbul.

Not much is known about Dad's stint in Worksop as a curate after ordination, but he enjoyed recalling that shortly after he took up the post he had called on the Lady Mayoress to introduce himself. He asked how she was and she said in broad Notts "Well, vicar, I feel like a rat's crawled up me arsehole and died there". More of Dad later.

Dad's eldest brother, Peter, was allowed to remain at King Edward VII School in Sheffield until he was 18, when he won a place at Wadham College, Oxford, following Fearnley's footsteps. After graduation he spent two years in the Royal Navy and joined the Colonial Service in Africa. Peter, with dark, aquiline good looks, was well served by his libido all his life. One of his girlfriends was the actress Deborah Kerr, of *The King & I* fame, who allegedly wanted him to marry her. However according to family legend he was dining her at the Ritz Hotel in London and when the Maître d' presented the bill he called Peter 'Mr Kerr'. Peter was not one to play second fiddle and the relationship petered out (pun intended).

Early on in Africa Peter developed a taste for the local talent, so much so that when he came home on leave in 1943, he told his mother Dorothy that if he did not meet and marry an English girl that trip, he was going to settle with a local girl in Nyasaland (now Malawi) where he was stationed. As luck would have it, I was christened while he was home. He was a godfather and Diana Hawkins, my mother's best friend at North Foreland Lodge, where they had both been at school, was a godmother. Peter and Diana were married three weeks later.

Peter spent much of his career in Africa or leveraging off his African connections until very late in life. During his time as chief advisor to the Governor in Nyasaland, a local medical doctor named Hastings Banda, decided to turn his hand to politics and became a thorn in the side of the British Government. At much the same time the Conservative Prime Minister Harold MacMillan decided it was time to let loose 'the winds of change' and set about divesting chunks of Empire.

Dr Banda's subversive activities had led to HMG exiling him to Sierra Leone, initially accompanied by Peter. Pretty soon the population of Nyasaland started to become restless and demanded independence, which HMG decided to accept gracefully, inviting Banda to form a government. Peter was instructed to act as intermediary. He proved such a success that he was invited to stay on after Independence as Banda's Chief Secretary.

When Peter retired, by which time he had been knighted, he was recruited by 'Tiny' Rowland of Lonrho, which had begun operating in 1909 as the London and Rhodesian Mining Company, to be their front man for its business in Africa. However in 1973 a group of Lonrho directors tried to oust Mr Rowland, claiming that he had bribed African leaders and violated international sanctions imposed on Rhodesia, now Zimbabwe. The affair prompted the then British Prime Minister Edward Heath's memorable comment about Lonrho being "the unpleasant and unacceptable face of capitalism" - to which Mr Rowland replied that he would not want to be its acceptable face.

At this point Peter decided that discretion was the better part of valour and joined Tyzack & Partners, an executive search company in London. In the meantime Tiny Rowland consolidated his wealth and position, and by 1983 he had identified Harrods, the Knightsbridge department store, as a takeover target. So confident was he of success that he invited Peter to become Chairman and Peter rejoined Lonrho in readiness for this crowning grand finale to his career. Unfortunately for Tiny and Peter, an Egyptian businessman named Mohamed Al-Fayed also wished to acquire Harrods, now known as 'Harrabs' on account of its majority customer base, and proved ultimately successful. Nevertheless Peter remained on the Lonrho board and gained a certain notoriety in the City as one of the oldest directors of a public company.

Peter was great fun, with a wicked glint in his eye for the ladies right until the end of his life. He and Diana led pretty separate lives and he always had girlfriends in abundance, none of whom seemed to resent their competition. He was often to be seen at Annabel's, the Berkeley Square nightclub. I used to pitch up there with company telling the doorman Uncle Peter was expecting me. I was invariably allowed in. Beats paying the membership fee.

He once took his daughter Stephanie and me to see the late Frankie Howerd, a famous and much loved camp comedian, perform at the London Palladium. At the end of the show Howerd told the audience to turn to the back page of our programmes, where we would find a bingo card. An assortment of prizes was wheeled on to the stage and we were told that the first person to 'make a line' was to shout 'Bingo' as loudly as possible. The caller went into action and soon Stephanie and I, who were sharing a programme, made a line and shouted 'Bingo' along with the rest of the audience – we all had the same card.

The next brother, Stephen, was commissioned in the King's Own Yorkshire Light Infantry after Sandhurst and saw action from the Normandy landings through until the end of the Second World War following the fall of Berlin. Some time in 1945, still in Germany he met and married a 'White' Russian refugee named Marie, about whom nothing more is known.

When Stephen retired from the army, at some point he was recruited by Lord Leicester, the owner of Holkham Hall in Norfolk, to restore a magnificent Victorian walled market garden on the estate. This he set about with gusto and great success with his son Andrew, who he hoped would take the venture over. Andrew, who had been a contemporary of Prince Charles at Gordonstoun, had been invalided out of the army due to a psychological disability as result of training with the Special Air Service (SAS). It is believed that he was unable to cope with their interrogation techniques, which included having a bucket placed over his head and hit with a hammer or similar at regular intervals. Eventually and quite unexpectedly Andrew elected to take his own life, and as result Stephen lost interest in the garden. He died relatively young. Marie predeceased them both.

As an aside, Andrew was a rather strange child. At the time of the Coronation in 1953 I was allowed out of school for the day and met him together with his younger sister Alexandra at my Aunt Margaret's house. Apart from watching the event on television, I have vivid memories of Andrew going round pinching everyone quite viciously and for no apparent reason. There are rumours that Prince Charles was bullied at Gordonstoun and I would not be surprised if Andrew had been involved. After Andrew died, his girlfriend had an affair with Stephen, which my mother thought was "quite disgusting".

David, my father's youngest brother, was Fearnley and Dorothy's only son to show genuine interest in joining the church, but he interrupted his training at King's College London to volunteer for the army soon after the outbreak of Hitler's war. After training with the East Yorkshire Regiment he was dispatched to join the British Expeditionary Force in Flanders as a 2nd Lieutenant. There his battalion fought a valiant rear-guard action against the German onslaught, but he was killed aged 21 on May 31, 1940, shortly before the fall of Dunkirk. His remains are buried at Houtem Cemetery in Belgium, about 10 miles east of Dunkirk, where the citation on his gravestone reads 'Remembered with Honour'. The War Office eventually returned David's personal effects, such as they were, to my grandmother, who always kept them in a glass cabinet in her drawing room. As far as I remember they consisted of his wallet, silver cigarette case and a few other small keepsakes. She always talked about him and had only happy memories. His death was reported in the local paper under the headline "Brodsworth Vicar's Son Killed'. The paper noted 'he was an extremely friendly and lovable man who would have made the best type of parson'.

Fearnley & Dorothy also had two daughters. The elder one, Margaret, was a thoroughly good egg, well – they both were, but Margaret (always known as Margie) was always exceptionally kind to me, particularly when my parents were abroad. I don't know much about her early life, but I can tell you she went to Malvern College. Now how that came about, history does not relate, but it stood her in good stead coping with all her trials and tribulations to come.

Margie was good looking, cool-headed and dependable. She married a very jovial and easy-going businessman named Bill Carlisle in the late nineteen forties. He was very overweight, enjoyed spreading copious quantities on marmalade as thickly as possible on his toast at breakfast and never declined a large gin or a glass of beer. By the time of the Coronation in June 1953, the Carlisles had two daughters, Nicky and Tina, and lived in a large villa called Cambridge Cottage with a big garden, near Ottershaw in Surrey. June 2 was a National Holiday and I was allowed out from prep school for the day. As my parents were stationed in Egypt, Auntie Margie took me out and we watched the Queen being crowned on a large black and white TV – a major event in all respects.

Later in the mid nineteen-fifties Bill, who worked for a multi-national mining company called Bells Asbestos – long before the toxic dangers of this product were publicly recognised - was transferred to manage their business in

Portugal, based in Lisbon. He had been born and brought up in Brazil and so spoke fluent Portuguese. Not long after the family had settled in to their new life, he had a coronary thrombosis and died at the age of 38.

There was a rumour, after Bill died, that his Portuguese manager wanted the top job and had asked a witch at Sintra, a small town not far from Lisbon, to put a curse on whoever held Bill's job until he himself was appointed. Whether the witch existed or there was a place people could go and ask for spells to be cast, history does not relate. In any event, Bill's predecessor and his wife had been killed in a car crash and the man before him had died in mysterious circumstances, so if any spell was cast it must have been pretty potent.

In any event there was no company compensation available and Bill had no life assurance, let alone private money, so the family came home pretty much destitute. Margie ran a cafe on the A3 for lorry drivers, to make ends meet. I went there once and was forever put off fat-cut chips after seeing a dog lift its leg into bucket of such chips in the kitchen. Margie gave this up after a short time and worked as a sales girl at Harrods, then as a rep on the road for Smith & Nephew, the pharmaceutical firm.

They lived in a flat in Queens Club Mansions in Barons Court, West London, then in a house in Addlestone, not far from Cambridge Cottage. She was always unfailingly kind, generous and supportive of me and I used to stay with the family regularly at weekends in the early sixties when my parents were abroad. Somehow Margie managed to keep her show on the road, thanks in no small measure to the love of her two girls, Nicky & Tina, which was always returned in spades. I know of no more a close-knit family. Margie suffered terribly from arthritis and died in her late seventies. She is remembered with great affection.

The younger of Dorothy's daughters, Rosemary (Rosie), was an entirely different kettle of fish. She was a party animal, with all the looks, charm and sex appeal to guarantee a good time. Fearnley, who was by now a Canon of Sheffield Cathedral and vicar of Brodsworth, near Doncaster, tried to keep her under wraps and highly disapproved of her relationship in 1948 with a young man five or so years her senior named Anthony (Tony) Barber. He was a newly-qualified barrister with a distinguished war record in the RAF, having experienced the deprivations of Stalag Luft III, the German PoW camp where the Great Escape took place. He was one of three sons of a local well-to-do family near Doncaster and his provenance should have appealed to Fearnley, but this was not to be. Given that Fearnley had married Dorothy when she was 18, what *was* he thinking about?

In the early 1950s Rosie married a man named Jack Surgenor, with Fearnley's approval, which was not surprising because she was expecting his child. Jack was a kind man but a bit of a Walter Mitty character and unable to settle down into permanent employment. He was a quantity surveyor and chose to drift between jobs on contract sites both in the UK and overseas, taking his wife and eventually two sons and a daughter – Christopher, David and Emma with him. As result my family never saw much of the Surgenors until Jack retired to Sussex in the early nineties, not far from my parents.

At this point Rosie's story begins to hot up. She saw in

the papers that Noel Barber, the author of *Tanamera* and other blockbusters, had died. Noel was one of Tony's brothers, so she took it upon herself to write a condolence letter to Tony. He had by this time had been ennobled on his retirement from a long career in banking, finishing as Chairman of Standard Chartered Bank and in politics, culminating in his appointment as Chancellor of the Exchequer to Edward Heath. In this role he received many brickbats, which were not entirely his fault but more thanks to Heath's one-eyed, dictatorial style.

Tony had been widowed a few years before Rosie's letter arrived and he asked her out to lunch. They began an affair, resulting in Rosie divorcing Jack and marrying Tony. Jack was very upset and went public in the tabloids, but Rosie was not for turning and Jack set up with someone else. However he never recovered from the trauma of his wife's infidelity and took his own life. Rosie, on the other hand, had a thoroughly happy second marriage. It was a great shame she had not been allowed to marry Tony Barber in the first place.

My mother and her family

Like my father, my mother – always known as Pam - was born in Buxton, in 1919. She had only one brother, Lincoln Adam, known as Mike, who was eighteen months younger. She spent much of her early life between Radlett in Hertfordshire, Buxton and a mansion flat in Sloane Square, London, where she remembers watching the modern Peter Jones department store being built – previously a two-storey building.

By all accounts her mother, Esmé, suffered from long-term ill health and by the time she was twelve my mother was never allowed to see her again. She died when my mother was 16 and a boarder at North Foreland Lodge in Kent, where one of her friends was Frederica of Hanover, the future Queen of Greece. Mother left school soon after Esmé died and spent much of the next few years looking after her father and Mike, who by this time was at Harrow.

For her 18th birthday my mother was given a rather splendid red MG TD sports car, which she raced around London as well as burning up the Peak District and Manchester, depending on where Alfred was doing business, with a galaxy of admirers in tow. However she apparently had eyes only for a trainee priest at a seminary near Newark, whom she had known as a child, and married him in October 1940. After my father had been ordained he became a curate in Worksop near Nottingham, but soon decided life as a local vicar was not for him and applied to join the Royal Army Chaplains Dept (RAChD).

My mother's only brother, Lincoln Adam Chandler, known as Mike, was 18 months younger than Mum. Both were brought up by nannies and really didn't see much of their parents. Mike went to Gibbs School, a day prep in Knightsbridge, and then Harrow. After leaving school he had planned to work for Vickers Armstrong, like his father and grandfather before him, but the Second World War put those plans on hold and he joined the army, ending up in the Royal Artillery in Burma.

He had a rough time in the jungle; he never discussed it, but like most young people of his generation he smoked and drank a great deal to cope with his wartime experiences. He had a phobia about never letting the petrol tank in his car fall to less than half full, on the premise that it might run out before the next petrol station. He also always put spent matches back in the box, originally to minimise the risk of discovery by the Japanese. This meant one always had to rootle through the box to find an unspent match, which could be quite annoying.

Towards the end of the war he was discharged on health grounds – part mental (stress), part physical (malaria) - and decided he could not face life in an office, so he took up farming. In 1947 he married a very pretty girl called Alison Williams and they had one daughter, Sue, who was about six years younger than me. Alison's father and my mother's father, Alfred Chandler, were in business together to the extent that William's business, the Galloway Water Power Company, built dams generating hydro-electricity, which was distributed over conductor cables manufactured and supplied by Alfred's company, Glover's Cables.

Soon after they were married Mike bought a small hill farm in Dumfriesshire called Craiganputtock, which consisted of a pretty Georgian farmhouse and about 1,000 acres. Its previous claim to fame was that it had been the home of the celebrated author Thomas Carlyle, who wrote many of his essays there. He was popular with your more erudite American, many of whom used to call and ask to see where he worked – in Mike's study. However Mike pretty soon got fed up with these unsolicited and unannounced calls and began telling his visitors that Carlyle like to write in the open up by the cairn, a pile of stones about a mile uphill from the house.

Holidays with Mike and Alison were fun, spent mostly

outdoors in all weathers, helping with the sheep and cattle, shifting stooks of corn to dry them in the wind and walking the farm with a .410 shotgun, later a 12 bore, looking for game. However Mike could be a bit unpredictable and I was somewhat nervous of him. He must have had a really tough time in Burma during the war. He had a penchant for 'black and tans', a mixture of beer and stout, and gin & 'it', 'it' being precious little French vermouth. Nevertheless he was kind in a gruff way and I always enjoyed being with him on the farm. Sadly his demons from the war became too much for him to bear and he took his own life while still in his sixties.

My parents were married in Buxton in October 1940 and the Best Man should have been Uncle Peter, but he was in Africa and his place was taken by a rather dashing Armenian fighter pilot and Oxford boxing blue called Noel Agazarian. Noel was later shot down and killed over the Libyan Desert.

Dad went back to the army after a brief honeymoon and my mother shuttled between her father's house near Taddington in the Peak District, not far from Buxton, and her in-laws' vicarage at Brodsworth pretty much until after I was born.

The Taddington property was called Preistcliffe. It was a pretty, low-beamed large cottage rather than a house and had originally been the main farmhouse in the area known as Preistcliffe Ditch. It was a cosy place with a large rock garden planted by Grandpa Chandler, with attractive views over farmland to the Peak moors. Grandpa commuted from there to Manchester in his Bentley or by train from Buxton. If he was going to London he often took us with him, and after the Cadogan Mansions flat was sold we stayed at the Mayfair Hotel, off Berkeley Street.

I was about three when Grandpa Chandler sold Preistcliffe and bought a place at Rudheath, near Knutsford. By this time he had married again. His bride was the receptionist at the Palace Hotel in Buxton, where he used to repair on his way home from the office for some refreshment. She was called Anne; I have no idea what her surname was, but her family was not held in any regard by mine. Grandpa referred to her as "a rose on a dung heap". When Anne died suddenly in 1947 her family materialised like vultures and tried to get their hands on as much of Grandpa's wealth as they could. Happily their success was limited to some furniture and pieces of my grandmother's jewellery.

Not long after Anne's death Grandpa was diagnosed with prostate cancer. He sold Rudheath to spend the final months of his life living in the Queen's Hotel in Eastbourne, where he died in 1949.

For the next fifteen years or more the only home of any permanence was the vicarage at Brodsworth, a mining village five miles northwest of Doncaster in the West Riding of Yorkshire. For many years the living at Brodsworth was one of the most valuable in the land, because it rested on top of a rich seam of coal mined at Brodsworth Main. Brodsworth Hall, which dominates the area, was built in the 1860s by Charles Thellusson, who was the eventual heir to a famously disputed fortune, over which a protracted, very public battle was fought in the High Court for almost 60 years. The dispute partly inspired Jarndyce and Jarndyce, the interminable case at the heart of Charles Dickens's *Bleak House*. When Thellusson finally inherited the Brodsworth estate and the rich seam of coal that lay beneath it, he built the Hall.

By the time grandfather Fearnley arrived, in 1934, the condition of the Hall had begun to dilapidate, partly as result of settlement caused by tunnelling, partly because Thellusson's fortune had been seriously eroded, leaving his heir Captain Grant-Dalton and his feisty wife Sylvia living there in restricted circumstances. Happily they were not restricted enough to prevent her from having a large tray carrying a comforting array of alcoholic beverages at the ready in whichever reception room, and there were many, she chose to receive her guests. When the captain died Sylvia married his cousin, who must have been lurking when I went there as a child, but I remember only Sylvia.

Everyone in the vicarage party was invited for refreshment after Sunday Matins, and that was always an occasion. The Hall was magnificently tatty both in and out. The furniture and furnishings were much the same as they had been the day the Thellussons had moved in the previous century. When Sylvia died English Heritage assumed responsibility for the place and were delighted to find an Victorian country house in its original state with no attempt at modernisation: holes in the carpets, threadbare curtains, high quality furniture but shabby. As a child I rather dreaded having to go there but the experience is still vividly remembered.

The vicarage was purpose-built to accommodate Fearnley and his family on a hill opposite but some distance from the church, and I went to stay with my grandparents there frequently until Fearnley died in 1968 and Dorothy moved south.

CHAPTER 2

A post-war childhood

I was born at 10pm on Wednesday May 19, 1943 at the Doncaster Infirmary. My mother had been walking near Brodsworth that afternoon and was chased by a bull. She made good her escape, but the effort started my arrival. May 19 was also the day poor Anne Boleyn was executed in 1536 and on a lighter note Oscar Wilde was released from Reading Gaol on that day in 1897. Wednesday's child, as the old nursery rhyme goes, is full of woe. Funny that.

I was named David first in memory of my uncle David, who had been killed in the retreat to Dunkirk, because I was first grandchild on either side. However my parents preferred to call me Richard, which has always caused confusion. Evidently Alfred Chandler insisted on calling me Richard as he didn't care for the Welsh or Jews, to both of which "David" has connections. The situation was compounded because my father's family objected to David being my second name and as the initials DRY spelt 'dry' and my nappies were always wet, my mother added Bill after a godfather. So I'm blessed with David Richard Bill – DRB Youens. Once when I was about twelve I was flying somewhere and a stewardess asked if Dr B Youens would identify himself to the crew as there was some sort of emergency. Initially I had some difficulty persuading her I wasn't a doctor – yes, I was twelve.

Dad was with the 8th Army down south and we did not meet for some weeks when he obtained leave. The parents had no home of their own, so Mum and I shuttled between Brodsworth and Taddington. Times were tough. All food was rationed. The war was not going well for the Allies, and D-Day was a year away. My parents saw each other rarely. Dad's boss, General Montgomery, C-in-C 21st Army Group, wanted all his soldiers to have no family distractions in the run up to the Invasion. As it happens, Prime Minister Churchill and President Roosevelt agreed to a draft of D-Day the same day I was born.

Dad landed in Normandy on June 7, 1944 - D-Day+1 - the day after the first assault on the beaches, with XXX Corps, part of the 2nd Army, and was transferred several months later to be Senior Chaplain to the Guards Armoured Division soon after the breakout from the Normandy Beachhead. My mother had little idea what was going on apart from Dad's heavily censored letters. Dad never spoke about his war. His commanding officer in Palestine in 1947, General 'Bolo' Whistler, told me many years later that he had been recommended for a Victoria Cross for rescuing wounded soldiers from a minefield while under enemy fire.

In the event Dad was awarded the Military Cross based on his general war record and his citation said that whenever the action was 'sticky' he invariably arrived in his Jeep.

He was with the first group of soldiers who liberated Brussels and was befriended by a wealthy Belgian family called Wellens, who always sent presents at Christmas until they died in the nineteen-sixties. He had a driver called Albert and during a lull in the fighting they went to inspect the battlefield of Waterloo. I have never been, but evidently there is – or was – a lookout with paintings of the action above whichever window you looked through. On their way back to camp, Albert was very quiet. Dad asked him why and Albert's comment was that Wellington did not appear to have had much aerial support.

In the meantime Mum and I languished up north and even after European hostilities ended, Dad was little seen, because he was part of the army being assembled in the Middle East for the invasion of Japan. However the Allies anticipated massive resistance and millions of casualties on both sides, which they were anxious to avoid, and they elected to drop atomic bombs to try and bring the enemy to their senses.

In this they were successful.

Egypt, 1946-1947

Soon after the war ended Mum and I went out on the RMS *Mauretania*, a Cunarder converted into a troopship, to join Dad in Egypt. Needless to say I have little recollection of this period. At some stage we lived in a rented house in Ismailia, a town on Lake Timsah near the Suez Canal, which was being guarded by British troops. We shared the house with another army chaplain called Dick Hambly, his wife Megan and son Michael. Michael could not speak very clearly and I had to translate for him. Megan was frightened of birds. For one meal, the cook – yes, we had servants - suggested pigeon pie. When he presented it he cut into the crust and a couple of live pigeons flew out. Megan had a fit. How cook laughed, but he had to find alternative employment.

Dad was sent to Palestine soon after we arrived, while we were left behind because of Zionist terrorist activity. We did however go and see him in Jerusalem. We had left the King David Hotel minutes before it was blown up by said Zionists killing 91 people in July 1946. The attack was ordered by Menachem Begin, who went on to become Prime Minister of Israel – as one does.

The local situation in the Middle East continued to hot up and eventually families were evacuated, with difficulty. Dad managed to wrangle Mum and me a passage home on another troopship, the *Empire Windrush*. The only problem was we had been given duff information as to when she was due to sail. When we arrived on the quayside at Port Said she had cast off and was already under way. Another army chaplain, Ken Oliver, was with us to see us off, as Dad was who knows where, and Ken was not to be put off. He commandeered a launch and we set off in hot pursuit. He managed to attract the attention of the crew, who threw a rope ladder overboard and we climbed up the side of the hull to clamber aboard. Evidently I hung round my mother's neck for the climb, like a monkey – but all she was worried about was the launch crew admiring her frilly knickers. Well, that's her story.

Germany, 1947–1949

Dad came back to England soon after us and was promptly posted to Germany, which was still in ruins. The Allies had divided what spoils there were between them. The British occupied the industrial north from the neck of Denmark south to Cologne. Dad was based in Bad Oeyenhausen, the British HQ, and we lived nearby. What you wanted you commandeered, and Uncle Stephen, who was also based nearby, saw to it that we wanted for as little as possible.

We lived in a mansion with a huge hall where the parents held dances – yes, dances. I can remember peeping between the banisters to see what was going on. They also had a magnificent drop-head Mercedes which had belonged to a German general, and they were driven everywhere by a prisoner of war chauffeur, a Count, who needless to say had never been a Nazi and loved the Brits.

We were posted several times within Germany, including Hanover and Celle, where I developed at a very early age a life-long fascination for the female form. We had a live-in (German) cook and housemaid. The cook was a bit of a battle-axe. The housemaid was rather different – a pretty blonde 20-year-old, who had been part of a Nazi programme called Lebensborn, essentially to procreate a pure Aryan race. My mother had been told that she had been coerced into relationships with Aryan SS officers and had a child, which had been removed from her at birth.

This experience may have unsettled her more than anyone realised. In any event she used to take me up to her room in the attic and 'mother' me against her rather wonderful, unfettered breasts. Needless to say I have vivid recollections of this experience. One day I was playing in the garden when I ran over a piece of wood with a nail sticking out of it, which pierced my foot from sole to instep. I made quite a fuss. My parents were out and the maid suggested to the cook that she knew a way which might calm me down. When the cook learnt what this might consist of, she told my mother when she returned and sadly the maid was never to be seen again. Such a pity.

On another occasion I was returning home in Hanover with my parents in the rear of an armoured staff car. It was snowing heavily and the driver did not realise we were travelling along tram tracks. As we approached a bend in the road a tram arrived in the opposite direction and we collided at some speed. I was thrown against a metal bar running along the back of the front seat and smashed my nose quite badly. Some nuns from a nearby convent smeared my bruised face with butter and somehow we went on our way. I must have gone to a doctor the next day but as the damage did not appear life-threatening, that was that. However throughout my youth I suffered from ear-related problems. I was treated by several eminent Harley Street specialists to not much avail and nearly died at school from mastoiditis complicated by meningitis aged 16. When I was 20 I went to see HM the Queen's Ear, Nose & Throat surgeon, a man called Miles Formby. He took one look up my nose and asked me if I had ever broken it. I told him about the accident in Hanover all those years before and he said there was a small bone lodged across the back of my septum, which was the root cause of my troubles. He removed it a few days later under anaesthetic at University College Hospital and I had no more trouble for many years.

Aldershot, 1949–1951

Dad was posted back to the UK in 1949 to Marlborough Lines, Aldershot, which included Mons Officer Cadet School, a Sandhurst for National Service officer cadets. I was now six and memories are a bit clearer. We had a house (army quarter) by the church with a large garden. The church was a rather splendid timber building originally used as a hospital for wounded soldiers returning from the Crimea and been named after Florence Nightingale. Sunday services were always packed, standing room only.

The Regimental Sergeant Major was an enormous man named Ron Brittain, who was reputed to have the loudest voice in the British Army and scared the living daylights out of new recruits and senior officers alike. He was a religious man and got along well with my father, so much so that he or Mrs Brittain would come and babysit when the parents went out or, I would sleep over at their quarter.

Years later I attended a dinner at Grosvenor House where RSM Brittain was Toastmaster. He looked magnificent in his red tails with a fine row of medals, and I introduced myself for him to announce me to my hosts. Youens is not an easy name to catch first time, but when he heard he straightened up immediately and said "Remember me to your father, sir". Not only did he remember Dad, he remembered looking after me too, or said he did. Good man.

I had two friends, Maurice and Herbert Webb, to play with. They lived at Mons, where their father worked in the Officers' Mess. There was a television in one of the Mess rooms and on Sunday afternoons we were allowed to watch Annette Mills singing with her puppet Muffin the Mule.

Annette was the sister of John Mills, the actor, and I used to think she was quite beautiful. However the Webb boys somehow got hold of a magazine called *Health & Efficiency*, which was a euphemism. The magazine was full of nudes, as in nudists. Move over, Annette.

While the parents were based in Aldershot I was sent to what is now known as a primary school, in a large shed and run by a very tough old spinster called Florence Seed. The school was called – Miss Seed's. Now there's a surprise. Here we were taught the rudiments of reading, writing and arithmetic as well as a smattering of history and geography under her watchful eye. Christopher Cazenove, the actor, was a fellow pupil and according to my mother we used to play together.

One day I was sent out of the class for some misdemeanour and found myself in a room with two or three other villains, including a divine twelve-year-old called Shirley. Someone cocked a snook at me and I cocked one back, but unfortunately Miss Seed walked into the room at that moment and my snook was, inadvertently but actually, for all practical purposes, cocked at her. She went ballistic (although come to think of it, ballistic was somewhere in the future) and beat me hard on my open palm with a ruler. I can see her now and shudder at the recollection, although I must have reformed my character by the time I left for prep school; Miss Seed came to our wedding.

During a visit to Brodsworth in 1950, the Aldershot quarter was burgled and all my mother's jewellery was stolen, along with some silver which included a tea service given to her great grandfather by the first Duke of Wellington – yes, the victor of Waterloo, although how he came to pass it along remains lost in the mists. None of the property was recovered, but the burglars turned out to be our soldier servants, called Butters and Flon, who were apprehended and sentenced to a spell behind bars. Unfortunately they had sold the goods on, but allegedly could not remember to whom. We had only just arrived at Brodsworth when the police called with the news of the burglary and we had to turn round and drive back through the night. I remember it was a new moon and my father said it was bad luck to look at a new moon through glass – the car window – and mother saying gloomily it was too bloody late.

Travelling around the UK back then, with no motorways, was a major undertaking. No town was bypassed and road direction signs, which had been dismantled during the war to confound invading troops, were yet to be replaced. In order to drive from Aldershot to Doncaster, you had to drive up the A30 into West London, up Park Lane to Finchley and on to the A1, which went through places like Grantham and Newark with traffic lights or policemen on point duty (directing traffic) all along the route. There were stretches of dual carriageway, but they were few and far between. Much of the traffic was commercial, as there weren't many private cars, and the roads were always very busy. The parents must have been seriously exhausted when we eventually arrived back in Aldershot, let alone depressed.

Mum eventually replaced her jewellery at Garrards the Crown Jeweller in Regents Street, now long gone and part of Aspreys. Among the goodies was a pair of sapphire ear studs, which she eventually gave to Annabelle (my wife far in the future). She showed them to a jeweller in Colombo (now Sri Lanka) when we were there on holiday 30 years later and he said they were glass. Since sapphires are principally mined in Sri Lanka he was probably right. Makes you wonder what the Crown Jewels are really made of.

CHAPTER 3

Prep School

In September 1951 I was sent to Eagle House Preparatory School, near Crowthorne in Berkshire. My parents delivered me at the gates into the care of the Headmaster, Paul Wootton, then set off for Southampton and a troopship back to Egypt on a new posting. I had been kitted out in brown Clarkes' sandals and long grey socks with red tops, Y-front underpants under dark blue corduroy shorts, a mid-blue shirt, red tie, blue wool long sleeve jumper and a dark blue blazer several sizes too big, so it would last; all supplied by Swan & Edgar, a long-gone department store on Piccadilly Circus in London. The building is now occupied, on the ground floor at least, by Virgin Records or some such emporium.

Feeling sad and lonely, having been abandoned and never having been away from home before, I wandered round the grounds for a while before being approached by a huge man in short trousers, who demanded to know who I was and who was my 'guardian' (a cousin named Binnie Nicholson, who had not yet arrived).

"I'm Richard Youens and my guardian is Binnie Nicholson, sir," I told him.

"Well, there are some things you need to know," the huge man said. "You're Youens, your guardian is Nicholson and I'm Whitfeld, not 'sir'". Then he turned to a boy about my age playing not far away with a Dinky toy and called him over. "This is a new boy, Hood. His name is Youens and Nicholson's his guardian. Look after him until Nicholson arrives." And with that he was away. It later transpired that he was a prefect called Michael Whitfeld and many years later we met again and became friends; we still are.

Hood, whose Christian name turned out to be Robin – what do some parents think about when they name their children? – took me under his wing and we stayed friends for the five years I attended Eagle House. After we left I never saw hair or hide of him again, but I did hear he joined the Rhodesian police.

I spent my first night in a small dormitory with four other boys. The only memento of home was the old car rug on my bed, which had belonged to my late Chandler grandfather and had kept him warm in his drophead Bentley. Frankly this was a bit upmarket, as the other boys all had tartan rugs and I felt rather self-conscious, but there was not much I could do about it. Toy animals were forbidden, but I smuggled in some form of woolly chicken, which I could hide in the palm of my hand. However this was soon discovered and confiscated. All right – rather pathetic, but by the time my children went off to prep school a soft animal was pretty much de rigeur.

I had great difficulty sleeping that first night and hid under the bedclothes trying to imagine I was anywhere else other than where I was. This desire was multiplied, and then some, by a rude awakening the following morning by a bell, followed by a dash downstairs in our pyjamas and dressing gowns to the changing room. There the headmaster awaited us, also in his pyjamas and dressing gown, standing by a large sunken bath above which were two cold showers going full blast. We were made to strip, stand in line and wait our turn for torture. When it came, we were alerted by a clap. Then we had to jump in under the shower and wait for the next clap, when we could escape. The intervals between claps seemed forever, but were probably five seconds – a very long five seconds. This practice occurred first thing every morning winter and summer for the next five years.

Eagle House wasn't exactly a barrel of laughs from start to finish. My parents sent me there because some of my mother's cousins had gone there. I don't think they looked at anywhere else. It was a gloomy Victorian pile in semi-suburbia, with quite attractive grounds and excellent playing fields where we played rugger in the winter, hockey in the spring and cricket in the summer. In the winter if the ground was frozen we played 'Cruisers', which consisted of teams, convoys of cargo ships made up of the slower boys, escorted by more athletic destroyers trying to avoid the submarines who were the fastest of the lot. It was a glorified game of touch and I was usually a cargo ship, but it was good fun nevertheless.

The Headmaster, Paul Wootton, and his attractive wife Anne became good friends with my parents, and my mother was still in touch with Anne for many years. Anne's good looks never deserted her, even in her nineties. Needless to say I developed a crush on her very early on.

The French master, John Watson, was quite superb. We never spoke to him in English the entire time we were at school. If we did, he ignored us. I had a smattering from holidays in France and Miss Seed's and I went from there. As result of Watson's high standards, I passed into the top French set at Sherborne, but I have gone downhill ever since. Watson received international recognition in 1960 when the UK came second in the Eurovision Song Contest, with Bryan Johnson singing *Looking high, high, high*. Watson wrote the lyrics and the music. You can watch it on YouTube – a far cry from the woman with a beard who won in 2014. He was also a member of the Magic Circle, and once or twice while I was there he put on a brilliant conjuring show.

The other master I particularly liked was Peter Huxtable, a quiet bachelor who taught English with great flare. For whatever reason, I don't think he ever married, but we boys were convinced he was having an affair with Anne Wootton. On the other hand, if he was homosexual, he was very discrete. I used to see him years later with mutual friends, who ran a restaurant in nearby Eversley, and he was always full of fun. I would hesitate to say he was 'gay'.

The Matron, Mrs Lydall, was 'nice looking' and in her fifties. She always wore a proper nurse's blue uniform complete with starched white apron and headpiece. She was very well liked by everyone, but she left rather suddenly after I had been there a year. She was replaced by Miss Howes, a skinny, po-faced spinster, who thought my fingernails were too long and always cut them to the quick. Nasty old bat. She was fired after a few terms and somehow Mrs Lydall was persuaded to return, much to everyone's relief. All the while we had an assistant matron called Mrs Illingsworth who was more of a motherly soul. Well – more grandmotherly, come to think of it.

I made quite a few friends at Eagle House, but none has remained with me except two. One was Michael Whitfeld, the prefect who had sorted me out when I arrived, and who much later had boys with my son Christian at Ludgrove. I commuted with him from Reading to the City in the 1980s and 1990s. The other was Keith Benham, who used to make a pile of his mashed potato, dig a hole in the top, fill it with gravy and call it Lake Titicaca. He went on to be senior partner of Freshfields, the City solicitors, and married an outstandingly pretty girl called Meri, lucky chap. Her mother ran a family flower business called Moyses Stevens, very upmarket and still going strong.

My best friend while I was there was George 'Nutty' Almond, who lived near Henley-on-Thames and whose parents regularly took me out from school with him when mine were abroad. His father, Patrick, was the top Henley doctor (GP) and his mother, Ursula, was a nurse. They lived in a big house called Bowling Close on the Fairmile, the Oxford road out of town. It's now a housing estate. Nutty went on to Radley and then Oxford, where he sent himself down after a few terms. Last time I heard of him he had bought a horse near La Linea in the south of Spain and ridden it back to Henley, but that was in the sixties.

Nutty had a friend called Richard Betton-Foster, always known as BF. He was rather scruffy, in National Health spectacles. His parents lived on the Isle of Wight and he said his father was a civil servant, which apart from being an oxymoron, covered any number of options. When my bride to be and I announced our engagement in the papers at the end of 1971, BF saw it and made contact. He came to the flat where we were living for a drink. He was still scruffy, wearing National Health spectacles and now a beard. He was not well received by my bride-to-be and has not been seen since.

Other boys who were friends included Hugh Sayers, who was ADC to Sir Richard Sharples, the Governor of Bermuda. They were both assassinated by a couple of local Black Power supporters in March 1973. Both men were apprehended and subsequently hanged – the last to meet such a fate under British rule anywhere. Then there was Ed Mainwaring, who became a very popular radio DJ known as Stewpot or Ed Stewart (his mother's maiden name).

Robert Scott was chairman of the Manchester Olympic Bid Committee, which campaigned unsuccessfully to host the Olympic Games in 1996 and 2000. He was also Chairman of the Committee, which won the bid to host the Commonwealth Games of 2002 and was knighted for these sterling efforts. I am sure there were others, but I've lost track.

My time at Eagle House was anything but distinguished. Apart from playing for the XV a few times, winning a prize for making a model of The White House and passing Common Entrance to Sherborne, that was about it. Even passing the CE came as a bit of a surprise.

Shortly before I left I was called into Paul Wootton's study and asked what I knew about sex. I must have looked completely blank, because he kindly went on to explain the reproduction process. Up until then such matters had never occurred to me. I had always been fascinated by the female form but assumed it was to be admired from a distance and the idea of penetration seemed somehow rather gross. My reaction was to ask if that was the case, how exactly was Jesus conceived? Paul had no answer to that and I was invited to leave the room. I was however rather intrigued with the whole idea and brought it up with Hamish Clifton-Brown, with whom I set the scoreboard during cricket matches. Hamish was rather worldlier than me and soon set the record straight.

Prep school holidays

By the time school broke after the end of my first term, my mother had been evacuated back to England from Egypt and, with no home of our own, we went to stay with her aunt and uncle, Teddy an Emmy Sharp, who lived at Greywalls, a big 1920s mansion overlooking Morecambe Bay in Lancashire. Teddy was a keen gardener, which was lucky – he had inherited several acres of walled gardens as well as lawns, woods and rockeries, which he opened to the public in aid of the lifeboats. They had three children, all older than me – Jane, Peter and Nigel, who was closest to me in age.

Nigel had a big model railway in a loggia in the garden, which was endlessly fascinating. That Christmas my mother gave me a Hornby Double-O train set of my very own and I could hardly believe my good fortune. I still have it in its original boxes, along with the track, locomotives and rolling stock as well as stations, signals and other railway paraphernalia, which I collected over the next five years or so. It was all beautifully made, and despite being played with for hours on end it is still in nearly perfect condition.

After Christmas we went to stay at the Old Hall Hotel in Buxton for the rest of the holidays. My mother knew the owner, Piers Marnie, and his wife, and we had stayed there several times over the years – comfortable but pretty dull for an eight-year-old. Still – anything was better than Eagle House, or so I thought.

On Valentine's Day 1952, half way through my second term, my mother gave birth to Georgina. King George VI had died the week before (we boys all had to wear black arm bands until after the funeral) and she was named in his honour. She was going to be called Georgina Elizabeth, but that was considered on reflection to be a bit over the top. Needless to say I did not meet this bit of serious competition until several weeks later. She was almost nine years younger than me and we never really connected, particularly when my parents were keen to thrust her down my throat at any opportunity, which I much resented.

Dad remained in Egypt, but Mum rented some converted cowsheds at Fullbrook Farm in Elstead, not far from Guildford, and hired a Scottish nanny called Isabel Bissett. We must have spent the Easter holidays there, but we may also have spent some of the time with my mother's brother Mike at his farm in Galloway, just over the border into Scotland.

A summer in Egypt

By the time the summer holidays of 1952 arrived, the parents had been reunited, with baby Georgina, in Fayed, an army town on the Great Bitter Lake, which in effect connects the north with the south sections of the Suez Canal. Most of the houses were very basic – even the senior officers' quarters. Very few had flushing lavatories. My parents' place had two.

I was flown to Cairo in a BOAC (British Overseas Airways Corporation) Argonaut, which was state of the art in those days. However it was not possible to obtain the necessary visas because of prevailing red tape, so the British High Commission agreed to grant me temporary diplomatic status, which meant I had to remain on British soil at all times. Fayed had this status anyway, but I had to travel in BHC cars between the airport and Fayed, about 130 miles all of which went without a hitch. I don't suppose even the Egyptians would have thought I was a threat to their security, but it was all pretty exciting stuff.

I spent several holidays in Fayed and became quite blasé about air travel. In those days parents had to sign a disclaimer, so that if anything went wrong the airline was not at fault as long as they weren't negligent.

I thought nothing of this until flying back for school at the end summer 1953, the aircraft's engines began to fail one by one and we were lucky to make an emergency landing at Rome Fiumicino late at night on the one remaining engine. We had to evacuate the aircraft once it had stopped on the runway surrounded by the emergency services, and were eventually bussed to a hotel in Rome at dawn, there to await a replacement aircraft from London, which arrived about 12 hours later. In the meantime I had no money for food or drink and was told to stay in my room until summoned for the return trip to the airport. When we eventually took off the stewardess brought round soft drinks and gherkins. I ate three or four ravenously, only to bring them back up over my neighbour minutes later.

A very popular great uncle named Reg Drury, married to Marjorie, one of Grandpa Alfred Chandler's sisters, met me at Heathrow, and when we unpacked my bags, the bottle of Cointreau I was bringing as a thank you had been broken and all my clothes were sodden with the stuff. Uncle was very disappointed.

In those days long-haul flight passengers were processed in a large Nissen hut on the north perimeter of Heathrow. Immigration and Customs were for all practical purposes combined. One time I was coming through not far behind a large foreign looking woman wearing a fur coat. The Customs officer asked to see the coat and the woman protested loudly but eventually took it off. The officer produced a pen knife and slit open the lining to reveal rows of watches, no straps, sewn on to the inside of the coat – which must have been very heavy. Cue police etc.

The Commander-in-Chief of the Middle East Land Forces, to which Dad was attached, was a cousin of my mother's called Cam Nicholson. He had several bungalows for visitors in his compound, one of which he lent to my parents when they first arrived and were waiting for their 'quarter' (house, in army terminology) to become free. A neighbour, albeit briefly, was Edwina Mountbatten, wife of Prince Louis. She and Mum became friendly, although Lady

M clearly had an ulterior motive as she talked Mum into washing and ironing all her best clothes, rather than leave them to the mercies of Cousin Cam's local staff.

Cyprus summer

For a change of scene in the summer holidays of 1953, a friend of my mother's called Bill Humble lent the parents a house in Northern Cyprus. The house was about 10 minutes' walk from the Mediterranean near the pretty fishing village of Kyrenia. Kyrenia's main claim to fame apart from the harbour itself was the Harbour Club, set back in one corner of the circular quay. It was here that the singer Anne Sheridan, one of the Forces' Sweethearts during the Second World War, spent her summers with her husband, who owned the place. As result the bar and restaurant were thick with army officers and their wives and my parents were there most nights.

We stayed in Kyrenia for about three weeks, during which on the morning of September 10 an earthquake all but destroyed the village of Paphos about 80 miles south west of us. Even at that distance we felt the tremors. I was lying awake when the ceiling light started to swing alarmingly. I thought I was dreaming to begin with, and raised the alarm. There were cracks around the base of the house but it had escaped any serious damage.

Christmas in Tripoli

By Christmas 1953 the parents had been posted to Tripoli in Libya, on the North African coast of the Mediterranean.

In those days oil-rich Libya was ruled by King Idris, supported by the British and American Governments, which meant it was protected by both countries' troops. We lived in a large flat on the Lunga Mare, a boulevard overlooking the harbour.

One holiday I was taught to ride by an NCO in a cavalry regiment, the 14/18th Hussars, based nearby. Neither of us enjoyed the experience much. Another time I was put in the cockpit of an American jet fighter at Wheelers Field, their massive air base outside town. My mother warned me that if I touched anything the wretched aeroplane would take off immediately. Convinced she was right, I did not enjoy that experience much either.

On the plus side - before World War II Libya had been under the 'protection' of Italy and their leader, Mussolini, before he lost the plot completely and went totalitarian, devoted considerable resources to excavating some of the remains of cities along the Libyan coast built by his ancestors the Romans. The best known is Leptis Magna, about 90 miles east of Tripoli and now a World Heritage site. We were lucky enough to visit the ruins several times and had the place pretty much to ourselves. It was fascinating to wander the streets and imagine the ancients going about their business in the same circumstances in which we found ourselves. The unforgettable experience did wonders for my Latin. Well, all right, it didn't, but it did breathe a bit of life into the language for me.

At one time while we were in Tripoli, Lord Mountbatten paid a courtesy call in whatever ship he was flying his flag at the time, and gave a cocktail party on deck for the locals, including my parents. He pulled Dad over and, wrongly assuming Dad knew everyone, told him to introduce him to the many guests. Dad evidently started off quite well, then began to run out of steam, coughing to cover the names of those being presented to the Great Man, whom he could not identify.

After a bit Lord Louis took him to one side and asked how many more Col & and Mrs Cough and Brigadier & Mrs Splutter he was going to meet. Dad apologized and said he simply couldn't remember everyone. He then said, "By the way sir, I'd very much like to meet the ship's chaplain. What's his name?"

Lord Louis said, "well, we just call him 'Chaplain'".

"But what's his name?" Dad persisted.

"OK, Padre," said Prince Louis Mountbatten of Burma, Admiral of the Fleet and the last Viceroy of India, with a hint of a smile, "I think we're quits."

The parents' flat had almost the same telephone number as a swanky French restaurant in town called *Les Trois Chefs*, which was always booked up days in advance, and often people would mistakenly call to book a table. After a bit Dad became rather fed up with this and decided the next time it happened to pretend he was the Head Waiter, confirm a table and recommend some 'specials'. He then called the restaurant and booked a table for him and Mum to dine and watch what happened when the other 'guests' arrived and departed tableless and very cross. Needless to say they dined out on the event for months afterwards.

Back to England

In the autumn of 1954 Dad was posted back to England

after the best part of four years in the Middle East. It must have been quite a shock to find him based in the less than exotic Shorncliff Barracks near Folkestone, Kent. The army provided rented accommodation in the form of a mansion with large grounds and a forest called Reindene Wood, near Hawkinge. It was pseudo Tudor, beamy and a far cry from the flat in Tripoli, let alone any of other places I had lived before. We had a very happy Christmas and Easter holidays there but I went back to Eagle House in May 1955, never to see the place again.

Having been told he would be in Kent for at least two years and my mother having made all the curtains throughout the house, within less than six months Dad had been posted to the Royal Military Academy, Sandhurst, about three miles from Eagle House. Talk about coming full circle. I could have done with the parents being on call back in 1951 but my world had moved on and I really did not need them on my doorstep now.

RMA Sandhurst

As Senior Chaplain to the Academy, Dad was allocated a substantial Georgian house in the Chapel Square, with a good-sized garden. Even though he went on to become Chaplain-General, he always said this was his best posting. He loved working with the officer cadets and clearly they loved him, because many of them tell me so to this day. We were at Sandhurst for three very happy years. In those days the cadets' training course was two years as opposed to six months as it is now and the cadets had holidays which coincided with mine, so I had the run of the place, which included playing on the obstacle courses and frequently falling in the Wish Stream as well as the lake in front of Old College built by French prisoners taken at Waterloo.

The Commandant was General Pooh Hobbs, whose daughter, Sarah, eventually married Ewan Graham, son of the assistant Commandant, Brigadier Freddie Graham, both good friends then, never to be seen since. The Adjutant was an Irish Guards major named Tony Mainwaring-Burton, who with his wife Edwina became my parents' lifelong best friends.

One of the adjutant's duties was to command the officer cadets' passing-out parade at the end of their term at Sandhurst. This event was known as the Sovereign's Parade, although the Academy seldom actually paraded in front of her. Tony yelled his orders while astride an enormous grey horse called Daster. At the end of the parade he had to ride Daster up the steps and into Old College. On one occasion as he mounted the steps Daster lifted his tail and did what horses do, much to everyone's amusement.

The Academy Sergeant-Major was RSM John Lord, a brave veteran of Arnhem, where he had been put in the bag for the rest of the war. Despite being a God-fearing disciplinarian who could spot a misdemeanour at a hundred paces, he was hugely admired by the cadets and instructors alike. He was offered a commission but preferred to remain in the ranks, albeit as the most senior Regimental Sergeant Major in the Army. His wife was utterly charming.

Prince Edward, Duke of Kent, was a cadet in his last term when Dad took up his appointment, but they became friends, particularly after he married Katharine Worsley, who took a shine to Dad and corresponded with him regularly. Another cadet at that time was King Hussein of Jordan. RSM Lord was alleged to have addressed him on arrival at the RMA: "Stand up straight, you horrible little king, sir". The King clearly took no long-term offence. When the BBC featured the RSM in a *This is Your Life* programme, the King attended.

CHAPTER 4

Sherborne

In September 1956 I went to Abbey House, Sherborne, Dorset, the school I was to attend for the next five years. The housemaster was MM (Mickey) Walford, a great sportsman in his day, a triple Blue at Oxford (cricket, rugger and hockey) and Great Britain silver medallist in the 1948 Olympics, losing to India in the hockey final. He was also a bachelor and his spinster sister, Joy, helped him run the house.

We new boys were instructed to arrive the day before term started to get acclimatized. The school uniform list was at Harrods and we had to wear a thick grey two-piece suit, winter or summer, and a white shirt with a detachable stiff (starched) collar, which had to be attached with studs front and back, as well as cufflinks. The tie had to be set in the open collar, after the back stud had been attached to the shirt, then the collar was attached at the rear, folded down with the tie still in place and finally both ends of the collar were attached to the front stud. The next hurdle was to tie the tie without getting the collar dirty. Black leather lace-up shoes completed the standard day-to-day wear. The suit jacket had three buttons at the front and for the first three years we had to have all three done up at all times. Anyone caught otherwise was in serious trouble. Despite these drawbacks, it was all quite exciting and grown up after Eagle House.

We were paired off – me with Christopher Irons, a squeaky-voiced boy with sticking out ears from the Isle of Wight, whose younger brother Jeremy went on to stage and screen success. I think he and I were allocated together because we arrived last. Otherwise I probably would have linked up with Alastair Grayburn, with whom I had played on the beaches of Norfolk during the war. His uncle had also been in Abbey House and had won a posthumous VC at Arnhem in 1944.

Alastair was paired with Robert Kemp, who had a rather racy bike with straight handlebars and was therefore a bit suspect, particularly as he had not been to a prep school. Nick Willans, whose father, Godfrey, had written the *Down With Skool* books illustrated by the cartoonist Ronald Searle, was paired with Bill McLintock, who had been bought up on a farm about 15 miles away and had a bit of a Dorset accent. The last two were Mike du Pré, whose father was the Finance Director of Gillette, the razor blade people, and David Spedding, who was to become my best friend later on at school – both he and Mike. I saw a lot of him during the holidays as well. David's father was army. His mother was arty. A mismatch if ever there was one, and they were soon to split.

When the rest of the school arrived we had already established ourselves in the Day Room, where about 30 of us were based for the first two years. We each had lockers for our possessions and tuck (extra food). The lockers were secured by a hasp, held in place by a locker peg – bloody thing: it had to be a twig in the shape of a perfect Y about 3" long. We had to go out into the woods in our spare time and find a suitable twig, peel off the bark, cut it to shape and sand it down. If it didn't meet the approval of "The Boxing Party", the senior boys in the Day Room, it was split and you had to start all over again. The Boxing Party was a gang of four of the most senior boys in the Day Room, and a pretty mean bunch they were too, led by George Inge, who went on to become chairman of Savills, the estate agents.

Fixed to the wall in one corner of the Day Room stood a big, square timber-sided box about 4ft high and 3ft square into which all dry waste was placed. Beside it was a smaller freestanding metal bin into which all wet waste was placed. There was a flap at the bottom of the timber box about 1ft high through which the waste was removed.

If a boy was irritating someone more senior and wasn't put off by casual admonishment, the irritated senior could plead his case with the Boxing Party that the irritant should be 'boxed'. This involved capturing the pest and pushing him head first into the box, putting the metal bin on top of him, climbing into the bin and forcing the pest to struggle out through the flap. However it seems that a year or two earlier some poor wretch managed to break his neck in the box and the practice had been dropped. Today the health & safety boys would have a field day, not to mention the lawyers.

Soon after my arrival, life at Sherborne became less

exciting and rather tedious, especially when we were told we had to pass a New Boys' Test after the first three weeks. This consisted of having to learn the history of the school, the school songs, the Lord's Prayer in Latin, the full names of all the housemasters, where their houses were (fair enough) and the names and initials of the School Prefects, to name but some of the subjects. Irons and I proved pretty hopeless at this and I failed twice and was beaten twice by the Head of House, OJC Parry-Jones, a tall crinkly-haired martinet with milk-bottle bottom glasses. My mother met him years later and said he had become a doctor and was very nice – no accounting for some.

All new boys were required to 'fag' for the prefects for their first three terms. This meant cleaning their shoes and boots, tidying their study, cooking coffee, baked beans etc. and generally running errands. I think the prefect blessed with my services the first term was Desmond Cameron. No idea what became of him.

We slept in dormitories of 30+ boys on horsehair mattresses on iron frame beds. At 7am each morning a bell was rung and we had to leap out of bed, go down stairs, immerse ourselves in a cold bath under the eye of a prefect, wash, go back upstairs, dress and make our beds. Light punishment was usually 'Calling', which involved going through the entire cold bath and dressing process twice in five minutes, reporting to the prefect who had doled out the penalty. He, needless to say, was still in bed, as he had half an hour's latitude in which to arise.

Breakfast was at 7.30am and usually consisted of porridge in the winter and cereal – cornflakes – in the spring and summer, followed by something hot, including kippers, but no choice - you ate what you were given. Chapel was at 8.30am and Abbey House was a stone's throw from the main school, so we did not have to walk far, then four or five lessons started around 9am through to lunch at 1pm. After lunch we played rugger in the winter, rugger and hockey in the spring and cricket in the summer – compulsory for everyone. Tennis, squash and fives were additional options in our own time. Lessons again from 4pm to 6pm. Free time to 7pm, then supper followed by 'Hall' – homework, bed at 9pm and lights out at 9.30pm.

Thanks to John Watson at Eagle House, I passed into the top French set, which was taught by Hughie Holmes, a charming man with a shiny bald head, who greeted us with the words 'vous êtes la crème de la crème', from which point my French proceeded downhill. The other masters who taught us in those early days are a complete blank, except 'Uncs' Gourlay, who taught us Latin in a small dungeon under the chapel. Uncs was pretty scary until you got to know him. If we could not answer a question, he would whip his gown around his face with just his eyes showing and cry "aha – foiled again!" I think he must have been a Zorro fan.

There were no lessons in the afternoon on Wednesdays and Saturdays, and apart from Chapel we were left pretty much to our own devices on Sundays as long as we showed up for meals or were out with our parents. We were allowed three such weekend outings per term – from Saturday after school for lunch until the evening after supper and after chapel on Sundays until 6pm: no chance of escaping for a night.

On Monday afternoons we played soldiers, sailors or airmen – our choice – as members of the School Combined

Cadet Force (CCF) and affiliated to the Devon & Dorset Regiment. This involved, the weekend before, preparing our uniform, which consisted of heavy serge battledress in the spring and winter or more lightweight drill in the summer, along with webbing and a slouch cap with badge.

The webbing consisted of spats around the ankles and a belt. All fastenings and the cap badge were brass, which had to be polished and the webbing 'blancoed', which involved covering the clean webbing with wet khaki cake to a uniform finish and leaving it to dry the night before. If spread too thick it broke up, too thin and it was uneven, so it had to be just right or extra parades. If you were a fag you had to do your prefect's gear as well including his boots, not to mention your own. The toecaps had to be like mirrors and the effect was achieved with great difficulty by melting polish, spreading it over the toecap and buffing it to an even surface before polishing it to a lustrous shine.

Most of us signed up for the military section, which was run by Michael Earls-Davis, who had been a major in the Second World War, and his Colour Sergeant was a prefect named John Wilsey, who seemed to take this role very seriously indeed. So much so he joined the Devon & Dorsets after Sandhurst and went on to become a full general, having served as General Officer Commanding in Northern Ireland. I on the other hand remained a private cadet for most of my career in the 'Corps', rising to corporal for the last couple of terms. Much of our time was devoted to parade ground drill with Lee Enfield Mark IV rifles from the Boer War, but they were perfectly serviceable, to the extent of firing blanks on exercise.

I had been in the choir at Eagle House and was volunteered for the school choir on arrival at Sherborne. We were required to sing the chorus of Verdi's Requiem at the beginning of December, in the Abbey. This meant hours of extracurricular practice, the only reward being the pleasure of singing in this spectacular building with one of the finest vaulted roofs in the country.

OJC Parry-Jones, he who beat me twice for failing my New Boys' Test, really had it in for me and I was press-ganged into becoming a member of his troupe to sing in an inter-house competition. There were eight of us – trebles (me and du Pré), altos (Irons), tenor and basses forming the Abbey House 'Glee' and much to everyone's astonishment – we won the cup.

As I was the youngest boy in the House, I was obliged to make a speech at the end of Winter Term 'House Supper'. This was a dinner attended not only by all members of Abbey House but also a number of Old Boys of the House and other guests. Happily I did not have to write the speech - that was the task of one of the prefects - but I did have to learn it off by heart. Just to make it interesting it had to consist of the longest words he could find in the dictionary. All I can remember is the opening 'Unaccustomed as I am to such skielist verbage at such a juvenescent age...' Needless to say I was scared stiff. I was first up after dinner and, fortified by a couple of glasses of Whiteways cider, I somehow managed to struggle through.

I cannot say that my first term at Sherborne was an unqualified success, but there was a lot going on and I survived, as did my fellows, and somehow we soldiered on through the next five years. However it is that first term which is seared in the memory. The rest made little impression and I was delighted when the time came to move on, probably because classes were a struggle and my only sporting success was being a member of the winning inter-house hockey cup in my penultimate term.

Girls at school

At some stage during my first term, my housemaster, Mickey Walford, called me into his study and produced the Green Book, about which I'd heard but not seen. This session was basically a rerun of my interview in a previous life with Paul Wootton at Eagle House, but with PICTURES - well all right, drawings. However Mickey made it quite clear this was all theory and practice would mean expulsion.

In these circumstances girls were a bit of a distraction, mainly because they were strictly off limits. In fact for the entire five years of our life at Sherborne, we were expected to assume the attitude that they simply did not exist. Not surprisingly to those of us with red blood coursing our pubescent bodies, this was a red rag to a bull and we were obsessed with making their acquaintance, in our imagination at least, at every opportunity. Sadly that did not amount to much, but it fuelled our conversation. We were a bit like the dog chasing a bus; we would not have had much of a clue what to do if we had managed to attract the attention of the objects of our admiration. Just for the record – carnal relations in the fifties were permissible in polite society within marriage only. Well, that was the theory. The sexual freedom of the late sixties onwards was restricted to most people's imagination, unfortunately.

One girl who had the admiration of the entire school was Gillie Steele-Perkins, who attended Sherborne Girls, the sister school just outside the town. Here the uniform was a brown serge suit in winter and green dresses well below the knee in summer. Somehow Gillie managed to look entirely delectable in both. If anyone was lucky enough to catch a glimpse of her in the high street (Cheap Street) he was everyone's hero and was expected to describe her in detail to the rest of her admirers. Alas, poor Gillie was unable to carry her good looks into her second marriage, which was where I caught up with her again, as Mrs ffrench-Blake and the wife of a spook. She was a sobering example of the effect of good living, booze and fags. Such a shame.

When I was about sixteen, one of my house mates – Mike du Pré – came back to school after the summer holidays with a cunning plan he had hatched with a girl he had met called Carol Cockleigh, who lived near his parents in Staines. Carol was a pupil in Thurston, one of the girls' school houses, and the idea was to put the names of some of her friends in a hat. Mike and his friends would pull them out and start corresponding with them – to what end remained to be seen.

I pulled Sue Ottaway's name from the hat and wrote off to her, introducing myself very politely, explaining age, height, interests, where I lived (Gibraltar, at that time) and so on. As there was a house rule that any letter postmarked Sherborne was automatically opened by the housemaster, we had to ask our correspondent to arrange with a friend elsewhere to act as intermediary by sending the letter in a stamped/addressed envelope to them to forward on.

Poor Sue had to follow this rigmarole, but she did not object and back came her response in the form of a photograph of her posing on a garden wall in a rather pretty dress. She was not only attractive but had a wicked sense of humour. On the back of the photograph she had written 'to my dearest, darling, delicious, delectable...and so on to the bottom, surely with the aid of a Thesaurus...Dick' (as I was called at school). How I wished she meant it.

In any event the correspondence hotted up after this and we had a lot of fun, without ever meeting – until one day about nine months into this romance, we finally did run into each other by chance, outside the Abbey Bookshop in downtown Sherborne one Sunday morning. We shook hands and chatted rather shyly, or at least I did, for a few minutes before each of us beat a hasty retreat to gather ourselves. Undaunted, we carried on our correspondence and I invited her to the Leavers' Dance at the end of my last term. More of that later.

Holidays from Sherborne

For the first two years of my Sherborne sentence my parents remained at Sandhurst. In the summer of 1957 we took a house on the north Cornish coast, on the recommendation of a friend of the parents called Jock Burns. He had commanded a battalion of the Scots Guards in Egypt when we were there in 1947 and he and his wife Joyce had remained friends. The house was somewhere near Polzeath, yet to be discovered by the glitterati in those innocent days. Unfortunately for us it rained every day all day and after about a week we up sticks and left, never to return and never to summer holiday in the UK again.

In the autumn of 1958 Dad was posted to Gibraltar. Great excitement. We were to drive there during the summer holidays and take our time, in style, in a new Mercedes. Dad decided to upgrade his mode of transport and was torn between an Alvis – long since on the scrap heap together with almost all British car manufacturers, thanks to the curse of the unions and weak management – and a Merc. However his mind was made up, curiously enough, by the salesman at Avis' showroom in Albemarle Street, London W1. Dad told him his dilemma and the man said for him it was a 'no brainer': a Mercedes every time. Small wonder Alvis is no more really.

Dad flew to Stuttgart in Germany to take delivery of this two-tone (very trendy in 1958, I can tell you) motor, and drove to Ostend to collect his family for the long trip to Gibraltar. Our first stop was Brussels, where the 1958 World Expo was in full swing. I had been looking forward hugely to spending a few days inspecting all the pavilions – particularly the Russians', which had the replica of a space satellite, which they had successfully launched into orbit the previous October. However after a morning on site, with my sister complaining of boredom, my parents gave up and had to drag me away in disgust. To this day I still resent missing such a wonderful opportunity to fire up my imagination as to what I might do when I grew up – well, that's my excuse for still wondering what might have been.

From Brussels we drove through Luxembourg and down the Rhine into Italy and along the Côte d'Azur to Le Rayole, a small village on the Mediterranean, and a hotel called

L'Hermitage, where we had been the previous summer after the disastrous stay in Cornwall. The hotel was owned and run by a pair of homosexuals, who the mainly British clientele thought were a bit of a joke, but they kept themselves to themselves and troubled no one – or so we thought.

One night my sister Georgina was taken sick and slept with my mother, and Dad took to her bed in my room. Late that evening the door to my room opened and one of the owners entered, unfamiliar with the change of occupation. Dad was a light sleeper and awoke immediately, saw the man standing there in shock and, realising his wicked intentions, roared at him to clear off. I hope he told him to 'bugger off', but history does not relate. Needless to say the story was round the hotel the next morning and the fellow was never seen again during the rest of our stay.

While most fair-minded people of whatever sexual persuasion would probably consider whatever consenting adults do behind closed doors is their business alone, thanks to affirmative action by aggressive groups like Stonewall, homosexual activity is taught in primary schools as an acceptable lifestyle. However these two consenting adults in Le Rayole did not contain their activities to behind closed doors and having read Somerset Maugham's biography I suspect many homosexuals are predators of young boys as well as young men. Therefore it is not an acceptable form of lifestyle to be encouraged; indeed it should be discouraged and accepted only as a last resort. Western society behaviour is coming closer and closer to that of Sodom and Gomorrah and we all know – or we should - what happened there.

After a couple of weeks at Le Rayole we set off again for

northern Spain for a couple of days at another beach resort on the Costa Brava, horrible even then, before striking inland to Madrid and down to Malaga, via Granada and the Alhambra Palace with its wonderful adjoining Parador. There were no duel carriageways in those days, let alone motorways and progress was slow – and hot; we are talking August here; there was no air conditioning, and certainly not in cars. We eventually pitched up in Gibraltar, having driven through smelly little fishing villages like Estepona, on about the 10th September, a few days before the start of my 'O' level year.

The three-hour flight back to Heathrow in a BEA Viscount (almost a jet but not quite) was particularly memorable thanks to my travelling companion, a lovely girl called Sarah Dean-Drummond. She was the height of sophistication, about a year or two older than me – a very pretty brunette with neat legs and feet in black leather high heels. Her shoes are seared into my memory as the sexiest I had ever seen: each had an opening above where her toes attached to her feet – there's even a name for it now: toe cleavage. It took me about a week to come back to earth. I used to read about her in the society pages and hope she had a happy life without me.

The Burns family

Back at school a couple of months later, a letter arrived out of the blue from someone called Joyce Burns. It was she whose husband had recommended Polzeath to Dad, but I knew nothing of that. She said she had known me when I was about three in Egypt, when she and her husband had met my parents. Anyway it seemed they had all met up again in Gibraltar, when she had been staying with the Admiral, and as she lived near Sherborne, would I like to come out for the day one weekend? This seemed like a pretty good idea and I wrote back, accepting with alacrity.

The day duly arrived and Mrs Burns came to collect me in a black MG Magnette – very smart - and took me back to Godminster Wood House, near Bruton, where life was to move up several gears and I was to return time after time over the next ten to twelve years – well, until I married.

Joyce's husband Jock had commanded a battalion of Scots Guards in Egypt in 1947 and then retired from the army some time later to farm his family estate, called Cumbernauld, between Glasgow and Edinburgh. Not long after he had established himself along came the Glasgow Corporation and compulsorily purchased the place lock, stock and barrel to build a new town. Jock had no choice but to haggle over the price and bought Godminster Wood with some of the proceeds together with a bungalow with a lot of land attached overlooking the ocean at Trebetherick on the north Cornish coast.

They had two daughters, Figgy (Felicity), who was horse mad and would have been about 12 and Mugs (Marion), who was 10 – blonde and extremely attractive with a clear complexion and a surprising presence in someone so young; I was very taken, even if she was 10. Anyway I had a very agreeable day out, despite it being a wet November Sunday, and was not looking forward to going back to dreary old Sherborne. However Joyce suggested a cocktail for the drive and produced a gin and orange (Kia Ora orange squash). I was feeling no pain and in fact was quite pleased with myself on arrival back at Abbey House.

Gibraltar

By the time I went back to Gibraltar for the 1958 Christmas holidays my parents were installed in the chaplain's quarter, which consisted of a house and garden backing onto the Convent, the Governor's official residence, on Main Street, Gibraltar's main drag. The officer in charge of the army garrison, a Brigadier Snow, lived in a quarter on the other side of the Convent, so the parents were at the epicentre of Gibraltar glitterati.

The Snows had a son called Peter who later came to fame as a television broadcaster and political commentator, and who invented the 'Swingometer' a device used at election time to reflect changes in voting profiles to try and forecast the likely result. This was all in the future. I was invited to their Christmas party. I knew no one, and being quite shy was reluctant to go. So Dad gave me some Dutch courage in the form of a glass of vermouth. It was quite disgusting (without gin) but had the desired effect and off I went – ever the party animal, never to look back. Needless to say there was a very pretty girl about my own age there called Caroline Church, and any residual memory of Sarah Dean-Drummond was quickly forgotten. A song which was all the rage at the time was the Platters singing an updated version of 'Smoke gets in your eyes'. Every time I hear it, it brings her all back.

The Snow party was the start of a friendship with several sons of Royal Navy officers based on the Rock, including Nick Rowe, Robin Schiffner and Hugh Powlett. Nick was at Wellington and went on to be hugely successful in business both in London and New York after a brief spell in the Navy. I was his Best Man and he said I was the worst Best Man he had ever had. So far he has only had one and anyway I was somewhat distracted at the time with my own wedding days away, not to mention a fiancée in a bolsh because I was elsewhere and not dancing attendance.

Robin and Hugh both made the Navy their career, Robin as an engineer who retired as an admiral and became Lord Lieutenant of Devon. Hugh's father was the senior naval officer in Gibraltar (C-in-C South Western Approaches, great title) and lived in a magnificent house called The Mount. Hugh became a submariner. In the spring and summer we would swim and generally socialise at Rosia Bay, the small harbour where Nelson's body was brought after the Battle of Trafalgar and now disused apart from recreational purposes. If the weather was foul at any time of year, and anyway in the winter, the meeting place *de choix* was a bar called the Copacabana on Main Street, where Carlsberg lager and lime juice would be taken – very refreshing. It's still there and hasn't changed one iota.

Nick had a girlfriend, whom we all fancied, called Carol Hinves (pronounced Hinviz) and one summer's afternoon I invited her for a paddle in someone's canoe. We paddled out of Rosia Bay into open water and set off south – direction Morocco. I thought I must have been paddling quite strongly because the land to port was passing rapidly by, but I did not give it much thought, so entranced was I by the company I was keeping. But within minutes, thanks to a very powerful current the presence of which I had completely failed to appreciate, we were in the middle of the Straits of Gibraltar and the African coastline was approaching fast. As luck would have it a Spanish fishing boat saw us, or rather saw Carol in her rather fetching bikini, and pulled alongside to offer some welcome assistance.

Carol was invited aboard and it was suggested that if we wanted a tow I should remain in the canoe. They seemed friendly enough, and it never occurred to innocent me that their interest was other than polite fascination for the female form at close quarters. Luckily that was all it was, and we were soon cast off outside Rosia Bay to make a somewhat sheepish return to jeers and catcalls from a lot of rotters in the cheap seats and a severe dressing down from Mother Hinves, who was a well-nourished battle-axe.

In those days cigarette smoking was considered the height of sophistication and while cigarettes were jokingly referred to 'coffin nails' no one took serious notice of any possible health risk. Everyone smoked. A red tin of Benson & Hedges untipped cost 1/10d, about 9p today. I thought they were pretty good. My father, who smoked, was not best pleased that I had taken to the taste of tobacco and said that B&H cigarettes were for the fairies. Real men smoked Players' Perfectos Finos, which were twice the size of anything else on the market. He suggested I try one, hoping I would be thoroughly sick and kick the weed before it became a habit. I must confess I did feel a bit queasy after the first drag, but soon got the hang of it. Thanks, Dad. It was 10 years before I decided I had had enough of Virginian tobacco, but that's another story.

In the meantime things pottered on at Sherborne. I took my O Levels in the summer of 1959 and much to everyone's surprise I passed six, failing only Physics with Chemistry. That was partly due to fusing the laboratory while I was fiddling around with a Whetstone Bridge – whatever that was. I was quite pleased with myself, not without some justification, because I never managed to have much success in the exam room thereafter.

Anyway I spent the rest of that summer's holiday after the results arrived in a haze of glory. By this time my parents had moved from Main Street, Gibraltar, which my mother loathed because drunken sailors would insist on throwing up on the front step, to a 'hireling', a rented quarter up Europa Road called Lancaster House for reasons unknown, with magnificent views across the bay to Algeciras and the mountains of southern Spain. It had a huge balcony, the scene of many happy parties of all ages.

David Spedding came out for a couple of weeks and we used to party at night and recover in the mornings listening to Cole Porter on my Dansette record player. Songs like 'A Pretty Girl is like a Melody' and 'Dancing Cheek to Cheek'. Hot stuff I can tell you. Well, the dreadful Beatles and the equally wretched Rolling Stones were still at school. Elvis Presley was up and about but had limited appeal – to me, anyway.

Spedding was not one to let the grass grow under his feet as far as the local women were concerned. The Naval Harbour Master, a man called Herrick, had a particularly pretty daughter, Diana, aged about 13, whom David fancied like fun, but her father was not impressed and gave my father merry hell for inviting David to stay.

A rather more exotic acquaintance I made while we were in Gibraltar was an English boy a bit older than me who lived with his mother in La Linea, just across the border in Spain. He was called Colin Cresswell and his mother was a rather glamorous White Russian. I don't think they had much money, although Colin went to Rugby, but they did have two eagle owls, which lived with them in their drawing room and flew out of the window to prowl around at night. They were over two feet tall with fierce eyes and fearsome talons and they crapped all over the floor. I think Colin and his mother eventually gave them to London Zoo. Coincidentally I heard several years later that Colin had gone on to marry Leila Gregson, a very sexy sometime girlfriend of Spedding, who kindly passed her on to me, albeit rather briefly.

The next time Spedding came out was the following spring holiday after I had been close to death's door that February of 1960. I had had a great deal of trouble with my ears and sinuses ever since the car accident in Germany in 1946, mainly aching and a lot of discharge. I had been going to an ear nose and throat specialist in Harley Street called Bedford-Russell – quite the leading man in his day. Every morning I had to lie on a bed with my head over the side and put salt water down each nostril, leave it there for two minutes, then insert a large nozzle attached to a rubber bulb into each nostril with the bulb depressed. By releasing the pressure the contents of my sinuses were supposed to be discharged. Yuk. I did this every day for about two years until my mother thought I should see someone else and I was referred to another ENT wizard called John Musgrove and he came up with some alternative treatment.

At death's door

In any event, towards the end of February 1960 I was due to go up to London to see Musgrove and was feeling miserable with a filthy headache. I went into my study, which I shared with Spedding and du Pré, to collect my things before setting off for the station, only to be attacked by both of them with pillows and general mobbing up, probably because they thought I was a fraud and off for a good time. Anyway after a couple of bashes with a pillow to everyone's surprise I must have passed out, and the next thing I knew I was in the school sanatorium, but not for long. The matron decided something serious was amiss and had me taken to the local hospital for diagnosis.

By the afternoon she suspected I had contracted meningitis, possibly caused by an infected mastoid. The local doctor did not have a clue, which was not surprising as this condition was rare and is rarer still today. I was carted off in an ambulance to Weymouth Hospital, where there was a competent ENT surgeon called Whittaker. He operated at once to clear the mastoid and I had to undergo a lumbar puncture to draw off spinal fluid from around the brain, with no anaesthetic - jolly painful, in fact I had to have it done twice in the same spot (ouch x 2).

I was to stay in hospital for two weeks and my first visitor was my grandmother all the way from Brodsworth, which was my first indication that something had really been wrong. However when Granny walked into the ward, she didn't ask me how I was or anything. She asked if I had heard the news.

'What news?'
'Princess Margaret's got engaged, and guess what?'
'What?'
'It's not to Billy Wallace!'
'Who is Billy Wallace?'

'Don't be ridiculous.'

By this time I was beginning to wonder if there had been anything wrong with me after all and I was off on the road to recovery.

The first my parents heard of my incarceration was by letter from Mickey Walford, my housemaster, on receipt of which my mother started bouncing off the walls, cursing Mickey for not telephoning them. Mickey evidently thought he had done everyone a favour by keeping my situation low profile – despite the school having to pray for my recovery, which was much appreciated although I had no idea at the time.

The flights between Gibraltar and London were always booked up weeks in advance; why British European Airways (BEA), who had the state monopoly on the route did not think to put on extra flights is anyone's guess. Hurray for privatisation. Anyway every flight always had two seats reserved until the last minute for the Governor or other diplomats and as luck would have it the Governor did not need his, so Mum was able to take it to come and visit her sickly son, who was not so sickly by the time she arrived, so it was all a bit of an anti-climax.

After I was discharged we went by train to Doncaster for a few days R&R at Brodsworth until my condition had recovered enough to cope with the pressurisation of flight. We then made our way back to Gibraltar by way of a night in London. Mum suggested taking in a show – my choice, and I suggested *Irma la Douce*, a musical about a prostitute in Paris, all though I kept schtumm about this for fear of it being vetoed.

I don't think Mum cottoned on to begin with but when some male members of the cast lined up outside Irma's house, jiggling their trouser pockets so to speak and singing '*Irma la Douce, the perfect pocket Venus, who helps all Paris to relax, Irma la Douce, we have to share between us for just a thousand francs including tax*', it was all too much. My mother grabbed me by the hand, saying 'come on we're leaving, this is disgusting', and leave we did, climbing over several members of the audience, much to their annoyance. Instead we ended up watching the movie *Gigi*, a musical, which could in today's climate have been interpreted to be about paedophilia.

As result of this episode I missed about half that spring term and had an extra couple of weeks in Gibraltar with not a lot to do. As compensation David Spedding was invited out and we went back to our old routine. Dad must have been feeling flush because he took us all to stay for a week at a new hotel along the Spanish coast, called the Golf at Guardalmina. It was a very grand affair as far as we were concerned and amazingly good value at a pound sterling a head per day, including breakfast, lunch and dinner.

Needless to say there were several other families staying with some fresh young daughters who engaged our interest, although Spedding had a great deal more success than I did – or so he said. There is a photograph of him standing by a pool with a towel over his head with just his long nose poking through in an album over the caption 'The Arab' in my mother's hand. Prescient when he was to become one of the Foreign Office's leading Arabists before assuming responsibility as head of MI6.

Back to Sherborne

Back at school for the summer term of 1960, there was not much in the way of excitement except outings with the Burns, cricket with the Abbey House roving team, which was called the Duckhunters, playing several of the local villages. We would set off on our bikes with gear hanging round our necks and usually end up being soundly beaten. The local yokels took great delight in duffing up us public school boys, and bully for them. It was all in good spirits and they always produced a huge tea, served, needless to say, by some rather comely yokelettes.

Other sporting entertainment included taking up golf. My mother had some old hickory-shafted clubs, including woods with striking plates made of animal horn, and a few metal-shafted irons, all of which she passed on to me along with some very ancient balls. Thus armed I would set off, again on my bike, with an equally ancient golf bag over my back, and pedal up a 1.5 mile hill to Sherborne GC, usually with Spedding and McClintock. It was a pretty ropey nine-hole course but we struggled round it. We did not have much clue what we were doing, but it did sow the seeds of a lifelong pleasure, even if the quality of my game now is much the same as it was then.

It was round about that time that someone at school went to see the local Catholic priest to discuss the merits of Catholicism compared with the teachings of the Church of England, which after all had only come into being thanks to Henry VIII's desire for a male heir, not to mention the charms of Anne Boleyn. The priest turned out to be a charming man of the world in his sixties named Father

Andrache, whose considerable intellect was complemented by a keen appetite for spaghetti bolognese washed down with plenty of scrumpy, the local rough cider, while listening to Wagner and Prokofiev.

Quite soon a gang of us used to go and see Father, usually on a Sunday, and spend the day discussing everything under the sun while devouring bowls of spaghetti bolognese washed down with plenty of scrumpy while listening to Wagner and Prokofiev as well as enjoying the fragrant weed (cigarettes, in case you were wondering). Among Father's new fans were Spedding, Alastair Grayburn, who was also in Abbey House, and Dick Eyre in Westcott House as well as several others.

Father had no money and we had precious little, but we always bought the food as far as I remember and Father supplied the scrumpy. We had a lot of fun and must have gone back to the house in the evenings reeking of booze and fags. In my last few terms I went to see Father at least two or three times a week. He was a marvellous pressure release valve and peerless company.

Acquiring cigarettes needed a certain amount of subterfuge with the help of the local tailor's shop. Provided we gave them some business, there was a young assistant who would nip round to the nearby tobacconist and buy us packets of Senior Service.

I am sorry to say that all these distractions affected my attitude towards studying for my 'A' Levels, let alone the regulated life at Sherborne, for which I developed a deep resentment. I longed to escape, but I still had another year to go.

Goodbye Gib, hello Knightsbridge

At the end of the summer of 1960 Dad was posted back to London, and we took our leave of Gibraltar with much regret. We had had a very happy time there. It was a fun place to grow up, but as New Yorkers say of their splendid home town – a great place to live, but I wouldn't want to visit.

Dad went to work at what was then the War Office, now the Ministry of Defence, and was located in Lansdowne House on Berkeley Square. He had to find his own housing and took a lease on a flat on Harriet Street, between Sloane Street and Lowndes Square. If you have to live in London, that's not a bad place to be. Dibdins the Jewellers was on the ground floor as was the Gloucester Pub – all long gone.

Sloane Street then was blocks of genteel flats, some with shops on the ground floor, including a good greengrocer, Truslove & Hanson the bookshop and Cobbs the Butchers on the corner of Basil Street – none of the designer emporiums selling wildly overpriced clothes and shoes that saturate the area today. The first night we moved in my mother gave me a pound note and told me to buy some steaks in Cobbs. She was very cross when I returned with four steaks and no change. That was the first and last time I was sent shopping.

The holidays were a bit lonely to begin with as none of my friends lived in London. Spedding and du Pré would come up on the train from Henley and Staines, but otherwise it was quite quiet. Mum tried to relieve the monotony by asking the daughter of one of her old school friends to stay. She was called Sally Pond, and while she was pretty we did not find much in common. Much of the time was spent at perfunctory studying and in the cinema in Kensington High Street.

Last days at Sherborne

Come June 1961 the end of my schooldays was in sight, with just the hurdle of 'A' Levels to overcome. The end of the previous term saw my only success on the sports field – I was a member of the team, which won the inter-house hockey cup. How about that? When David Spedding was appointed to Head of MI6, the press were keen to find a photograph of him and the best they could come up with was our team photo, which some sneak had obligingly provided. I suspected it was a fellow named Robin Maconchy, since he was quoted widely in the papers at the time as knowing David. I do hope I'm not doing him an injustice.

It was about this time that the CCF held a 'night operation' on a military training area near Weymouth. I was instructed to set an ambush for the 'enemy' and lay in wait with my section. Soon after my vision had adjusted to the dark I saw not far away the glow of several luminous watches, which I assumed belonged to the enemy and ordered my section to attack. When the smoke cleared the watches turned out to be glow-worms and pretty soon I was demoted from corporal back to private. This debacle did not affect the interest in military matters of one of the boys in my section, Iain MacKay-Dick, who went on to Sandhurst and was commissioned into the Scots Guards. He ended a distinguished career as General Officer Commanding the Household Division – in charge of the Queen's Birthday Parade (Trooping the Colour), then GOC London District.

IT'S ALWAYS FRIDAY

Towards the end of every June, Sherborne School commemorated its foundation by Edward VI with a Commemoration Weekend, known as Commem. Leavers celebrated the end of their schooldays with a dance in the gym, known as the Commem Ball, to which parents were also invited (groan). Inevitably mine came. My date was the delectable Sue Ottaway, my adopted 'lonely girl', with whom I was corresponding at least once a week and of whom I had become very fond; she was a very good egg. We started out from the Burns' house, where we all changed. Darling Sue had borrowed an off-the-shoulder number from her elder sister which suited her to a tee. I was bowled over, as well as being transfixed as I wondered how it stayed up and how I could find somewhere to find out.

The 'somewhere' was one of the squash courts, but by the time it occurred to us that we ought to be rejoining the party, our absence had been noted by 'the Chief', as the Headmaster was known, and a search party was on the prowl. By the time we made it back to the party, my parents were mortified by my raffish behaviour, not least because the Chief was a friend who had been to stay with them at Sandhurst several times, and Dad gave me a piece of his mind in no uncertain terms in the street outside Abbey House under the fascinated gaze of most of its inhabitants. I was overcome with the humiliation of my circumstances. How poor Sue felt didn't bear thinking about. This wretched incident occurred just before my exams started and for a long time I was very distracted – upset for Sue and with my father. I still want to curl up with embarrassment at the memory, over fifty years later.

No longer a schoolboy

By mid-July 1961, Sherborne was done and dusted and I was glad to board a train and head for London, with no idea what to do next apart from wait for my 'A' Level results, although I was filled with foreboding that they would be a major disappointment. Sue was courageous enough to accept an invitation to come and stay at the flat, but while I still fancied her like fun, somehow the magic was not there anymore and that was the last time I saw her, until about thirty years later when she came up to me at a function at Grocers' Hall in the City and introduced herself. I am ashamed to say I did not recognise her, but she was still very attractive.

Not long after leaving school I went to a party in Henley with David Spedding and his gang. I travelled by train from Paddington to Reading. In those days the carriages had doors which could only be opened by a handle on the outside. The luckless passenger nearest the door and ready to alight had to pull down the window and fix it down by hooking a leather strap attached to the top of the window on to an eye on the middle of the door just below the bottom of the window. Sounds complicated? Well on this occasion it was all too much for me and I failed to secure the window properly. As result, just as I put my head out of the window to open the door, the window shot up and hit me hard in the face, breaking one of my front teeth – blood everywhere.

David and his mother Joan were meeting me and said I looked like Dracula, so having told British Rail what had happened I was wheeled off to the Spedding dentist in Reading to be cleaned up and a temporary cap fitted. I eventually had a permanent crown installed and was awarded £30 for my pains by BR. Not enough, as it turned out. The crown was forever being replaced at ever-increasing expense.

While waiting for the 'A' level results, Alastair Grayburn, whom I had known as a child during the war and later at Sherborne, kindly invited me to stay with his parents at their home near Aldeburgh on the Suffolk coast, where we golfed and partied. Grayburn Senior was a jobber in the City, a profession that matched stock buyer to stock seller but ceased to exist with the 'Big Bang' in October 1986 when the Stock Exchange went 'on line'. He had also been in Abbey House along with his brother John, who, as mentioned earlier, had won a particularly gallant Victoria Cross during the Battle of Arnhem and whose actions were immortalised in the film *A Bridge Too Far*.

In any event I must have been a very fickle character. No sooner was Sue Ottaway out of sight than I met a very sophisticated blonde from Thorpeness a mile or so up the beach from Aldeburgh, also partying, and I remember having a happy time walking her home on a couple of occasions late at night. I never saw Alastair again after that visit. He became a doctor and was killed in a car accident in Kenya some time in the late seventies.

From Aldeburgh I travelled by train to Burntisland on the north shore of the Firth of Forth to stay with friends from Gibraltar days, followed by a visit to Brodsworth on the way south and then with nothing better to do, I accompanied my family for a wet fortnight on the Brittany coast. It was there that my dreaded 'A' Level results arrived, and as I had feared I had only managed passes at 'AO' Level.

Now what to do? Well the parents rallied round. Dad said I had to have 'A' levels and I should cram for them. My friend Nick Rowe from Gibraltar had been in the same fix a year before and he attended Davis Laing & Dick (DLD as it was known), a crammer of some repute in Bayswater, when he succeeded where Wellington College had failed.

The 'Crammer' and beyond

By this time Dad had been posted to Germany and the flat in Harriet Street had been sold. I was considered too young to live in a bedsit so, come mid-September 1961, I was billeted in a rather scruffy but perfectly adequate hotel in Pembridge Gardens, a stone's throw from the crammer in one direction and Notting Hill Gate tube station in the other – perfect. I spent three months at DLD studying for the same History and English 'A' Levels as at Sherborne, but following a completely different syllabus. It speaks volumes for DLD that I obtained good passes in both subjects in less than a third of the time. I suspect that the original failure was partially thanks to the quality of teaching at school, the confined atmosphere and the effect of the Commem drama, which by now I accepted was somewhat of my own making.

DLD was by no means all work and no play, oh no. There was a fellow student called David Brazier, who had been at Lancing, and was hoping for a place at Cambridge on the back of his prowess on the squash court. He played for Sussex and the England Under-Twenties. I thought I was a reasonably competent squash player and invited him to play at The Senior, Dad's club in Pall Mall, where I played fairly regularly under the watchful eye of the resident professional,

Ali Akbar Khan, a Pakistani international. Ali Akbar's face was a picture when I turned up with David – not surprising really; I was completely flayed just knocking up.

There were quite a few other party animals at DLD, including a wicked character called Wayne Sonnis, who lived with his mother on the river in Barnes, and was either a huge success later in life or in prison. My mother gave me the use of her Fiat 500, which she called Buzzy (short for the Buzz Box), in which I had learnt to drive, and this was the gateway to freedom. I managed to get thirteen people in and on it one night, before being stopped by the Law.

Needless to say there was a very pretty girl in my class... this one was called Maryann Jupp, and she lived with her widowed mother in Pinner. She used to stay back at DLD doing her homework in the evenings and I would do mine at the hotel. She would then come up to my room and we would test each other on what we had learnt, or at least that's what I told the management.

It was on a trip out to leafy Pinner to stay with Maryann and her mother that I managed to write the Fiat off. Some clown had broken down in the middle of the Edgware Road in a very ancient Austin. He had his flicker (indicator) out to turn left, but was stationary, so I decided to pass him on his inside. At that moment his car came to life and he pulled over and into the poor old Fiat. The Austin was made of solid steel, whereas 'Buzzy' the Fiat was all paint and ended up a squashed heap on the side of the road. There was hardly a scratch on the Austin, damn it, but the driver was an awkward so-and-so. Years later I went to a meeting in the West End of London. During the introductions one man looked at me and said 'Yes, Mr Youens – we've met before, in less happy circumstances'. He did not enlarge and I did not take the bait, but I always wondered if he was Austin Man.

Christmas 1961 was spent in Germany with the parents, who were based in Rheindahlen, a purpose built army base not far from Düsseldorf, which was the headquarters of the British Army of the Rhine. There were plenty of parties, although I was a bit younger than the young officers, who were mostly dashing, or they thought they were, and had the pick of the women.

The women included Caroline Stares, whom my mother claimed had been my first girlfriend when I was three and she was four, the first time we went to Germany soon after the war. Caroline hardly threw a glance in my direction with plenty of more interesting distractions, some married. Sally Charles, Georgina Pilitz and Rosie Turner-Cain are names which also trip off the tongue. Sally was to appear frequently over the next fifty years, Georgina I shared a flat with for a few weeks in 1964, more of her later, but Rosie disappeared off the map early on – more's the pity, as she was the most attractive of the lot with a flawless complexion.

It was around this time I met my future Best Man, Mike Dewar, whose father was also stationed in Rheindahlen. Mike was a cadet at Sandhurst learning to become an army officer, and he went on to serve with distinction before retiring to form his own public relations business as well as forever appearing on TV and radio as a commentator on military events around the world. He was one of a select few whose children's school fees were indirectly financed by the likes of Saddam Hussein.

After Sandhurst Mike won a military scholarship to Oxford, and I was lucky enough to attend many of the balls and parties during his time there. At one stage he shared a house with several other undergraduates including Charlie Messenger, Mike Houdret and David Gyle-Thompson, of whom more later. The walls in the only bathroom in this establishment were covered floor to ceiling with naked ladies of apparently very easy virtue and the cistern above the lavatory was best described as a mammary montage. That was all very fine, but at parties the place seemed to be permanently occupied.

CHAPTER 5

Switzerland

The plan after I left school had been to spend a year or two at a European university and Lausanne in Switzerland was the academy of choice, but that had to be put on hold on account of my exam results and the start date put back until April 1962. This meant after the Christmas break I had three months on the loose. It was in Rheindahlen that I had my first job as a rather half-baked store detective in a supermarket run by the NAAFI (Naval Army & Air Forces Institute).

I didn't last long as it was deadly dull wandering around pushing a trolley pretending to be a shopper in the hope of catching some villain. The women shelf stackers had a bit of fun sneaking the odd packet of Tampax into my basket in the hope of causing embarrassment. They were disappointed when they had to draw my attention to what they had done, and even more so when it was clear I had no idea what purpose Tampax served.

Happily the chap who ran NAAFI took pity on me and suggested I might like to go and work in Winterberg, a ski resort in the Harz Mountains where the army went for training and NAAFI ran a hotel-cum-mess for officers. I was assigned to work in Reception. This was a lot more fun, and so were the receptionists, Helga and Heidi. There were a couple of German waiters who took me under their wing and taught me the rudiments of skiing. This was no easy task in a pair of ordinary army boots on hickory skis wearing jeans and a mackintosh. There was little snow and a lot of rain, but I persevered and soon got the bug.

Lausanne University Finishing School

In no time it was April 1962 and I was packed off on the train to Lausanne, where I had been booked into a student hostel of sorts to the north of the town run by the wife of one of the university professors. There was a mixed bag of us lodging there, including a Swedish princess and Lawrence Levy, who became a good friend. We were all attending the Ecole de Français Moderne, which was attached to the Faculté de Lettres at the University. The place was stuffed with Brits, none of whom had the slightest intention of doing much work, and those foreigners who were there all wanted to speak English, so in effect a good time was had by all.

I became friends with John Dunn-Yarker, who was a bit older than me and had been teaching at an English prep school called Woodcote House before Lausanne. It seems he fell for the Matron; history does not recall whether she fell for him, but in any event he was asked to leave. As luck, for me, would have it his parents lived in a splendid château on Lake Geneva near Vevey and pretty soon I was invited to stay.

It was called le Château de la Tour de Peilz, and it came complete with its own marina as well as hot and cold running servants. Adrienne Dunn-Yarker, John's mother, was a formidable matron, who luckily took to me and made me very welcome. Her grandfather had been a doctor in the British Army stationed in Egypt at the turn of the century, and he had been instrumental in providing medical facilities to help the local government cope with a serious plague which was affecting many of the populace. As result he was given some largesse by way of thanks from the last Egyptian Pharaoh, King Farucq, and sensibly he decided to locate it in Switzerland, using part of it to acquire the château.

John Dunn-Yarker senior was a director of the General Trading Company, a high end gift and soft furnishing emporium which used to be near Sloane Square in London. John junior had younger twins, Marion and David, who also became friends. Apart from the château, the Dunn-Yarkers owned a very comfortable flat in Château d'Oex, a small ski village in the Gstaad Valley, about 90 minutes' drive from Lausanne. I was to become a frequent visitor, both at the château in summer and the flat in winter.

The waiters

In the summer vacation in 1962 I decided to try and find some work, and together with David Curtis, another toiler at the university, we found jobs as waiters at the Hotel

Victoria in Wengen, a ski resort in the Bernese Oberland of Switzerland. David went on a day ahead of me and I drove to Lauterbrunnen, where I parked the car. By this time I had been lent my mother's Mini Minor, which was a bilious shade of green and a grand little machine. On the map Wengen was about half a mile away but in practice it was 1,600ft up an almost sheer cliff and only approachable by a railway train operating on cogs.

David met me at the station. The scenery was stunning, with the peaks of the Mönch and Jungfrau mountains towering above us in the bright sunshine. Unfortunately David's face did not complement the view. 'It's a hotel for Jews' he whispered, in case any nearby might take offence. 'So what?' I asked in all innocence, not thinking Jews were any different to the rest of humanity, and that was in the days long before political correctness had ever been thought of. 'Well, you wait and see,' said my friend, giving me a very old-fashioned look, and we walked up to the hotel.

It did not take long to discover that there is a world of difference between highly religious Jews and easy-going Christians like ourselves – the hotel was a religious retreat and there were all manner of rules with which we had to comply, particularly during the Jewish weekend. The hotel was owned by a Swiss-German ogre, whom we had to address as Madame, but whom one day I came across in the kitchen stirring a cauldron of soup all the while shaving her chin with an electric razor. She looked as if she had been a guard at a concentration camp, and certainly behaved towards us like one.

David and I were on duty immediately and I made the first gaffe by greeting a guest on arrival into the dining room. He looked furious, went to wash his hands in a basin by the door, then made for his table, where he grabbed a bread roll, broke it and crammed some of it in his mouth. Still chewing and spitting crumbs in my direction he cursed me for speaking to him before he had 'broken bread'.

There was one sitting for dinner and a set menu, the first course being fish. Once everyone was seated David and I started to place individual servings in front of the guests. It so happened I was first to put a plate down in front of a man who immediately burst into song, well a dirge more like, directly at me. I almost dropped the other dishes I was carrying in shock, but it transpired that whoever was served first had to sing for his supper.

During the Sabbath none of the guests was permitted to 'work'. This meant they could not turn a light on or off, or even open a letter. Furthermore they could not ask anyone else, i.e. gentiles like us, to do the job for them. Instead if they wanted a light switched on, they would to say 'it's dark in here' and we would have to switch the light on. All the kitchens were below the dining room and in the ordinary way of things the food was delivered by service lift. However electricity was forbidden during the Sabbath, so we had to carry all the food up a narrow staircase. On one occasion I managed to drop a plate load of trout down the none-too-clean stone steps. We scooped the food back onto the serving dish and the guests ate it, none the wiser.

I can tell you this was not a lot of fun. We had hardly any time off and worked every day from about 6.30am until 10pm, no weekends. Well, after a fortnight of this nonsense we decided to up sticks and hand in our notice. When we collected our wages I was paid less than David and on enquiry I was told that I had failed to book a boiled egg for one of the guests on two mornings and what he would have been charged was deducted, with no allowance for the cost of the egg he didn't eat. I was not impressed and could have taken a dim view of Jewish people and their religion, but for what happened next.

The Levys

David's parents had taken a villa near Ventimiglia on the French-Italian border overlooking the Mediterranean, but they weren't due to arrive for several days. However I remembered that one of my housemates in Lausanne was staying with his parents at the Reserve Hotel in Beaulieu not far away, so we decided to drive down to the south of France anyway and call in on them, thinking we might be fed and they might know somewhere we could stay until the Curtis parents showed up.

What I had not thought about was that my friend was called Lawrence Levy and I suppose had I been less naive it might have occurred to me that Levy was a Jewish name. David and I pitched up at the hotel, which was a classy establishment, right on the seafront complete with pool, tennis courts and a very far cry from the Victoria in Wengen. We were welcomed with open arms by Lawrence, who was more than ready to party and took us to meet his family, including his pretty sister Miriam.

The senior Levys could not have been more charming or generous, and they invited us to lunch wanting to hear all about Lausanne from another prospective and what we had been doing since the end of term. Well, we bowled in all wide-eyed and innocent and regaled them with the stories of our experiences and were rather surprised they did not roar with laughter and commiserate. Instead they stared at us open-mouthed in horror and what transpired to be embarrassment.

'There is no reason why you should know' said Lawrence's father, 'but we are Jewish ourselves and I can tell you that while I have heard of some of the customs you're describing, it is certainly not the way most of us live and I don't want either of you going through life with a negative view of us as a race.' With that he excused himself and disappeared off in the direction of Reception to return moments later and announce, 'as your parents, David, are not due for another three nights, I have arranged accommodation here until they arrive and I hope you will be our guests'.

Needless to say we were delighted to accept and lived like lords for the next three days. The hotel was owned by the Clicquot champagne family and it was rumoured that the old widow at the corner table in the dining room was indeed the La Veuve Clicquot. We were very reluctant to leave when the time came. I have never forgotten their generosity and I don't suppose my friend David has either.

Provence

The Curtises were also very kind and generous and a good time was had by all in Ventimiglia, where I must have stayed for a week before deciding to head back to Switzerland, the Dunn-Yarkers then going home to Germany. The rest of that summer of 1962 passed in a bit of a haze. The Dunn-Yarker boys, John and David, came up to stay at Rheindahlen, where John took a fancy to my mother, much to my embarrassment. He had a thing about older women. Then in September we set off back down south in convoy to stay with a friend called François Mason and his attractive young wife Marie; they had a summer place near Ménèbres in Provence.

Provence was waiting to be discovered by the wretched Peter Mayle and his very successful efforts to gentrify the area, thanks to his book *A Year in Provence*. Back then all the local villages were populated by peasant farmers, the fare was basic and the local wines were one better than rough vinegar – hold on, they *were* rough vinegar. François and Marie were trailblazers, if they had but known it. They lived in a ruined farmhouse and we three boys shared a room with outside facilities. They were generous to a fault, and by way of a thank you we took them to a show in Cavaillon, a small town 10km away.

None of us had any idea what we were in for, but the show turned out to be a series of rather erotic skits, each a bit more saucy than the last, interspersed with some comedy routines. One story was about a doctor who had a patient with a worm in his stomach, which he could see by looking up the patient's rectum with a torch.

'Is there a cure, Doctor?' the worried man asked.

'Don't fuss. I've seen this before' he replied. 'I want you to go home and follow a strict diet. Every day at noon I want you to eat a baguette followed by a sausage. Come back in three weeks.'

The patient was a bit suspicious, but decided to follow the advice and came back in three weeks.

'Off with your trousers and up on the bench, face against the wall' instructed the doctor, 'knees up by your chin.' The patient did as told. Out came the torch and the doctor bent to his task.

'Yes, all is going to plan and the worm is fattening up nicely. He even winked at me. Keep following the diet – baguette followed by a sausage at noon and come back in three weeks to be here a quarter to noon.'

Well the poor patient was so far in he decided to play along, and back he came as instructed.

'Off with your trousers and up on the bench, face against the wall, knees up by your chin.'

The patient once again followed orders, the doctor bent to his arse, 'yes, it's ready' he said, 'stay right where you are and don't move'.

But after a while as the clock approached midday the doctor did not appear to be doing anything apart from shuffling around the surgery. The patient looked over his shoulder to see what was going on and immediately saw a fresh baguette on the bench and the doctor approaching him with a mallet in his hand.

'Whatever do you think you are doing?' he cried.

'Ah' said the doctor, 'in a moment I am going to ask you to eat the baguette and then we wait.'

'Wait for what?'

'Well I expect the worm to stick his head out of your arse and say "and the sausage?" at which point I'll hit him on the head with the mallet.'

This brought the house down and the audience must have taken five minutes to recover. It probably doesn't play so well from the page, but told in Provençal French by a very droll comedian we went on laughing for a week and I have repeated the story on occasions ever since.

Back to Lausanne, and a brush with royalty

After a week with the Masons, it was time to return to Lausanne and our studies. This term I was billeted midtown with a Grande Madame and three or four girls, two of who were Canadians and cousins. The pretty one was called Tracy, who turned out to be racy. Years later I happened to be browsing through an edition of Playboy Magazine, as one does, and came across a photographic spread of girls from Canada. There was racy Tracy, leaving not much of her glory to the imagination.

Apart from trying to apply myself to my studies in this distracting company, I was invited at weekends to stay with the Dunn-Yarkers at their chalet flat in Château d'Oex. John Dunn-Yarker, who had been brought up on skis, had not mastered the art and I, who had only started the previous winter, was at least the same standard. Luckily there was a third member of our gang called Patrick Starns, a Canadian who was highly skilled, and I was able to follow him down the mountains with some success.

Chateau d'Oex was home to several finishing schools for girls from good families - very few girls went to university in those days. Their main objective, after school, was to find a man, settle down, look after him and start a family, and these finishing schools showed them how. Where did it all go so wrong? In any event the village was packed with young ladies in search of companionship and I became quite friendly with an aspiring model called Liz Spence who had come all the way from Ripon, Yorkshire. More of Liz later.

We had the run of the Gstaad valley to ski, but by far the best area was called Les Monts Chevreuils, a long downhill run of about four miles over varied terrain and great fun. The main drawback was the antiquated ski lift. It consisted of an overhead steel cable moving at about 6mph, onto which we had to attach a belt, which hooked round our backsides and had to be held in place for the entire uphill ride of at least 20 minutes. That winter of 1962-3 was one of the coldest on record and we skied in temperatures way below zero. As a result one's hands tended to freeze however many times we switched our grip on the lift, it took some time once we had arrived at the top to thaw out sufficiently to be able to ski back down.

Not only were our hands frozen but also our faces. On one descent I fell on my ski pole and managed to dislodge the crown on my front tooth, the one I had bust at Reading Station two years before. The crown was lost in the snow. The dentist this time was a professor at Lausanne University called Dr Rabal, who was well past his sell by date and had not opened a dental manual since the war. I think we are talking the Great War here. By the time the new crown was ready, the skin on either side of the gap had grown over and had to be removed in order for the crown to be fitted. I assumed that Dr Rabal would use some form of anaesthetic, but no chance. He cauterised the skin with a hot wire. I can still smell the burning flesh.

One time on the slopes I met my ski instructor friend from Ménèbres, François Mason, while he was giving David Niven, the actor, a lesson. Niven lived in Château d'Oex and

I had already met his sons David and Jamie through the Dunn-Yarkers. François introduced us and I was very flattered to be told by the hero of *Around the World in 80 Days* that he had heard about me from the boys. He was as charming in the flesh as he appeared on screen. He was polishing up his skiing skills for his forthcoming role in *The Pink Panther*.

Some time later Patrick Starns and I were driving my Mini up an icy lane to reach the ski lift when two cars blocked our path. The rear one had Monegasque (Monaco) plates and I recognised Jamie Niven in the passenger seat, so we chatted while the car in front pulled off the road to allow us to pass. Jamie's car had chains whereas the Mini only had snow tyres, and I knew I would have a problem regaining traction, so I asked if he and his driver, who looked vaguely familiar, would give us a push. I put Patrick, who was a lot lighter than me, in the driver's seat and the three of us pushed him off. I leapt in and we were away.

Some time later that day I met Jamie again on the slopes and asked who his driver was. Prince Rainier, I was told. Well this man was probably one of the richest in the world, thanks to his Principality, and one of the most famous, having married a few years earlier the American film star Grace Kelly, one of the most beautiful women of her generation. And there he was happily pushing my humble Mini up a back lane in the Swiss Alps. Had I arrived or what?

At the end of the spring term I drove Patrick to Bonn, where his father was the Canadian Ambassador, dropped him off and carried on to my parents. We had driven overnight without stopping apart from fuel, and when I tried to climb out of the car on arrival in Rheindahlen and swung my feet onto the ground, my legs had gone to sleep and collapsed under me. I lay on the ground for what seemed ages until the circulation eventually returned and I was able to stagger into the house.

I stayed one more term at Lausanne, where I was achieving very little apart from having a good time with a very jolly crowd including a new girlfriend called Harriet Eeles, who came from Sutton Veny near Warminster, not far from where we live now. When I first met her, she was on the arm of a rather scruffy American, but that all changed when about 20 of us went for a long weekend in Burgundy with one of the professors. He took us on a tour of the cathedrals – Vézelay, I particularly remember, despite the distractions of Harriet, who was quite a catch - very pretty, with long elegant legs and a figure to die for. She was very bright too, so what she was doing with me, heaven knows. There are a whole lot of rather soppy photographs somewhere taken by Lawrence Levy – unless they have been destroyed by the First Wife.

CHAPTER 6

Looking for a career

By April 1963 it was time to think about a career, but I had no idea what I wanted to do apart from try and earn some money as easily as possible. My friend David Curtis from waiting the previous summer was also at a loose end. His mother gave us both an introduction to Harry Warr, a celebrated wine merchant and partner in the city firm of George, Idol, Chapman with offices in St Mary-at-Hill off Eastcheap and cellars in Wapping. He agreed to take us on as unpaid trainees to gain a taste, or not, for the business.

We pitched up on a sunny morning in early May at the company's cellars near the Prospect of Whitby, a pub on the river near the docks. Judge Jeffries, he of the Bloody Assizes, used to live nearby and there is a noose in the bar in honour of his custom. It was a pretty rough area, but the pub was popular with Americans looking for quaint England.

The wine cellars were just that - cellars, with bins of

bottles, each bin containing up to 144 bottles with the name of the vineyard, shipper and year written in chalk on a piece of slate hanging on a hook above. The wine was mostly claret shipped from various châteaux in Bordeaux by Eschenaur, a leading dealer in the area. Otherwise it was port blended and bottled by Dow's, who are still regarded as one of the best, although port has rather gone out of fashion.

There were several permanent members of staff, including a manager and two general factotums called Bert and Fred. Bert tried to convince me early in our acquaintance that you could tell how many women a man had 'known' by the number of wrinkles on his willy, and Fred's celebrated party trick when we were bottling port was to take a full bottle off the line and drink it in one go without falling over.

On Fridays at midday David and I would go to the company's office in the City to learn about wine, which mostly involved tasting about eight different varieties, trying to recognise the individual flavours and then identifying them by tasting them again, this time blind. We were supposed to spit the wine out rather than swallow it, which seemed to us to rather a waste, so by the time the sandwiches arrived we were a bit wasted ourselves. Eschenaur imported Château d'Yquem, the much celebrated pudding wine - I can still remember the taste 50 years later, so maybe I did learn something.

At that time I was sharing a bedsit in Cornwall Gardens, off Gloucester Road in South Kensington, with my school friend Mike du Pré, who was an audit clerk studying for his Chartered Accountancy exams with Peat, Marwick, Mitchell, now part of PricewaterhouseCoopers. We had a room on the fourth floor with a basin and a couple of gas rings. There was a communal bathroom and lavatory on the landing. The landlady lived in the basement and our room overlooked her patio.

One Saturday night Mike was away and Mike Dewar, my army friend from Rheindahlen, who was now an undergraduate at Oxford, came for the night. We had been out late and feeling jaded the following morning I started a fry-up for a late breakfast. Having cooked the bacon. I pushed it to one side of the pan and cracked a couple eggs into the fat. The second egg was very bad and the smell on top of a hangover was almost too much, so without a second's hesitation, let alone any forethought, I threw the lot out of the window. Unfortunately at this moment the landlady was hanging out the washing and her baby was lying in its pram. To this day I cannot remember quite how I managed to sweet talk her into letting us stay on.

It was round about this time - the summer of 1963 – that I met up again with Liz Spence, late of Château d'Oex, now training as a model, with assignments in London and elsewhere. I used to drive up to Ripon for weekend parties and sometimes we would meet at her parents' flat in Ivor Court near Regents Park. They kindly took me to a showing of *Lawrence of Arabia* at a cinema near Victoria Station, soon after it came out. Afterwards we went to an Italian restaurant, which may have been a first for Mrs Spence, who seemed a bit nonplussed by the menu. Eventually she decided on soup for starters and told the waiter she would have minestrone - but confused him, and the rest of us, by pronouncing it 'miner-stroan'. I know it was cruel, but I didn't know whether to laugh or cry.

RICHARD YOUENS

Discovering insurance

It must have been around this time I gave up on the wine trade and started answering adverts for various forms of employment. I ended up taking a job with an insurance company in Pall Mall, where it turned out the manager, Bob Braun, had played cricket and rugger with my father and his brothers in Sheffield. The company was called the Atlas Life Assurance Company and it was part of the Royal Exchange Insurance Group. I was interviewed at the Royal Exchange in the City by the Bank of England and opposite the Mansion House and thought I was joining a pretty upmarket business. Little did I know.

The Atlas was a small life and general underwriter whose main account was the Iraqi Petroleum Company's pension fund. How exciting is that? Having gone through the rigmarole of signing up, including a full medical and joining their pension fund, I decided I was honour bound to give it a shot. As I said earlier, I hadn't a clue what I wanted to do. Quite sad, but there we are. It worked out in the end.

One weekend in late November that year I was invited to stay with the Spence family at their home near Ripon and set off after work on Friday November 22 in my very loyal Mini Minor up the A1. The M1, England's very first motorway, was still under construction in 1963 and its open sections were no good to me. On arrival chez Spence the family turned out to meet me as I parked. They all had long faces and I thought some member of the family had died. In a way they had: President Kennedy had been assassinated a few hours earlier in Dallas, Texas. I can picture the scene outside Liz's house as if it was yesterday.

Kennedy was, to us young, the great hope of the future. With him, politics became interesting. His speech inviting Americans to ask not what America could do for them but what they could do for America was fresh leadership after Profumo's disgrace in the Christine Keeler affair and the dreary administration of Harold Macmillan.

My generation and older always remember where they were when they heard the news about Kennedy's death. Equally I can remember where I was (shaving at home in Singapore) when I heard Lord Mountbatten had been assassinated in Northern Ireland and (about to shave at home near Hungerford) when Princess Diana had been killed in Paris.

The Profumo Affair had caused great excitement earlier in 1963 and the press had a field day every day with new revelations about John Profumo MP, Minister of War and a member of Harold Macmillan's cabinet, who had dallied with Christine Keeler, a very attractive 21-year old lady of easy virtue. She was also said to be seeing a Russian diplomat, and since we were in the middle of the so-called Cold War with the Soviets, this was not a 'good thing'.

Christine had a friend called Mandy Rice-Davies who was in a similar line of business, also frolicking with the glitterati, but more of her later. Profumo denied any impropriety in Parliament, was found to be lying and fell on his sword. To his eternal credit he spent the rest of his life in sackcloth and ashes doing charitable works in the East End of London. His wife, a famous actress at the time called Valerie Hobson, stood by him throughout – which, according to my friend the actress Cherry London, no great admirer she, was quite out of character, but she probably didn't have much choice.

Harold Macmillan also resigned soon afterwards, allegedly on account of ill health. The Conservatives staggered on for another year under Alec Douglas Home, a lovely man but past his prime, and at the next election in 1964 Harold Wilson arrived on a Labour landslide.

While all this was going on I had started work with the Atlas Assurance Co. Ltd. in Pall Mall, London SW1 in their Life Department on £350 a year plus a London weighting allowance of £70. Imagine. The people were lovely but the work was dire. The department manager was a woolly-haired 30-year-old with a bushy moustache called Tom Bissell and I was the junior clerk. I suppose with a public school accent I must have been mobbed up, but everyone was friendly enough and we were all clock-watchers. The hours were 9 to 5 with an hour for lunch, with 3/- (15p) Luncheon Vouchers which were tax free, and with which one was able to buy some nourishment, but not much.

By this time I was sharing a basement flat in Norland Square off Holland Park Avenue, not far from Shepherds Bush. However before I moved from Cornwall Gardens I had split with Liz from Ripon, thanks to the intervention of my Aunt Margaret. You see I wasn't that loyal and had met up with one of David Spedding's exes, the afore-mentioned Leila Greyson, who was part of the Henley crowd. She knew which way was up in no uncertain terms. Anyway Liz was down for a weekend and I took her to meet Aunty Margie, who said 'How do you do, Leila?' Liz was unimpressed and after some discussion I had to admit my infidelity, so that was that.

My flatmate in Norland Square was some fellow I had met at a party with David Spedding in Henley - Charlie someone, fat, jolly and a couple of centuries after his time. Mention someone's name and he would exclaim "stap me vitals, is he still alive?" The flat was very damp, so much so that if you pressed a plastic glass to any wall it was full of water in no time. I jest, but you get the idea.

Some time in November 1963 my mother pitched up from Germany to inspect these quarters, took one look at them and removed me to a bedsit in the Finborough Road near Earls Court, where I stayed for about six months. The bedsit was perfectly comfortable but pretty depressing and when not on the tiles, which wasn't often due to limited funds, I studied for my insurance qualification, which was seriously depressing too, but I plugged along.

Outside entertainment mainly involved hanging out with a group of people from my Gibraltar days, including Carolyn Buttenshaw and Lindy Allen, at a pub in the Fulham Road called the Crown. Their group included some petrolheads keen on vintage cars and at one stage I was seriously considering turning in my Mini and buying an old Bentley. However my mother disabused me of that notion, saying that her father, who had several Bentleys, always found he was expected to buy the drinks. I stuck with the Mini.

Lindy Allen popped out of the woodwork recently. My son Christian and I had planned to golf in Norfolk and, as we needed somewhere to stay, the secretary of Brancaster Golf Club suggested a local B&B run by Lindy someone, not Allen. Unsuspecting, I called and made the arrangements. When I gave my name the Lindy someone said 'not *the*

Richard Youens?" In the end we never went - grandchildren ill or some such.

In May 1964 I hit 21. Dad was going to be in Berlin on business over the weekend of my birthday and invited me to join him and Mum there. The night of my birthday I was introduced to some officers in the Somerset & Cornwall Light Infantry who were kind enough to take me on the Town. I can't remember much about the evening except we went to Maxxims, a nightclub on the Kurfürstendamm, which was and still is the main drag in town. I thought the girls in the cabaret were quite stunning and then was quite stunned to be told they were all men - indeed the one who had particularly caught my eye because of her endless legs was an American GI. We moved on later to a place called Smokeys, where the women were real.

To celebrate my coming of age, my parents later threw a cocktail party for me in the army quarter of one of Dad's fellow chaplains, which was very conveniently inside Wellington Barracks and the nearest private house to Buckingham Palace. Sadly it has since been demolished to make way for progress. Afterwards we went to dinner in a pub called the Rose, no longer there, in Petty France just behind the barracks. It was one of my haunts and the chap who owned it was a friend. The food was good and I was walking on air with a new girlfriend called PJ Foxley-Norris; I always wondered what became of her.

Rent-a-gent

In the summer of 1964 I decided I had had enough on Finborough Road and moved in with five women in Doughty

Street in WC1, way off my usual beaten track. The connection was a girl I mentioned earlier called Georgina Pilitz, whom I knew from Rheindahlen. Two of the girls were nurses at nearby Great Ormond Street Hospital. They were all committed elsewhere. I was just there to help with the rent and slept on a sofa in the drawing room while I decided what to do next. One of the nurses was engaged to a soldier, whom she had known all her life, and neither of them had ever looked at anyone else. They were married soon after I met them and shortly thereafter he was killed in a road accident in Germany. Life can be very cruel.

Some time in July 1964 I walked into a flat-finding agency, subsequently referred to by us as 'Rent-a-Gent" in Beauchamp Place, off Knightsbridge, and they sent me to investigate a flat at the end of the street, landlord Mr Nicholas Hallings-Pott. I was interviewed over a glass of sherry, all very civilised, by Pott and his flatmate Martin Whitfield, both Wykehamists, and was taken on. The third floor flat was what New Yorkers call a 'cold-water walk up' – in our case a gas geyser in the kitchen supplied the only hot water in the place and there was no lift. It was on the corner of Pont Street and Walton Street, three floors up. There was a large living room, two bedrooms - one single, one double and the usual offices.

I was assigned the single room and moved in almost immediately, finally to move out in January 1969 four and a half years later. I say 'finally' because I was taken on the understanding that I was replacing a third occupant named Gerry Waterlow, who was on a six-month assignment out of town. He wanted his bed back on his return. Happily on his return in March 1965 he announced that he was to marry that July, and the lucky girl was one Diana Skyrme.

None of this meant anything to me, but it did when I met her. Diana was on the stage and appearing in TV commercials. She was from another planet: beautiful, elegant, rich and friendly but slightly aloof - jet set in motion. We were all agog. I moved out as agreed, but on the understanding I could have my bed back after the wedding. I spent the break in yet another bedsit, this time in Markham Square off King's Road, where a delightful girl called Jackie Ballantyne helped me with my homework.

Gerry and Diana were kind enough to include me in their wedding celebrations, where to my dismay everyone was in morning dress except me. Diana's family had a major involvement with Tate & Lyle, the sugar producers, and the wedding was a grand affair. Little did I know it but the Skyrmes were friendly with a local family called Methven who were all present, including their younger daughter Annabelle, aged 16, who was to become my own darling bride six-plus years later. Needless to say neither of us have any recollection of the other at the time, but that was all to change.

Forty years later when we were planning to move but hadn't decided where to, Diana insisted we looked at a cottage in her village of Rushall, near Pewsey in Wiltshire and we've lived there happily ever after. Sadly Gerry died of Alzheimer's disease a few years ago, but Diana is cracking on in great form. I've been very lucky with my friends.

The Inspector

As far as the day job was concerned, by this time I had been transferred from the Life Department to work in sales as an

'Inspector' – well, that's what it said on my business card: 'DRB Youens, Inspector, Royal Exchange Assurance'. I was up there with the greats. I was handed a bunch of Rolodex-type cards with the names of solicitors, bank managers and the like who had clients who needed life assurance (even if they didn't know it), and I was expected to call on them regularly to encourage them to sell Royal Exchange products to their unsuspecting clients for mortgage protection and the like. Can life get more exciting?

My new appointment coincided with the arrival of a new manager called Tom Hutchings from up north. He called me and all the other Inspectors into his office and explained that he wanted us to be the best of the best and be completely fearless about whom we were dealing with, be they prince or pauper. He did give us one memorable piece of advice when dealing with princes and the like. We were not to be put off and remember, 'even the Queen has to go to the toilet in the morning'. Never thought about that before.

By this time the Royal Exchange Group, which consisted of the said Royal Exchange Assurance, my alma mater the Atlas and two other cutting edge insurance companies, Car & General and Motor Union, had been consolidated into one office at 10 St James's Street and all the inspectors were in one room. I made several friends, including John Lewington, who was always making jokes, Peter Dixey, who I still hear from at Christmas - I am godfather to his son Andrew - and David Hawksworth. David knew Richard Stephenson, whose family owned Locks the Hatters almost next door, and the three of us used to slope off to lunch at the Royal Overseas League, a rather tatty club off St James's.

We inspectors were required to wear a bowler hat and carry a rolled umbrella when out on our rounds, provided at our own expense. Richard was kind enough to let me have a reject bowler from his shop at a much-reduced price. He also sold me a grey top hat for £3, which my son Christian still wears, me having inherited a black one from my great-grandfather.

Towards the end of January 1965, Winston Churchill died aged 90. Many, including me, consider him to have been one of the greatest Englishmen who ever lived, even if he was half American. He was quite properly awarded a state funeral, which included his coffin lying in state on at catafalque in Westminster Hall so Joe Public could file past and pay his respects. I joined the line at about 5am somewhere on the South Bank between the Westminster and Lambeth Bridges and was fascinated by the pageantry, including the four Life Guards standing at each corner.

Apart from these friends I cannot say that my nearly three years with the Royal Exchange, now subsumed into a French mega group called AXA, was full of fun, but life after hours was busy. Several mothers of debutante daughters expected me to walk their girls at hunt balls and country house dances as well as coming-out dances in London houses and (mostly) hotels like Grosvenor House, the Dorchester and the Savoy. Some were fun and others, particularly where I didn't know a soul, were pretty tedious. The English tend to travel in packs and if you're not part of a pack you're on your own.

Staying in people's houses before a country bash meant you met some of the other guests and sometimes found a kindred spirit, but the hospitality was usually very generous. I just hope I behaved. Corridor creeping added a certain piquancy and I don't think I was ever caught red handed. People also asked you to dinner at their houses before a dance in London.

One such evening I was dined at a house on Uxbridge Street, off the Bayswater Road, by people I didn't know from a bar of soap. The host, a man of all of 25, was giving a hard time to a fellow guest who probably deserved it, but I felt sorry for him. So having learnt that the host was a keen amateur jockey I asked rather pointedly if he had ever won anything, only to be told he had been third in the Grand National a week or two before. Back in your box, Youens. This man was called Christopher Collins. He had also managed to pass his chartered accountancy exams, coming fifth in the country. His father had told him if he came in the top ten he would buy him a business, and Christopher was MD of Goya, the cosmetics company. He went on to be a successful businessman, chairman of Hanson among others, and a member of the Jockey Club. Cocky bugger though, right from the start.

The lovely Jackie Ballantyne, whose mother was at North Foreland with mine, used to take me to parties, including Queen Charlotte's Ball: the highlight of the Season, where the girls were all in white and we boys were in white tie, which I usually borrowed from Derek Bingham, a friend from my days in Switzerland. We were the same build. I went again to Charlotte's another year this time with Sally Harvey, whose parents Bruce and Molly pretty much adopted me, what with my parents being in Germany. Bruce was a doctor in the RAF and they were stationed near Maidenhead, where they lived in a quarter.

I used to go and stay with the Harveys for the odd weekend and one such visit was preceded by a trip to Scotland which included a drive over the Devil's Beef Tub, a magnificent moorland bowl north of Moffat where the Scots herded stolen English cattle, but maybe not recently. Before setting off my Aunt Alison Chandler told me a gruesome story about two women who had been murdered in Lancaster, their bodies dissected and the parts tossed into a burn halfway up the Beef Tub. I mentioned this at dinner and Bruce Harvey said he had been a professional witness as well as acting as a police doctor in the case.

He had lived in Lancaster in 1936 and was returning home early one morning from a night shift at the hospital when he met an Indian fellow doctor in the street, who was a neighbour. This man appeared to be nursing a wound and Bruce asked if he could dress it, only to be shooed away. Some days later the Indian, named Buck Ruxton, was arrested on suspicion of murdering his housemaid and subsequently accused of killing his wife as well. He claimed that his wife had been having an affair so he killed her, the event being witnessed by the maid, so he bumped her off too. He then cut up their bodies in the bath, wrapped the parts in newspaper, a bit like fish & chips, drove up to the Beef Tub and threw the lot into the burn - to be discovered by some walkers a few days later.

The case was followed closely in the press. Ruxton was defended by the great (to be) Lord Birkett, whose advocacy failed to save him from the gallows and the bath used for the dissection is still used as a police horse trough at the local nick in Lancaster. Bruce Harvey was one of the doctors on the case and knew Ruxton a little from neighbourly contact.

Sally, his daughter, stayed loyal to the RAF and married a future Air Marshal and Governor of the Isle of Man and Windsor Castle, named (now Sir) Ian Macfadyen.

I had another girlfriend at about the same time called Penny, whose father was a successful RAF fighter pilot with 11 kills in North Africa. His name was John Lapsley and according to his daughter, he was known as John Thomas Lapsley because he had the biggest in the RAF. Make of that what you will. I saw quite a bit of Penny and even went skiing with her in Austria a couple of times, via the Snowsports Special, an overnight train to St Anton with a carriage converted into a bar-cum-dance car attached to the end. Every time we stopped at a station someone had to open the doors and let all the beer on the floor escape, otherwise we would have been wading around with the stuff up to our knees on arrival.

On one of these trips we fell in with another crowd at our hotel, including a rather sad Royal Marine officer called Robin Gardiner, whose wife and two children had been drowned in a ferry disaster in the Channel Islands a few years before. I was to meet him again many years later when looking round Elstree Prep School near Newbury, where he was a master, now happily married again with a new family. I lost touch with Penny in 1966. I think she went on to marry a farmer in Essex.

CHAPTER 7

The Apprentice Loss Adjuster

Some time in May 1966 I saw an advert in the personal column of the *Daily Telegraph* for people with insurance experience to work abroad. I was invited to send my CV to a Mr Graham Miller at an address in Charles Street, Mayfair. Well, my father's club, the Guards' Club no less, was in Charles Street, so it must be kosher and I applied. A letter came quickly back inviting me to call for an interview. The letterhead described the business as 'International Loss Adjusters & Surveyors' with offices 'at' Baghdad, Hong Kong, Johannesburg and heaven knows where else, but it all sounded very exciting.

I presented myself at the offices of Graham Miller & Co in Crutched Friars in the City a week or so later. Mr Miller, who looked a bit like a younger Winston Churchill, with bulldog manner to go with it, seemed interested in me and I had little idea about his business except that it was something to do with investigating insurance claims, about which I knew zippo. Having asked me the usual questions about my background, mainly irrelevant - ditto academic education and how much I knew about insurance (not a lot), he was on the point of saying 'don't ring us we'll ring you' when the telephone rang and the Lagos office manager was put through, a man I subsequently came know as Martyn Belben, a right chancer if ever there was one, but fun with it.

I could only hear one side of the conversation, but after a couple of minutes, Mr Miller said "hang on, I've got someone here who might be interested". He turned to me and asked, "what do you know about motor insurance?" I told him I had passed the exam paper in my studies and he told Belben. After some discussion he turned back to me and asked if I wanted to go to Lagos. Well Nigeria was not on my radar, as I preferred the more glamorous potential of Hong Kong or Johannesburg, so I declined and that was pretty much that. Mr Miller said he would be in touch and I departed.

After a few weeks and having heard nothing, I called him and reminded his secretary of my interest. She promised to call back and did so, to say Mr Miller could not remember me. He'd like me to come back for another interview. I was a bit put out, having always thought I was once met never forgotten, but agreed to another date. This time I seemed to have his undivided attention. He said he wanted to take me on as a trainee, but working with one of his partners as his assistant. I thought that sounded promising and accepted subject to terms.

Well, in those days 'terms' consisted of a salary and two weeks' paid holiday a year. None of your pension, health insurance, company car etc. At the time I was on £600 a year, so I said I couldn't move for less than £1,200, which he accepted, and I nearly fell over. I handed in my notice and started a month later. When I told my boss, Bob Braun, I was leaving he was quite cross. He said I had had a great future with the Royal Exchange and the adjusters 'would want their pound of flesh'. He was right there. More to the point, I drove Dad home that evening and he was also quite cross and nursing a hangover from a rather boozy lunch with Braun, which neither had thought to mention to me.

Dad had recently been posted back from Germany to London where he had been appointed Chaplain General, which meant he was in charge of all the Army chaplains, as well as being made an archdeacon. When he had asked my grandfather back in 1940 for Mum's hand in marriage he was asked if he intended to become Chaplain General. Dad told Grandpa 'yes' and he had now ticked that box.

One of the perks of his job was to live at Tattenhall, an ugly faux Tudor mansion on a busy corner of West Byfleet, a dormitory suburb in leafy Surrey. However it was not immediately available, so 'home' for the time being was Bagshot Park, a hideous pile on the A30 also in Surrey, which had been the home of the Duke of Clarence and was now the home of the Duke of Wessex - two sillier titles it's hard think of.

Having been hired by Graham Miller, I was walking on air. I had no idea what I had let myself in for, but who cared? I was 23 and wanted to make my way in the world.

I pitched up at 3-5 Crutched Friars on July 12, 1966 and was assigned a desk in the office of Jimmy Guild, one of Graham Miller's partners in the same suite of offices as GM himself. Jimmy was about 5ft 8ins, bald like a monk and aged about 50, which seemed to me to be in his dotage.

His secretary, Miss Pearce, was on holiday and I sat at her desk. Jimmy plonked several files on my desk and told me to read them to get some idea of what he did. As far as I remember, the first file I looked at was to do with the collapse of some cooling towers at Ferrybridge in Yorkshire. Well, I was a Yorkshire lad so I knew about Ferrybridge – hell, I had driven past the coal-fired power station every time I went to see Liz Spence in Ripon. Come to think of it, I even knew what a cooling tower was, though I'd never thought about it before.

In any event according to the file, several of these cooling towers had collapsed during construction thanks to a violent windstorm and its trailing vortexes created by the barometric pressures in the corridors caused three towers to vibrate. Get it? Evidently this was the fault of the design and/or construction and our insured was a man named Olaf Kier, whose business had been involved in the construction of the towers. All of this I discovered from reading the file. I did start wondering seriously what I had let myself in for.

At about 11 o'clock Jimmy (well, sir to me) looked up from his desk and asked if I spoke French. I said I did and he said 'well, you had better come with me to Paris on Wednesday. I need to settle a claim on Alan Bates'. Suddenly my life was completely changed. One minute I'd been flogging insurance in the West End of London. Now I was off to Paris for the day. Such a thing was quite unheard of in 1966. OK, the glitterati travelled at whim and so I suppose did captains of industry, but 23 year-old insurance clerks - definitely not. My flatmates were pretty sick when I told them that evening.

Alan Bates was a leading actor with a string of successes before and after *Zorba the Greek,* which had come out in 1964. He had damaged his leg jumping off a bollard in Paris while making a French film called *Le Roi du Coeur*, directed by Philippe de Broca. Filming had been delayed as a result, and the additional cost to complete principal photography solely as result of this mishap was an insured loss. We were to meet with de Broca and his wife Marie, who had produced the film, and agree these costs.

That same afternoon, the insurance broker on the account came to discuss the claim with Jimmy and in Miss Pearce's absence I was required to make tea. The broker's name was Robin Hillyard and he was to become a lifelong friend. Robin's job, with a firm of insurance brokers called Sedgwick Collins, was to sell film producers the necessary insurance cover, in this case called Film Producer's Indemnity, at the keenest price and place the risk with an insurance company. Robin's firm had a collaboration with another broker in Los Angeles called Albert G Ruben, who had an exclusive arrangement with the Fireman's Fund, a small but highly reputable underwriting company based in San Francisco.

The suppository

On Wednesday morning I set off for London Airport, as Heathrow was known then - Gatwick was for charter flights and Stansted et al were pretty much private and/or military. There was no tube line to the airport, one cabbed it or more cheaply took a bus from the West London Air Terminal located at what is now a big Sainsburys on the Cromwell

Road. You checked in there, went through customs and were driven in a coach directly to board the aircraft. My ticket for the open return flight to Paris was £10/12/6d (about £10.62).

We flew on a Vickers Viscount, a forty-eight seater turbo prop aircraft, operated by British European Airways (now merged with BOAC (British Overseas Airways Corporation) to become British Airways) to Le Bourget on the outskirts of Paris, where we were met by a production car and taken to the studios at Billancourt. On arrival Jimmy and Philippe discussed the merits of various issues and it was left that I would sit with the Production Accountant and come up with the appropriate numbers.

Needless to say I had only a glimmer of what I was about but it seemed pretty straightforward/I managed to fake it and we all parted good friends. Somewhere in the middle we stopped for lunch in a very Parisian restaurant, where we wined and dined in style. Philippe ordered an ice cream concoction, which arrived in the shape of an inverted cone with a maraschino cherry on top. He took one look at it and said 'merde, c'est comme une suppositoire ça!' Jimmy and I burst out laughing and he looked surprised, not realising the word was much the same in both languages.

We were done and dusted soon after lunch and headed back to Le Bourget. Having checked in we went through passport control and had half an hour or so to wait for our return flight. As we sat down Jimmy asked me to buy him a bottle of Teachers and 200 State Express cigarettes, and told me to buy the same or similar for myself - on the house, so to speak. He said it was a perk of the job for being inconvenienced by having to go to Paris for the day and a jolly good lunch. I didn't need any second bidding.

RICHARD YOUENS

The World Cup

About ten days later we heard from Robin's boss, Bob Dorning, that some props for a United Artists/Mirisch production called *The Bells of Hell Go Tingalingaling!*, had been damaged in transit to the location in Gstaad, Switzerland. Filming had to be suspended and then rescheduled to film around their absence until replacements could be found. Again the extra expense incurred on account of the delay would be a claim and it was our job to police the production company, approve their plans and keep the extra costs to a minimum.

It was the Friday before the World Cup Final and England were playing Germany, so Jimmy was most put out that he would miss the match. Not being the slightest bit interested in football, I couldn't have cared less, and we set off for Geneva, where we were collected by the Production Accountant, Paul Hitchcock. Paul went on to become head of production and general trouble-shooter for Warner Bros in Europe. He told us that this production was a mess. The director, David Miller, was hopeless, there were weather problems, they were way behind schedule and it was quite likely it would be closed down.

The film numbered among its cast Gregory Peck and Frances Bennett, who was hot in the UK thanks to her lead role in a soap opera about a magazine called *Compact*. More to the point, Jimmy had met her that spring in Greece where her daughter, Joanna Monro, had been working on a film as a child actor and Frances was employed as her chaperone. Joanna had been ill and Jimmy had his first taste of a film claim.

It was soon clear that Jimmy and Frances had got along famously, as she was all over him like a rash. I was agog, having never been up close with a 'famous' actress before, and here was I having dinner with her in the main restaurant at the Gstaad Palace Hotel, one of the smartest in Switzerland and world famous. Only trouble was I ordered lobster and came over all queer. I had to beat a retreat and was thoroughly sick, leaving Jimmy and Frances to their own devices.

I was fine in the morning and no doubt hung out with Jimmy and Paul until after lunch when we went off to watch the wretched football. There was a television lounge in the hotel, where seats had been reserved for guests including Jimmy and me. Most of the cast were billeted elsewhere and, as televisions were few and far between, most of them came to watch the match with us. England won, in case you're interested. In the end the film was shelved and never completed. A pity. The plot was quite original and the locations were magic.

These two exotic trips set me up with Graham Miller & Co and I never looked back over the next thirty years. My new colleagues were a bit suspicious of me to begin with, but I soon made friends and Graham Miller himself was a great supporter. When we came back from Gstaad on the Sunday after the match, the weekend had gone and I was not paid anything extra but that was fine.

I had to surrender my desk to Miss Pearce on the Monday morning, when she returned from holiday. She looked not unlike the Queen and they were/are about the same age. She was very attractive with a great figure and was very bossy. I like older dominatrices and lusted after her for years, to no avail. One compensation was I no longer had to make the tea. Miss Pearce is still going strong. She still lives in the same house in Pinner with her hubby, Graham, who used to manage the Norwich Union's office in Watford. Her Christian name is Yvonne, but to this day she has been and will always be 'Miss Pearce'.

Graham Miller and Jimmy Guild shared a suite of offices with their secretaries and me. Graham's secretary was a rather scary spinster called Miss Hall. We never called anyone in the office by his or her Christian names. It was always formal. Miss Hall was Graham's gatekeeper and kept everyone at bay, but she turned out to be a bit of a pussycat once you got on the right side of her and I'm good at that. She was Mildred Cleeve Hall and never married. Both she and Miss Pearce worked for the same people all their lives: hard to imagine today.

Miller, Guild and their two secretaries had originally worked for another firm of loss adjusters before the Second World War called Frank Brown & Co, where Graham had been a partner and Jimmy a staff adjuster. Graham by his own admission did not do very much at school or afterwards, except play a lot of bridge, mostly at Brooks, a club in St James's Street where he met Frank Brown. Evidently his skills convinced Brown that he would make a good adjuster and persuaded him to join his practice.

Harris & Co

There were a lot of dubious characters in the insurance industry then and doubtless there still are. One such in the thirties was a man named Leopold Harris, who did business acting for insureds and presenting their claims to insurers in return for a healthy percentage of whatever settlement was eventually paid. In the event of a major fire, usually first on the scene with the fire brigade was Leopold in his chauffeur-driven Rolls Royce, ready to scare the hell out of the luckless insured, convince him he would be screwed by the rotten insurers, but good old Leopold would save his bacon and more besides.

After trading quite legitimately for many years, business dropped off and Leopold decided to beef up his income by setting up dummy companies owning warehouses and the like, insuring them and their contents for well in excess of their true worth, then burning them down and pocketing the claim. Insurers suspected what he was up to but were never able to pin the rose on him, even though on one occasion their investigators examined extinguishment water-damaged bales of material wrapped in brown paper. When they unwrapped the bales they found fire-damaged textiles underneath, but they could never trace ownership back to Leopold Harris.

In the end a number of insurers and Lloyd's Underwriters got together and appointed a solicitor named William Charles Crocker to drop everything else and nail Harris. During his enquiry Crocker unveiled a real can of worms. It transpired Harris had officers employed by the London and some county fire brigades in his pocket as well as employees of the London Salvage Corp, not to mention some underwriters and adjusters. A man named Harold Deardon wrote a book called *The Fire Raisers* which told the detail of the story.

No one came out covered with glory. Underwriters asked if any of the adjusters was above suspicion and Crocker replied that Frank Brown & Co was the only such firm. As result Frank Brown was inundated with business, including rather surprisingly claims arising out of the Spanish Civil War. Leopold went to prison and served thirteen years, only to return to his old profession. I met him several times, as well as having to do business with his sons, who were good fun - particularly Henry Harris.

The Origins of Graham Miller & Co

When the Second World War broke out Jimmy Guild immediately joined up. However loss adjusting was a preferred occupation, meaning adjusters were exempt from military service and Graham Miller, and others, concentrated their efforts on settling war damage claims in London and elsewhere on behalf of insurers who then in turn recovered from the Treasury.

At the end of the war Jimmy was demobbed and rejoined Frank Brown, which was prospering mightily, mainly thanks to the efforts of Graham and his team, and this was recognised in the market. Graham took the view that he should have the lion's share of the profits, which was rejected, and eventually in 1956 he took off with Jimmy and the two secretaries, Miss Hall and Miss Pearce, to set up Graham Miller & Co in a couple of rooms in Bow Churchyard off Cheapside in the City.

They were instructed by a number of Lloyd's underwriters as well as some brokers, including Henry Head & Co, to take all their clients' files with them, which formed the nucleus of the new business. Henry Head was a top Lloyd's broker with much of the first-class business, both private and commercial clients, and they insisted that all their lead underwriters should use Graham Miller to adjust their claims. In these cynical days that would be deemed deeply suspect, but back in the fifties after the shock in the thirties of Leopold Harris' shenanigans, there was no suspicion of further corruption. In fact corruption in the top echelons of the insurance business was pretty much unheard of. Villains like Harris were few and far between. It didn't last long.

Graham's new business prospered and after about nine months Frank Brown's bookkeeper, Jim Riseam, applied to join as an adjuster. Graham agreed, on the understanding that he would go out to Johannesburg to set up the first overseas office. Jim accepted and opened a one-man band in downtown Jo'burg. There were a number of local firms who resented this interloper from London and persuaded their clients to avoid Jim like the plague. Being a parochial business environment, this tactic worked well until there was a major fire in a warehouse in Port Elizabeth. Every local insurer had an interest and as the warehouse owner was liable it was a question of establishing the value of the cargo and paying up. The insurers of the warehouse sat back and waited for the claims to come in.

In such circumstances, rather like the war damage claims, each insurer assessed his clients' losses, paid the claims and asked the third party to reimburse under their rights of subrogation - don't ask. The warehouse owner's insurers were under no obligation to accept their tenants' claims at face value, but that's what they tended to do:

established market practice. However Riseam persuaded the insurers of the warehouse to think again and let him check the individual adjustments, which he tore to shreds, to the delight of his client and the dismay of the surrogating insurers, let alone their adjusters, who were left with red faces.

All the Jo'burg insurers of whatever colour were reinsured in London, meaning London had the lion's share of the losses, and they all sat up and took notice of this new boy on the block. Jim soon had offices in all the main towns in the Union and Graham Miller & Co's wagon was rolling.

Not long after Jim had established himself he was instructed to deal with a messy personal accident claim where the insured had bought several life and personal accident policies quite soon after each other and then was found murdered in the back streets of Pretoria. Insurers were suspicious but there was no immediate evidence of fraud. The police arrested a suspect, who was convicted and sentenced to death, but there was no obvious motive let alone any connection between the two men.

Jim's enquiries revealed the dead man had business debts and a young family. He also discovered that the murderer had similar difficulties, but his wife had received a significant sum of money from an unknown source a few months after the murder. Jim came to the conclusion that the insured must have commissioned the murderer to kill him. Days before the execution he managed to persuade the court to stay the execution while he interviewed the condemned man, who eventually confessed and the various insurers were off the hook, although the man still went to the gallows.

Graham Miller's main clients were Lloyd's underwriters and the main competition was a firm called Toplis & Harding, which was an independent partnership but for all intents and purposes Lloyd's claims department for losses overseas. Nearer home claims involving the loss of fine art and jewellery were the domain of Antony Hart and his family business, but Graham Miller was knocking on his door. Tony Hart was reputed to meet his informers wearing a deerstalker and caped coat à la Sherlock Holmes. Whether this was true or not is neither here nor there, but the idea has always appealed.

In 1963 a bunch of villains managed to stop a Royal Mail train during the night in Buckinghamshire, hold up the crew and pinch the cash in transit, amounting to over £2.6 million. This became known as the Great Train Robbery and Tony Hart was appointed to deal with the claim. During the ensuing press furore, loss adjusters found themselves under the microscope and the general conclusion was that Graham Miller & Co was the biggest and best of the lot. Probably press hype, but it did not do the firm's reputation any harm.

Thomas Howell Selfe and Robins Davies & Little were the other two main players in the London Market but their business interests did not conflict with Graham's. Otherwise there were quite a few other adjusters in the UK but they weren't much competition. There is a professional institute in which all adjusters are represented but by all accounts they were, and probably still are, a dull bunch. Graham Miller used to refer to them as 'a bunch of clerks' – a bit like the grey men at the European Union.

Entertainment Insurance

It was about this time that Richard Ballantyne's syndicate at Lloyd's decided to underwrite Film Producer's Indemnity insurance in competition with Chubb and the Fireman's Fund both in the US. The man who adjusted the claims in Europe for the Americans was called Fred Geddes, a partner in Toplis & Harding, but although well liked he was not considered much of a rocket scientist. Ballantyne had identified a film production accountant called Ken Richards who talked a good story and wanted Graham to hire him, in which event we would have all the business. Graham went along and agreed to pay Richards £8,000 a year - a huge sum in those days.

Business followed but Ballantyne had a line on *Cleopatra*, which was more a celluloid record of Liz Taylor and Richard Burton's passion for each other. There were endless claims, which cost insurers a king's ransom, and in 1965 Ballantyne decided to close his book, leaving us holding the Richards baby. Graham fired him and Jimmy Guild handled the run-off of the account. One of Ballantyne's reinsurers was the Fireman's Fund - don't anyone think insurance is other that an incestuous business - and Jimmy's adept case handling came to their notice. As result the Fund started sending us business direct, and that's about when I came in on the act.

As an aside, Fred Geddes, who was the initial adjuster on *Cleopatra,* was taken off and James Crocker, the solicitor son of William Charles Crocker, of Leopold Harris fame, was asked to take over. James was the stepfather of my old school friend Christopher Seddon. Wheels within wheels? It's been that way all my life, as you have seen and will continue to see. Second aside – Ken Richards went on to become Sean Connery's financial adviser. Sean sacked him too.

Jimmy's first instruction direct from the Fund was the cast claim on the child actor Joanna Monro during the filming of *Brown Eye, Evil Eye*. This was another muddle and a wonderful man called Lee Katz had been brought in by United Artists, the LA studio and the film's distributor, to sort things out. Lee quickly realised Jimmy was new to the business and, instead of running rings round him, pointed him in the right direction, showed him how films were made and the pitfalls for insurers. They became firm friends and I was lucky enough to take up the mantle years later.

Back to the story: Graham Miller & Co had a reputation for being able to respond to claims on new classes of business, one of which was Contractors All Risks, the lead insurer of which was Commercial Union, and Jimmy had been closely involved in drafting their first policy. In the main this insurance cover was for fire, lightning and explosion as well as accidental damage to land based structures under construction.

In the autumn of 1966, after I had been with Graham Miller for a couple of months, David Babb, a claims broker with Leslie & Godwin, now part of AON, called with instructions to attend to a claim following the collapse of a telecommunications mast under construction by British Insulated Callenders Cables (BICC), my grandfather's old firm. Jimmy was busy and sent me off to have a look. I took a train from King's Cross and was collected somewhere like Stamford and taken to the site, where a 1,500 ft high cylindrical mast had toppled over during the night in high winds. Evidently the contractors had not secured it with sufficient guys for whatever reason. It was weeks from being handed over to the client, Associated Television, so that they could begin broadcasting in the area as well as earn revenue from leasing the mast to other broadcasters including the BBC.

I made notes, asked what might be the cost to rebuild and was told about £500,000 - a huge sum in those days. In addition BICC feared claims for late delivery and client's loss on earnings. I never thought to call this in to the office and went back to London and home for the night. When I told Jimmy about it the next morning he had a fit and we went straight back to site. I was a bit put out, thinking I had gathered the necessary information for an initial report.

Bahrain & Saudi

A few years before I joined Graham Miller, one of Toplis & Harding's partners, a leading light called Jock Sutherland, jumped ship and joined us. Jock was ostensibly an engineer, but without any formal qualification. Nevertheless he could turn his hand pretty much to anything and was good at digging us out of pits when we were in out our depth, as he did for me after a major fire at an oil refinery in Singapore, but that's another story. He was responsible for home foreign business, that's to say one-off jobs overseas where the risk has been written in London or where the local adjuster is not considered able to cut the mustard.

One such was a fire in a warehouse in Bahrain where several cans of Arabic films for local exhibition had been destroyed. The insured, the British Bank of the Middle East, now swallowed up into HSBC (who isn't?), had lent a local distributor the money to buy the films, which were rubbish with no hope of exhibition and the fire was manna from heaven. Lloyd's were on the receiving end and Jock was instructed. The loss was a piffling £4,000 but needed investigating. There was also a claim on some night-time landing equipment for the nearby Dammam airport under construction in the Eastern Province of Saudi Arabia, so the expense of two on-site investigations was justified.

Jock arrived in my office, asking Jimmy if he could borrow me. Jimmy agreed and Jock said, "How would you like to go to Bach Rayen?" in his broad Scots brogue. Well I had no idea where he was talking about and even less about what do with the two claims, but I volunteered immediately. I only had winter weight suits and this was August 1967, so I needed to go and buy some summer clothes for the trip. So I went off to Tropiccadilly, a shop on Piccadilly specialising in tropical clothing, owned by Airey & Wheeler. I explained that I was going to Bahrain and asked them to kit me out. I left the store with a couple of empire builder shorts, some Aertex shirts just like the ones I had worn at prep school, some long khaki socks and a pair of suede boots, aka brothel creepers.

I set off from Heathrow flying at the sharp end, thanks very much underwriters, in a BOAC Vickers VC10 ('Try a little VC Tenderness' was BOAC's slogan). After a stop in Rome I was the only passenger in First Class and the lovely stewardesses did their best to get me plastered, so I was feeling quite refreshed when we landed at about midnight local time. I was the guest of the local Lloyd's agents, Gray Mackenzie, and someone had been detailed to collect me and take me to their mess - there were no hotels in Bahrain except The Gulf, which was the preserve of passing air crews. Whoever collected me had had to leave a party to do so, and took me back there. I have no recollection of the rest of the evening but I do remember my room at the mess was very hot and sweaty, with just a ceiling fan.

The next morning I had a 10am appointment with Northern Assurance, a big Graham Miller supporter, who had insured the films – reinsured by Lloyd's, which had been destroyed. The local manager was an Indian called Freddy Vas who was horrified by my attire. He said I could not be seen in a Muslim country with bare knees and took me immediately into the nearby souk, where a tailor ran me up a pair of long trousers for a few dinars. Then he took me down to the docks, where the warehouse was located in which the films had been stored.

Freddy was very disappointed that I had not brought a deerstalker hat and magnifying glass with me and stood over me waiting for me to make some intelligent comments on the cause of the fire and what I planned to do about it. The heat in the warehouse (known in those parts of the world as a 'godown') was well over 100c and the humidity must have been 95%, so I was keen to complete the business and escape as soon as possible. I had been briefed that celluloid had a tendency to self-combust. There was no evidence of other fire damage in the area and so the obvious conclusion on cause was spontaneous ignition, which is an excluded peril under any fire policy, ergo loss not covered.

That afternoon I took a 20-minute flight to Dhahran in a Gulf Air Dakota DC3, which must have seen war service. After the aircraft took off an Arab two rows in front of me stood up, moved into the aisle, squatted down and moved his bowels in a significant fashion. There was no cabin crew and after landing we passengers had to negotiate around this steaming pile in order to disembark. When I mentioned this to the Englishman from International Aeradio, my next insured, he said it was not particularly unusual.

This claim involved damage to delicate aircraft landing guidance equipment, which had been shipped out from Pye of Cambridge where it had been made. It had been offloaded with a clean bill and the packing cases were only very slightly damaged compared with the destruction wrought to the equipment inside. I asked to see the docking facilities and was driven about two miles along a causeway out into the Gulf where the port was located. I was impressed by the speed at which the lorries in both directions travelled, completely ignoring the 'sleeping policemen' along the way, and the manager and I agreed that this was probably why the equipment was in such a state.

That evening I was put up at the Dhahran International Airport Hotel, which sounded quite smart but was anything but. Having dumped my kit and had a shower the manager collected me and took me back to his place for supper with his family. I complained about my non-alcoholic Tuborg lager at the hotel and asked how he coped without booze and he told me not to worry. After I had met his pretty wife and young family he asked me what I would like to drink. I asked what was on offer and he said I could have whatever I fancied, so I said a gin and tonic would do nicely. He then took me into the matrimonial bedroom and pulled out a bottle of clear liquid from under the bed where he had a private still, put some in a glass, added a few drops of whatever, ice and tonic and hey ho, welcome to Siddique, the local moonshine. It was not too bad, but you wouldn't want to make a habit of it.

Back at the hotel I piled into bed and went to sleep, only to wake up a few hours later to find ants all over me. I leapt out, ripped off my pyjamas and ran into my en suite bathroom to brush off the ants, only to find an Arab sitting on the lavatory. He scuttled off immediately through another door I hadn't noticed, which led onto the corridor, and above it was a WC sign. I was not much amused. Sleep was in short supply for the rest of the night and I was glad to be going home the next day.

Once back in London I made some enquiries through our agent in Amman, Jordan, to see if the films which had been destroyed could be replaced, which they could at considerably less than their insured value. I then went to see the Northern's claims manager to ask what he wanted to do. He was well within his rights to deny the claim for lack of coverage, but the BBME was an important client and he decided to offer to replace the films without admission of liability. I went to see the BBME, whose man was furious because this was a bad loan, he knew it, and had hoped to walk away effectively having had the loan redeemed by insurers. He was between a rock and the proverbial hard place and in the end accepted in cash the amount Northern would have paid to replace the films, about £1,500 as far as I remember. I was a hero with the Northern for a while.

Munich Olympics

Jock's department was heavily involved in construction

insurance and one major contract was the 1972 Olympic Games facilities in Munich, which included infrastructure such as surface and sub-terrain mass transit as well as the stadia etc. All this was insured directly in London, as the Germans had no such local insurance market.

We had staff constantly on the go between London and Munich and we had some pretty weird claims, such as a seafood restaurant built inside a massive fish tank so diners ate with fish, including sharks, manta rays and so on swimming all around them. The restaurant owners put in a claim for theft of sharks - in the middle of downtown München. They had stocked up the tank with fish, whose numbers were reduced overnight. They restocked and still the numbers reduced, and the only conclusion was the obvious - the fish were all eating each other. Underwriters declined to pay on the basis of inherent vice.

Early in 1968 I was asked to go out and deal with some claims which needed settling and asked if I might be allowed to send in my reports and take some holiday. It so happened I had a girlfriend called Serena Brett who was working as a chalet bird in Saas Fee and she had some spare space in her chalet. My request was granted, so apart from the cost of flying to Geneva from Munich, renting ski equipment and the *abonnement* I had an almost free two-week skiing holiday. One should always be grateful for small mercies, not to mention accommodating girlfriends.

Royal visit

In April the Queen and Prince Philip came to Bagshot Park for Matins in the chapel and Dad preached. The royal couple sat in the front on the right and Mum, my sister Georgina and I sat on the left. Needless to say the place was packed. Dad looked a bit nervous but he had met the Queen many times and was one of her Honorary Chaplains, so he was used to being in her limelight and was on top of his game. Afterwards we all assembled in the hall and were introduced. Prince Philip asked me what I did. I told him I was a loss adjuster and without missing a beat he said, "Well, it's an ill wind which blows no one any good!" How we all laughed. When I told Don Cass, an American broker, about it the next morning he said, "If he'd said that to me I'd have said '*rude noise* to you and the horse you rode in on'". I suppose I felt better, but you have to hand it to the Duke, he's always been consistent.

Wylfa Power Station

Jimmy Guild had a penchant for dealing with claims on nuclear power stations under construction, usually for our friends at the Northern Assurance, now in my story part of the Commercial Union (which has long since been lost in the maw of AVIVA), whose insured was English Electric, now part of GEC, later to become part of Marconi. He had piles of files on claims at Trawsfynydd Nuclear Power Station in Wales and in July 1968 there was a fire in the reactor room of another such generator at Wylfa on Anglesey.

We caught a train at Euston to Holyhead and went along to the restaurant car for a late lunch. No restaurant car, but there was a bar, drinks only. Jimmy liked whisky, Teachers for preference with American Dry Ginger, but not much. We must have consumed the best part of a bottle between us by the time we arrived late that evening in Holyhead.

We checked in to the hotel, where there was only one room left, which we had to share, and went in search of the restaurant, which was closed. We managed to persuade the manager to rustle up some sandwiches and we proceeded to split another bottle of whisky before retiring. When I woke the next morning Jimmy was already up and smoking his pipe, which only added to my misery. We were taken out to site and had to climb 60 feet up several ladders on the outside of the main hall to reach the reactor housing, without any safety harnesses in a howling gale and then climb down again. Well that's one way to clear a hangover. On the way back in the train we had to try and work out what the potential cost of repairs would be so we could give insurers a reserve. In the end we decided £265,000 was about right and six months later the claim was settled for £259,000, which means the estimate was frankly a complete fluke.

Darling Julie

The next morning I arrived in the office to find that there was a problem on a Paramount production in Paris called *Darling Lili* starring Julie Andrews and Rock Hudson and directed by Blake Edwards of *Pink Panther* fame. There were so many claims on this film that I had a Citroen DS 23, now a classic, plus driver allocated to the insurance account, which was a bit embarrassing when the claims were submitted. Blake Edwards was busy seducing lovely Julie, whom he eventually married, and Rock was busy seducing boys in the bars all over town. I had no idea he was homosexual, having been brought up on him and Doris Day being all over each other in one film after the next.

Furthermore this was the summer of a German hothead with red hair called Daniel Cohn-Bendit, 'Danny the Red', revolting against the regime of Charles de Gaulle. French students were rioting all over town causing mayhem and the French Government kicked him out. You could do that in those days. Needless to say today Danny is now an MEP and a Green leader.

Jimmy dealt with most of the claims on *Darling Lili* but I handled one involving scenes in a night shoot which were destroyed by Technicolor during processing. They inadvertently ignored specific instructions to force develop, ie leave the negative in the developer longer than usual. The scenes were dark and had to be reshot.

By this time the unit had relocated to Brussels because the situation in Paris was too dangerous and the scenes were reshot in the Palais de Justice doubling as a railway station with Jeremy Kemp chasing Julie through crowds of extras in period costume at a cost of $100,000. Whole feature films are made for less. I needed to talk to Blake before they reshot and had to wait outside his caravan on the set for 20 minutes while he finished lunch. Lunch being Julie. I was sick with envy.

Paramount presented their claims, totalling over $4,000,000, and everyone involved decided the best plan of action was to meet somewhere where we could work uninterrupted. Kilkea Castle outside Dublin was chosen and completely taken over by us, 'us' being various Paramount executives including a highly cerebral accountant named

Jason Brent, with whom Jimmy got along famously and they became personal friends. Lawyers from Paramount were also out in force. Ed Hamby, the Fireman's Fund underwriter, represented insurers and came from Los Angeles together with Scott Milne, the broker from Albert G Ruben, and his man in Europe, Don Cass. Then there was Jimmy and me.

We pitched up on a Sunday evening and worked through the night and most of Monday, me toing and froing between Kilkea and the production offices in Dublin where all the accounts were kept. By Tuesday we had the bones of a deal and sometime during the night there was an agreement, which had to be audited. That was down to Jason and me. By Thursday evening we were done and dusted. All very exciting for a simple 25-year-old.

When I was in Dublin I stayed at the Gresham Hotel, as one did in those days, and on one of the evenings while I was there I arrived back from the production company's office at about eight o'clock to find quite a rumpus going on in the bar. As I stood in the lobby wondering what to do, Richard Harris, the well-known dissolute Irish actor, staggered out looking well refreshed and in some disarray, having got the better of a couple of other patrons who had discovered they had issues with him. Years later I met him again at the Savoy Hotel in London and he had lost none of his aggression.

CHAPTER 8

The film business

It was around this time we started to become involved in Italian film business, which heretofore had been the preserve of Fred Geddes of Toplis & Harding. He was an adjuster of the old school. He always wore a three-piece suit and smoked endless cigarettes, which he held between his lips, talking all the while. As he did so the ash would grow longer and longer, so much so that his listeners would ignore what he was saying and watch transfixed waiting to see how long before it eventually fell onto his waistcoat, which was so covered it looked like the side of a volcano. It was his party trick to cause distraction during negotiations and I'm sure it must have worked on many occasions. People are so gullible, yes, me too. I was distracted along with everyone else.

One of the first jobs I had in Italy involved the actress Charlotte Rampling, who was allegedly suffering from a gynaecological indisposition, at a location in Orvieto an hour and a half's drive north of Rome. The claim was notified late one evening while Robin Hillyard, Don Cass and I were having dinner together with our local doctor named Frank Silvestri sitting outside the Café de Paris on the Via Veneto, and this is where I met Geddes, and Frank, for the first time.

The next morning, feeling rather tired and sorry for ourselves, Robin and I set out in a taxi for Orvieto with Frank meeting us there. He found us sipping large espressos trying to get our act together and I asked him to examine the patient and be quite certain of his diagnosis. Conditions pertaining only to the female, including pregnancy and disorders connected such as menstruation, are excluded perils, so any claim for the extra cost caused by delay in filming as result is not covered.

Now Frank was an excellent doctor, but he did not seek controversy. His value to insurers was that he knew most of the stars and they liked and trusted him, so if he told them they were fine they'd go back to work even if they were not absolutely chipper. Sometimes this had its uses, sometimes it didn't, but Frank was the only game in town. In any event off he went to see Charlotte and came back an hour or so later to declare "she's got glands up her snatch". I kid you not. This was hardly a technically clinical diagnosis, but I decided it fell within the exclusion and we told the production company they were on their own.

They weren't best pleased, but they accepted the situation and managed to film around her anyway, so there would have been no claim. The problem for insurers with many Italian producers in those days was that they saw insurance as a means of generating a contribution to their budget, or at least to recover the insurance premium. It was a game. Both sides knew the rules and it kept you on your toes.

One of the greatest villains was Dino de Laurentiis. We had masses of expensive claims for damaged negative on *Waterloo* and only discovered years later that he had one crew using a faulty camera at the battle locations in Russia and much of the damage was deliberate. Needless to say he had several camera crews in action simultaneously, so he never reshot scenes but claimed anyway. Italian production accountants sometimes kept three sets of books: one for the producer with a true record, one for the taxman with grossly exaggerated costs and one for insurers which was somewhere between the two.

Copenhagen

There was the occasional break from business on trips. I had a very happy evening the first time I went to Copenhagen, thanks to the hospitality of a family called Larssen whose elder daughter had somewhat hurriedly married my old school friend Mike du Pré, and I was godfather to their lovely daughter Nina Miranda. Mike's cousin Jacqueline, the world-renowned cellist, was a godmother.

Larssen father collected me from my hotel and took me on a tour of the city centre with his younger daughter sitting in the back of the car, a blonde bombshell aged 12 and serious jailbait. As we approached the main square opposite the Tuilerie Gardens he pointed to a statue of two Vikings blowing their horns and told me that according to legend you could hear their horns playing whenever a virgin passed them. As we drove by he turned to me and said, "I didn't hear anything. Did you?" I was slightly shocked, but the daughter just laughed. This wasn't the first time.

Tehran

Just before Christmas 1968 a claim came in on a production on location near Tehran called *The Invincible Six*, about an attempted theft of the Iranian crown jewels, starring Stuart Whitman and Elke Sommer. I flew out on Pakistan Airlines and sat next to an engineer called Robin Mitchell who was working on the reconstruction of Persepolis to celebrate 5000 years of Iranian history. He and I were staying at the same hotel, the Hilton: in those days there were only two, well – only two of any repute. We agreed to meet the following evening and we talked late about the merits of our respective jobs.

A couple of years later I pitched up for a meeting with Powell Duffryn in Slough and ran into Mitchell as I was leaving. To my dismay I learnt that he had decided to become an adjuster himself, but had joined a competitor, when we would have been delighted to have him. The day we met in Slough was January 1, and my appointment was at 9am. New Year's Day was not a holiday then.

Back to Tehran again at the end of the year. I can't remember what the job was all about this time, but the film director was a Russian émigré called Jean Negulesco, who was a bit of an eccentric. We got on quite well and he asked me up to his penthouse suite at the Hilton for dinner one night. When I arrived there was a wood fire burning on the marble floor, over which his wife or whatever was roasting lamb. Luckily smoke alarms were still in the future.

The business must have taken some time to conclude because I did not arrive back into Heathrow until late on Christmas Eve, then the cab taking me to the flat in Pont St collided with another vehicle on the Chiswick flyover, so I had to abandon the driver and share another cab, which had been held up, into town. This was a Tuesday evening and I was back in the office on Friday. No chance to skive off even for a day.

Goodbye Pont Street

My days at 66a Pont St, the cold water walk-up where I'd lived happily for the past five years, were drawing to a close. Both Nick Hallings-Pott and Martin Whitfield had found themselves girlfriends who had agreed to marry them and the weddings were scheduled for a Friday (London - Pott) and the next day Saturday (country - Whitfield) in mid-February 1969, so it was time to move on.

Pott married a sailor's daughter called Jean Collet, who had looked after us on a skiing holiday two years before in Verbier, us being Pott, Whitfield and Ronnie Hicks, an occasional fourth occupant of the flat, who was a wine merchant. I had managed to dislocate my left thumb colliding with Pott the first day on the slopes and spent the whole two weeks skiing with the thumb in plaster because the local doctor could not reposition it in his surgery and had to take me in his car down to Martigny to fix it under gas. A horribly claustrophobic experience, but everyone including Jean was very sympathetic. I asked her out to dinner but was promptly turned down. Her boyfriend, Nigel Barttelot, was due in town that evening.

I was not the only one in the wars that holiday. Ronnie had a collision with the postman, who schussed into him at great speed. Ronnie was quite badly bruised. Postie dislocated both shoulders. Ronnie's skiing was a painful business at the best of times but this was agonising, not only for him but for anyone watching.

One afternoon the rest of us were waiting for the ski lift at the bottom of a run called Tortin, the end of which was a steep slope known as the Wall of Death. It was great sport waiting to see if anyone fell over coming down it, because usually they could not stop until they reached the bottom. Most skiers made it at least halfway before coming unstuck but that afternoon just after we boarded the chairlift a skier shot over the top of the Wall and crashed all the way to the bottom. Yes, it was poor old Ronnie. We had no idea he would be mad enough even to attempt Tortin, but that was Ronnie for you.

Pott in the meantime had met and fallen head over heels for a Franco-Egyptian beauty called Francine, who lived in Geneva, and he spent several months after the holiday chasing after her over long weekends in Switzerland, but in the end they called it a day. I then re-met Jean Collet shopping in Safeway (a supermarket now long gone) on King's Road and invited her back to the flat. She and Nick took up and here we were a year or so later with them engaged. Time, as I say, for me to move on.

I had made friends several years before at Oxford with a future very successful entrepreneur called David Gyle-Thompson who, as luck would have it, was looking for someone to take one of the rooms in a mansion flat in Drayton Gardens, which was owned by Charlie Cope. The other inmate was Anthony Palmer, who was a bit younger than the rest of us and was training to become a Chartered Accountant.

Robert Redford

I took up residence in Drayton Gardens early in January 1969 and shortly afterwards went to Kitzbühel in the Austrian Alps, where Robert Redford was expected to arrive a week late to start filming on *Downhill Racer*, because he had injured his knee falling off a skimobile at his ranch in Utah. *Butch Cassidy* had not yet been released, but it was expected to be a blockbuster and Redford was already rather full of himself when I met him at the splendid Goldener Greif Hotel.

The film started late and there were delays because Redford was unable to be filmed ski racing for some time while he recovered. This meant a double had to film some of the scenes, to be intercut with actual footage of races, including the Hahnenkamm above Kitzbühel as well as the Lauberhorn in Wengen and other races through the season. As result I had a lovely time monitoring progress by pitching up at whatever location on a Thursday, working as little as possible on the Friday and skiing the rest of the weekend at virtually no personal expense.

Hans Brinker

At the same time a production of *Hans Brinker*, about the

little Dutch boy who allegedly stuck his finger in a hole in a dyke, thus saving his country from a potentially catastrophic flood, ran into trouble because the boy actor playing the eponymous role was ill. The insurer was a competitor of the Fireman's Fund in the US called Chubb, with whom we did not have any prior contact, and their underwriter once rang at about 3am asking me to put different stamps on the envelopes containing our reports. I kid you not. It was the only time I ever worked for Chubb and they were not a barrel of laughs.

This claim proved to be a nightmare because the weather kept changing and caused havoc with continuity. The producer was a piece of work called Allan Buckhanz, and the broker was on another planet. A simple claim became very complicated and Buckhanz, who had a rather unattractive habit of blowing his nose on his napkin at dinner, was finding every opportunity to load it up with unrelated expenses. It was eventually settled in Hamburg. All I can remember was sitting on a low sofa and having to work with papers all over a coffee table for hours on end. I was bent double and in agony when the meeting ended, trying to stand up. The insurers were not best pleased with me because they thought they were paying too much. They were probably right.

Song of Norway

I got the call to deal with a cast claim in Norway on a musical, well an operetta, based on the works of Grieg, on the very morning, Valentine's Day, of Pott's wedding, which was inconvenient to say the very least. I could have postponed going until the next day, Saturday, but that was Whitfield's do, so I decided to make the judgement of Solomon and miss both. I flew to Oslo and caught a train to Lillehammer, a small (then, the Winter Olympics were held there 25 years later) ski resort, mainly cross-country, as it was low lying.

The temperature was -14c and the air was moist in the form of frozen ice particles, which were being ingested by the crew, and one artiste, called Toralv Maurstad, was sick, hence my presence. Well the bugger was at a production party when I arrived and the first thing I had to do was to send him to bed. To be fair he had been off for two days and was feeling a lot better, but he made me miss two weddings, so - bed.

On the Saturday he could not work in exterior, but was expected to be fit enough to resume all his duties on the Monday. I decided I had better hang about until Sunday at least to be sure he would work Monday. I had been warned the place was cold and had taken a thick tweed suit, which had belonged to an uncle, après ski boots and a sheepskin coat, but it was still bitter outside and the icy air made things very unpleasant.

That evening I went down to the bar and met up with the crew as well as some of the artistes, including Harry Secombe, the Welsh singer and comedian, whose fame stemmed from his part in 'The Goon Show' that mad comedy radio programme with Peter Sellers, Spike Milligan and Michael Bentine. Harry was an opera singer manqué with an amazingly powerful voice, and very funny. He was kind enough to invite me to join his table for dinner along with an actress called Elizabeth Larner, and told the producer that after he had finished with me I'd pay whatever he wanted. After dinner we returned to the bar, where he started to sing. I was sitting beside him and the volume he created was painful, but it was a very happy evening.

Sometime in June, Toralv went sick again and this time production was on location near a place called Arlesund, north of Bergen in the heart of fjord country. I was told that someone would meet me at Arlesund and take me from there. I must have ridden almost every form of transport that day, except a horse: a tube to Gloucester Road to get some kit from Drayton Gardens, taxi to Heathrow, a flight to Oslo, a change of planes to Bergen and on to Arlesund. On arrival there was no one to meet me, so after a wait and still no show I decided to take the bus into town and find out if anyone knew where the production was located.

Someone on the bus said that Toralv had a house in Arlesund, a pretty one-horse town, well fishing village, at the head of what appeared to be a fjord with a few islands scattered about. Anyway after alighting from the bus at the harbour, my new best friend hailed someone who was testing a speedboat, called him over and explained my predicament. Mr Speed Boat told me to climb aboard and he'd take me to Toralv, who lived on one on these islands. This time round he was down with 'flu' but fit enough to offer me dinner, after which he promised to arrange transport to the production company, which had been alerted to my arrival.

At about 9.30pm my transport was announced and I was rowed out to a seaplane riding 100yds away in open water, engine idling. This being midsummer in the land of the midnight sun, we set off in broad daylight over the nearby mountains and down into Gieranger Fjord, which is considered to be the most spectacular of the lot. If ever there is an advert encouraging the punters to visit Norway, there is almost always a shot of Gieranger. Well, viewed from a seaplane flying through the fjord I wouldn't dispute its reputation for a minute. I was quite enthralled by the astonishing sight of waterfalls cascading on either side as we passed between massive cliffs with mountains beyond until we came to the head of the fjord and landed on dead calm water perfectly reflecting the scenery, which made the pilot's job of judging where the water was exceptionally difficult.

Romance in the air

Back at home I was well settled in to the flat in Drayton Gardens and having a very jolly time. Jackie Ballantyne was still lurking and came round for dinner one night, looked at Gyle-Thompson and immediately decided he would be just the job for one of her flatmates, Penny Fearnley, a doctor's daughter from Devizes. Well she got that right and David & Penny are now proud grandparents.

A few floors above us lived James and Edith Bull. He was a leading radiologist and recognised as such all over the planet. He had a sister Mary, whose daughter Lavinia had married Mike Dewar, my soldier friend from Germany; and I had been his Best Man the year before. Edith was a bit of a battle-axe but very good company once she knew you. They had a daughter called Sarah and the point of this story is that Sarah's best friend was a girl called Annabelle Methven. Sarah had an intimate soirée on April 9, 1969 at her parents' flat and as the Dewars were attending I was invited too. So it was that I met, albeit briefly, my future bride for the first time. We had in fact been guests at Gerry & Diana Waterlow's wedding back in July 1965, but she was 16 at the time and did not register on my radar - any more than I on hers.

Dabbling with 007

I had always been a fan of Ian Fleming and the James Bond novels, and thought Sean Connery was the personification of 007, but 1969 was the year Sean opted out of the role and George Lazenby was cast in his place. The new film was *On Her Majesty's Secret Service* and in the final scenes Lazenby marries Diana Rigg, who is conveniently topped off by Irma Bunt, baddy Telly Savalas' equally evil assistant, played by Ilsa Steppat. Ilsa lived in Berlin and liked the odd sherbet. At the beginning of May she tripped in her flat, fell and cracked her shoulder - cue a cast claim, because the end of the show had not yet been filmed and would now have to be delayed.

We were alerted on a Friday afternoon and Ronnie Wilkinson, who was the London version of Frank Silvestri, called the doctor in Berlin treating Ilsa, a Professor Dumrich, to find out his diagnosis and prognosis. As result Ronnie concluded Dumrich had not been near a medical book since before Hitler became Chancellor, so I arranged to fly to Berlin the next morning with an orthopaedic surgeon. I went home to my parents near Esher for supper and to stay the night before going on to Berlin next morning.

I arrived to be told by my mother, no film buff she, that a man named Cubby Broccoli had called asking me to call back. Cubby was the main man behind the Bond films and his daughter, Barbara, took up the mantle when he died. Anyway Cubby asked me which flight I was taking in the morning and said he'd meet me in the VIP lounge at Heathrow as he was coming too. I pretended I always used the lounge and would see him in the morning.

When I checked in I told the clerk I was expected in the VIP Lounge she smartened up her act and I was duly taken there to find Cubby already ensconced with Charlie Forte, the hotelier. During the flight Cubby explained that he had arranged for a girlfriend of Ilsa's to fly up from Munich and meet us in Berlin because part of my plan was to fly Ilsa back to London for treatment and Cubby thought the girlfriend's presence might be helpful.

On arrival at Tempelhof airport I was given a message to the effect the orthopaedic surgeon, who was supposed to have been on the same flight with us, would be arriving after lunch, as was Ilsa's friend, so Cubby and I went off to the Hilton to check in and eat. It was at this point that Cubby explained that the friend did not know Ilsa from a slice of cheese, but was in fact his girlfriend. Oh, OK.

I rang up the Air Officer Commanding Berlin, who was a friend of Dad's, told him what was happening and asked if it would be possible to bring Ilsa back to London in one of his aircraft the following day. He seemed to think that was frightfully sporting and agreed to make the arrangements.

We went back to the airport and when the surgeon arrived he took me on one side to explain that he had brought his nurse, except she really wasn't a nurse. Oh, OK - hello gooseberry. Then the girlfriend arrived. She was obviously quite a player, a petite blonde with an hourglass figure and a beguilingly wicked smile. We all set off for the hospital and everyone went in to see Ilsa, except me, who kept in the background. The surgeon said he was not happy with the treatment and made several recommendations but thought it unlikely she would agree to being transferred to London. Cubby said he'd talk her into it in the morning and took us all to dinner, including the 'nurse'.

As none of us had much idea of where to eat, Cubby simply asked the hotel concierge which was the best restaurant in town and to book us a table. We were given a private room. Cubby sat at the head of the table, with his girlfriend on his right and me beside her with the other two opposite. Everyone ordered steak au poivre for mains and Cubby ordered the finest claret to go with it, which of course none of us could taste.

Towards the end of the meal I felt a hand creeping up my thigh and had the greatest difficulty maintaining conversation with a straight face. At the end of the evening I was feeling no pain and suggested we all went dancing, and while the girl seemed more than keen, Cubby was not amused. In fact he gave me quite a ticking off on the plane going home - something about trying to pinch another chap's girlfriend was considered rather underhand, or words to that effect.

The following day it was soon clear that Ilsa was refusing to budge, and the RAF had to be stood down: news which the AOC received with much disappointment. A couple of days later I met with the Associate Producer, an old friend called Stanley Soppel, and the film's director, Peter Hunt, who was an editor, directing his first major production. It was agreed that we would somehow rewrite the final scenes to shoot with Ilsa but in such a way that her condition was not obvious with skilled editing. As result there was no claim. A bit of trivia: evidently Diana Rigg couldn't stand George Lazenby and before filming the love scenes she would chew a clove of garlic. Poor George.

Sadly Ilsa died of a heart attack only four days after the film was released.

CHAPTER 9

A man of property

Out of the blue Charlie Cope, our Drayton Gardens landlord, decided to go to Cirencester to learn farming, and we were all turfed out in late June 1969 so he could let the flat. David Gyle-Thompson was in the real estate business and it so happened he had a basement flat at the King's Road end of Sloane Avenue which was empty, so he and I moved in on a short term basis, probably for a few weeks, and then we moved to another of his short lease places just north of Regents Park. My only recollection of the place is that we were there when the Americans landed on the Moon on July 20.

My mother became rather concerned with my nomadic lifestyle and decided it was time for me to have somewhere of my own: very kind of her. There was a family trust fund and the trustees gave me a budget. As result I bought a two-bedroom flat in Chesham Street, between Eaton Square and Pont Street in London's Belgravia. Very lucky me.

It was a maisonette on the ground and basement of a block, which had been refurbished by some property developers-cum-estate agents called Andrew Milton, based in nearby Milner Street. The bedrooms and bathroom were on the ground floor and there was a living room and a kitchen, with an eating area at the far end, in the basement. The 57-year lease cost £9,000.

I moved in towards the end of September 1969 with someone called Geoffrey Burnand, who I had met ushing at Marion and Peter Chamberlin's wedding the year before. He had just come out of the army and was starting out with a firm of stockbrokers in the City.

In those days pre-privatisation, if you wanted a telephone you had to apply to the General Post Office and wait on their pleasure - no competition. When eventually my turn came, the clerk I was dealing with asked where I wanted the phone installed. I gave my address and he asked which flat, because he had lived there before the place was developed. It transpired he had lived in my flat and very kindly assigned me the number BELgravia 3344, Belgravia being the local neighbourhood. BEL became 235 when automated dialling was introduced. 'BELgravia double three double four' was very easy for the girls to remember and always made a good impression.

In those days more people smoked that not, and I was no exception. I had started smoking cigarettes at school and in the holidays aged 16, when we were in Gibraltar where a packet of 20 was less than 10p (1/10d in old money). Jim Guild, with whom I shared an office, smoked cigarettes, a pipe and anything else legal he could put a hand on, so I was pretty much kippered from an early age.

However this came to an end on October 16, 1969, when I chucked Virginian tobacco at about 3am. I had earlier invited one such girl (see penultimate paragraph) called Carolyn Davies to supper at the flat. Geoffrey was away for the night. I must have worked myself into a bit of a state about making a move on Carolyn and smoked far too many cigarettes in the process. The only move I made was to take her home after a fruitless evening, and I woke up in the middle of the night feeling like death warmed up. As result I never smoked a Virginian cigarette again, but I did smoke Gaulois and cheapish cigars instead, although I haven't smoke anything for 20 years plus.

On Remembrance Sunday 1969 Dad was on parade at the Cenotaph in Whitehall along with the rest of the Great and the Good, starting with the Queen, of course. His family were invited to watch from a Home Office balcony and to drinks afterwards as guests of the (Labour) Home Secretary, Roy Jenkins. Mr Jenkins was standing at the door greeting people with a tray of drinks. Mum, who only reads the hatches, matches and dispatches in the *Telegraph* and does the crossword in about 20 minutes, accepted a glass of something and swept past thinking he was some flunkey, which seemed to amuse him. A socialist with some sense of humour is a rare bird. Most have their heads up someone's backside, usually their own.

There were not many people there and plenty of room to walk around. Harold Wilson, the PM was there, looking well refreshed, along with Ted Heath, the leader of the Conservative Opposition, Mrs Thatcher, who was Shadow

Minister of Education and very glamorous with it, Denis Healey, probably the worst ever Chancellor of the Exchequer until Gordon Brown came along, and most of the leading politicians of the day. It was fascinating to see them all at close quarters.

The rest of the year hurried past in a blur of nest-building at Chesham Street and I would like to say fighting off the girls now I was a man of property, but the only one who springs to mind was Gilly Twiss, whose father was Third Sea Lord and lived in a flat over Admiralty Arch where the drawing room looked down The Mall. She was good fun but committed to some lothario called Julian Beale, who was lurking in Australia, and I was her last hurrah, which probably suited us both.

When I went skiing in Klosters in February 1970, I was told by Gilly to look out for a couple of girls there, working for Deborah Kerr the actress, who had allegedly loomed large in my Uncle Peter's life during the war. One of them was a delightful creature called Sarah Footitt, who could float my boat any time but she had been warned off by Gilly, damn it. Mean or what? Especially when Gilly was about to fly off to Oz and marry Julian, which she did and I never saw her again for years. Not so Julian. He has been around one way or another ever since.

Meeting Mandy

Early in May 1970 a claim was notified by an independent production on location in Israel. It was a low budget Western called *Madron* and starred Leslie Caron of *Gigi* fame. I checked into the Tel Aviv Sheraton and met up with the producer, Manny Henigman. After we had established our credentials he invited me for a drink, which seemed like a good idea. He said "come on, I'll take you to Mandy's". I looked blank and he said, "You know, Mandy Rice-Davies' place". Well Mandy, you may remember, was at the heart of the Profumo Affair in 1963, mentioned earlier in this narrative, and here she was running a night club in Tel Aviv, having married an Israeli business man.

She met us on arrival, clearly a good friend of Manny and doubtless hoping for a part in the film. She was very attractive and funny, living up well to her press and we had a jolly time. The next day I went off to the location miles away in the desert and didn't get back until midnight, so I thought I'd go and check up on Mandy. When I arrived she was in a huddle with Winston Churchill's grandson, also called Winston and a bit of a drip I had always thought. So apparently did Mandy, because she dumped him and joined me at the bar for the next couple of hours. I always wondered if I was on to something there, well - maybe not.

A girl in a different league

In May 1970 I invited an ex of my sister Georgina called Jonathan Hubbard-Ford to supper at the flat with others. He said he'd love to come but had already asked a girlfriend out for the evening, so I said to bring her too. I asked another girlfriend called Sarah Pollock (golly there seems to have been rather a lot of them, now I remember) to help cook the meal but she couldn't come at the last minute so I invited Caroline Stares.

The evening arrived, the doorbell rang and I opened it to find a girl almost falling into my arms – well, there was a small step down into the hall from the outside lobby. She quickly recovered her composure and announced that she was Annabelle Methven and that we had already met – at a party in Drayton Gardens. She was followed in by Jonathan, looking slightly bemused. When we were washing up after everyone had gone, Caroline said "you're going to marry that girl" and do you know - she was right.

1970 was a very busy year for business in Italy. I was constantly whizzing to and fro, for weeks at a time. United Artists were backing an Italian producer called Alberto Grimaldi and he was making the most of it. Apart from spaghetti westerns, he made quite rude films including *Satyricon*, *Canterbury Tales* and *Last Tango in Paris,* to name a few. He was up to every trick in the book and kept us on our toes I can tell you, much like Dino de Laurentiis.

In September I was asked to a private viewing of a film called *A Fume of Poppies* in a small theatre in Wardour Street by the producer, a madman called Ted Ritter. We must have had some claims on it but I've no idea what. Anyway he was keen I should see his masterpiece. I knew from what little I had seen of the script and the rushes that it would be rubbish, but did not see why I should suffer alone, so I invited Annabelle to come along as well, and the rest is history. The one saving grace of the evening was taking her to Mario & Franco's Trattoria Terrazza in Romilly Street, Soho. I suppose it was a bit passé by then but still popular and pricey. I don't think I had ever spent so much in a restaurant on my own account, so I must have sensed I was in a one-way street.

IT'S ALWAYS FRIDAY

That was it really, although the friendship with Annabelle took its time to develop and we did not marry for another eighteen months. She was, and still is 40 some odd years later, very pretty. She is good fun to have around, laughs at my jokes, is highly domesticated, loves animals, is a meaner dancer, my best friend and I'm a lucky boy.

CHAPTER 10

Settling claims

One of the original Lloyd's underwriting syndicates was Herbert de Rougemont. In the sixties and seventies one of the underwriters on the syndicate was Bob (known in the Market as 'Flash') Gordon. His underwriting 'box' in the Room at Lloyd's, a bit like a couple of high-backed church pews facing each other with a table in between, was located close to the Rostrum - a sort of indoor gazebo with a bell suspended from its rafters. The bell was recovered from the wreck of HMS *Lutine*, which had sunk carrying gold insured at Lloyd's in 1858, and has hung there ever since. It is tolled on momentous occasions, more recently 9/11 and the London 7/7 bombings as well as at the beginning and end of the two minutes' silence every Armistice Day.

Bob Gordon always respected his box's premier location by wearing a fresh rose every day in a tiny silver vase clipped behind the buttonhole on his suit. He specialised in 'specie' risks. That is to say gold, precious metals, gems, cash-in-transit and so on, and as a favour to some of his broker clients he would cover their personal effects as well. One such client was a man named John Wallrock, chairman of a long-gone broker called JH Minet, who submitted a claim for the loss of his wife's engagement ring, which was insured for £8,000. He contended that the ring was in his wife's checked luggage and must have been stolen by baggage handling staff somewhere in transit between Nice Airport and Heathrow.

Bob Gordon instructed us to investigate and Graham Miller decided he had better handle the case. Graham and Bob were good friends and did a lot of business together, but they specialised in giving each other a hard time. On this occasion Graham concluded that there was a strong possibility that the ring had been lost or stolen in France and told Bob he was sending me down to Nice to make local enquiries. I was duly dispatched with instructions to have people armed with metal detectors to check the grounds of Mrs Wallrock's mother's villa somewhere above Villefranche, where the ring was last seen. I was also told to find out what investigation the police had made and offer a ten per cent reward for information leading to its recovery, as was the custom.

I was collected at Nice airport by Madame's chauffeur in a big limo and driven to the villa, while the chauffeur protested his innocence and that of his wife, Madame's cook for twenty years. On arrival Madame treated me with haughty contempt, complaining that Lloyd's was wasting time and money; the ring had been stolen in transit. I poured on the charm as best I could and asked to be shown where the ring had last been seen. Having called her daughter in London to enquire, she took me up to a bedroom suite, where daughter and hubby Wallrock had slept, and offered me some coffee. This arrived almost immediately, along with a large brandy. By this time it was about 3pm and I thought I had better have a hunt around before going to see the police etc.

Well, you've probably guessed - I found the ring in a matter of minutes. I pulled open a drawer in a chest, heard a clang and found what looked like a socking great diamond ring in the drawer below. However I had left my briefcase downstairs and could not remember the description on the insurance schedule. I nipped below, recovered the file and lo, the description matched the ring in my hand. Madame was arranging flowers in the kitchen when I walked and asked, "Does this look familiar?" Well the staff were delighted, but Madame was understandably embarrassed and called her daughter to give her the good news.

I was a bit nervous in case Customs found the ring and suspected me of stealing it, and I did not want to lose it, so I tied some string though the shank and hung it around my neck like a necklace inside my shirt. This trip was on a Friday and I had originally planned to spend the weekend with my parents near Esher, but I now had business in Stockholm on the Saturday so I had decided to stay the night with them anyway. However by the time I arrived they had gone to bed and the next morning I had to leave early before they got up.

Before setting off I put the ring for safe keeping in my stud box on the spare room dressing table, then when I arrived at Stockholm I membered my parents were selling the house. Worried that some viewer might pocket the box I called home, very complicated in those pre IDD days, to ask my mother to hide the box. She was horrified, as the ring was worth more than the house.

Happily all was well and I pitched up in the office on Monday morning with the ring back round my neck. The first thing Graham Miller asked, rather facetiously, was "well, did you find the ring?" I opened my shirt button and showed it off with a flourish. He was delighted and went round to Lloyd's soon after it opened to tell Gordon. Gordon's reaction was to the effect that he did not expect to be charged anything other than expenses. Graham told him he thought we were entitled to a small fee for my trouble, and by the way Youens had advertised a reward, which he was entitled to claim (£800), but he thought he could persuade me not to claim as long as Gordon agreed to settle our charges. After some discussion and I'm sure a certain amount of leg pulling, Gordon agreed, and that should have been that.

However when we put in our fee invoice, the insured, John Wallrock, who was also embarrassed at having put underwriters to such expense, decided that he had better broke it himself and went to see Gordon. During the ensuing conversation at the box, he commented that he was surprised to see that Gordon had sent his adjusters around Europe First Class. Gordon was surprised too and called Graham for an explanation.

Graham came in to see me and asked if I had gone First. I was able to show him the bill from Thomas Cooks, which clearly stated I had travelled economy. I then called Thomas

Cooks and found out that travelling on a Friday cost a premium over the other weekdays, of which clearly Wallrock was unaware. Presumably he and his wife flew to Nice midweek and he hadn't done his homework before complaining. I thought it was pretty cheap of him, since he had been all over me when I went round to his office and returned the ring. He even insisted on giving me a cigar. A few days later Gordon instructed us to deal with another claim for lost jewellery in Hampstead and wrote on the claims slip, "Try going there First Class!" I did that job too and found the missing ring in the lining of a handbag, so I thought I must be rather good at this sort of thing.

A few weeks later we were instructed to deal with the loss of a brooch given to the singer Lulu by her then husband, Bee Gee star Maurice Gibb. She met me at the door of her house in north London in a short dressing gown and fluffy high heel mules and showed me where the brooch was last seen, but no luck and I don't think I have found anything else ever since.

As a footnote to the Wallrock claim, some years later it became public knowledge that some underwriters had set up baby reinsurance syndicates into which they siphoned off some of their quality accounts and they invited some of their best supporters to participate in the benefits. Peter Cameron-Webb was one such underwriter and Wallrock was one of the beneficiaries. To his great credit, when all was revealed, Wallrock is thought to have reimbursed all the money he had received. But shame on Cameron-Webb, Peter Green (a past Chairman of Lloyd's) and the many others who were in on the scam.

Dogs and donkeys

Later, in October 1970, we had a claim on a spaghetti western made in Colombia and starring Bud Spencer and Terrence Hill. It was called *They Call Him Trinity*. The script was in Italian because the stars spoke no English, which was dubbed later, and the producer was a huge, bearded character called Italo Zingarelli, who had been a whizz at making cheap porn movies. A dog had bitten Bud on the behind and filming was delayed because everyone was worried the dog was rabid. Well that is what was reported to us, and without evidence to the contrary we had to accept.

I met Zingarelli at his offices. He spoke no English and my Italian was limited so I took our man in Rome, Massimo Volpe. Massimo was anything but. He was about five feet tall and the same again round. Zingarelli's man was much the same and they hated each other. While they sat and fought, Zingarelli produced a raft of magazines depicting ladies doing rude things with donkeys which was all new to me and we sat and admired the action waiting for our reps to sort themselves out, which in the end they did and everyone was happy.

This film made Zingarelli, and he never looked back. Neither did Bud or Terrence, with or without English, and they went on to make another and had another claim. This time it was damage to the negative. When I met Zingarelli to discuss the claim, he asked how much the insurers wanted to pay and I offered half what I thought the claim was worth. He bit my hand off and took me out to lunch at the Giarosta Toscana, a wonderful restaurant at the top of

Via Veneto - turn right and it's 100 yards down on the right. Massive amounts of antipasti, followed by pasta, followed by meat grilled on an open fire and so on. I'd been there before and recommend it to everyone. We had a happy time and that was that. Zingarelli turned his interest to wine making and, after he died, his son Sergio carried on the tradition. *Rocha delle Marcie* is the name of the business and the product is excellent.

Dinner in Dracula country

In the summer of 1971 we had a claim in Romania, which was then behind the Iron Curtain. It must have been a cast claim because I took Frank Silvestri with me and we met in Bucharest for a long drive to Brasov in the foothills of the Transylvanian Alps, where the unit was on location. The film was called *Pope Joan* with Liv Ullman in the title role as the only female Pope, directed by Michael Anderson, who had made *The Dam Busters* and *Around the World in 80 Days*. It also featured a saucy little actress called Lesley-Anne Down, who played the aristocratic daughter in a then current and immensely popular TV soap called *Upstairs Downstairs*.

The producer was a friend called David White and he took Frank and me out to dinner. David had heard about some restaurant up in the mountains, which was reputed to be worth the trouble. Liv plus boyfriend and the lovely Lesley-Anne wanted to come along for the ride, so off we went in a Russian 4x4 which was rather long in the tooth. The restaurant turned out to be a shack with wolves' masks hanging from the wall, in the middle of nowhere, patronised only by locals, all armed to the teeth, and they were deeply suspicious of us and menacing. The men's eyes looked up when they saw the girls and they licked their lips.

We had two choices: run for it or brave it out and try to make friends. We opted for the latter, went up to shake them by the hand and explain why we were there. No one spoke any mutual language but we must have made ourselves understood and everyone settled down eventually. The food was basic stew, made of - well, it probably doesn't bear thinking about (it may well have been bear), but tasty, and the local wine was surprisingly acceptable. Even so lovely Lesley proved very standoffish, no joy there at all.

Lunch with Sophia

A couple of months later Frank Silvestri and I went to a location near Monza for some reason or another. I have no idea what the film was called or what happened to it but it starred Sophia Loren, who must be one of the most beautiful actresses ever to grace the silver screen. In this show she was a nun. At lunch – still in her habit - she asked Frank, whom she knew well, and me to sit on her right and left hand. It's the only time I have ever had lunch with a nun, in or out of her habit, and with Sophia I was completely enchanted. She was a pin up in one of my exercise books at Sherborne and here I was at her side.

The Grocers' Company

There are many Livery companies in the City, all committed to good works in one form or another. They had started as trade guilds and the Grocers' Company had originally been a group of pepper merchants in the 1100s, who collaborated to monitor the quality and quantity of bagged peppercorns being imported into London. Their remit soon extended to other spices and while they were known as the Pepperers, this was thought to be too generic and so they became the Grocers since the spices were all imported by the 'groce', which later became 'gross'. The Grocers are for the most part a thoroughly nice bunch of mostly professional men and women, many of whose families have been members of the company for generations.

I mention all this because in November 1971 Annabelle's father, who I suspect was quite keen that I should either marry his daughter or let her get on with the rest of her life, invited me to a white tie do at Grocers' Hall, where he had been Master Grocer a few years before. It was a very grand affair to meet the newly-elected Lord Mayor of London, and I was having the greatest difficulty stopping my bow tie from spinning like a helicopter rotor. The man on my right was a rather pompous doctor called Simpson. He was keen to tell me he was an expert slaughterer of airborne game and had had 'Charles' to stay the previous weekend. "Such a pretty shot, you know." I looked at him in all innocence and asked "Charles who?" He looked very down his nose and said "Prince Charles" and that was that. I don't think we spoke again all evening.

A miscommunication

Every now and again adjusters are sent on a wild goose chase, sometimes of their own making, sometimes as result of confusion elsewhere. In December 1971 Jock Sutherland, one of Graham Miller's partners, sent me down to the French Riviera to deal with storm damage to a holiday village. A hundred and twenty-five cottages had been destroyed, along with a TV mast and a chimneystack. When I arrived in Nice airport the only car Hertz had left for me to hire was a large BMW saloon, which they kindly let me have at minimal rental and off I set to site, where I was met by the manager. No one else was about, this being out of season.

The man seemed quite surprised to see me at all, let alone in a rather smart car, and invited me into his house for coffee. I said that was very kind but time was of the essence and I wanted to get back to London that night, so please would he take me round the camp and show me the damage. This time it was my turn to be surprised when he said that the damage was limited to the chimney of cottage number 125, which had been blown down in a gale, taking the TV aerial with it. We restricted our fee to expenses only.

Long-Distance Call

Jock's department did quite a few claims for NATO projects under construction. One such was a hush-hush listening post in the mountains near Salonika in northern Greece. Everyone on site had to be positively vetted and no one else was available at short notice, so Jock sent me. My details were submitted to the Foreign Office and the next evening a man in a bowler hat and black coat and carrying a briefcase arrived at the flat in Chesham Street to ask a lot of questions. I fear I thought the whole business was a bit of a joke, but the next day my visit was authorised. There could not have been much positive vetting in that short time, but maybe Dad being Chaplain-General helped.

I had to travel via Athens overnight and stayed at the Hilton, where the bar on the top floor had a magnificent view over the Acropolis. I found myself chatting to a Dutchman who was a fellow insurance man with the American Insurance Group otherwise known as AIG, a smoke and mirrors outfit if ever there was one, but phenomenally success nevertheless. When we parted company we exchanged cards and his name was Constant Pardon. There was not a lot to see when I arrived at the NATO site but the Project Manager was very friendly and insisted on me calling Annabelle by satellite telephone, something quite unheard of in those days when it was all you could do to make a local call.

IRA sorted – not

A week or so before Christmas Marcel Ophuls, a documentary film maker of some renown, was hospitalised in Belfast while making a film about the life of a British squaddie coping with the so called 'Troubles'. I think it was called *A Sense of Loss*. Marcel's problem was haemorrhoids, something with which I was, and still am, only too familiar. I went to see him in his ward in the Royal Victoria Hospital and commiserated. I walked back to the Europa Hotel, famous for being bombed by the IRA, to be welcomed by the doorman, who told me I was completely mad and not on any account to walk around Belfast with or without an escort.

His concern was well placed. That evening the General commanding the British Army in Northern Ireland, Sir

Harry Tuzo, whose daughter had shared a flat with my old girlfriend Serena Brett, was rash enough to announce on national TV that the IRA had been contained and hostilities were as good as over. Within hours all hell was let loose all over the city and I had a bird's eye view from the top of the hotel. Bombs were going off all over the place, buildings on fire and police, army and fire engines skidding in all directions. Quite exciting really. Marcel started filming a week late, but as his condition was pre-existed inception of the insurance policy I don't think we ever paid any claim.

I mentioned earlier that Graham Miller had three partners, one of whom was Jim Riseam, who had opened in Johannesburg and established a network of offices in the Union. He was always having wife problems and came back to Europe in 1969 to escape the latest. With Graham's blessing he opened an office in Zürich, from where he handled a large and profitable book of offshore business. He was a very capable businessman and loss adjuster. I always thought he would succeed Graham Miller in due course. We always got on well and I liked him a lot. One morning in 1971 we heard he had been taken ill in Caracas, with a blocked colon. Sadly he never recovered from the surgery. He was only 48.

Foot in mouth

During the late summer of 1971 United Artists backed Bernardo Bertolucci to direct Marlon Brando in a two-handed drama called *Last Tango in Paris* with an unknown actress, Maria Schneider. Brando had a son, Christian, who was always in trouble, and during a break in his schedule in Paris Brando had flown back to LA to see him. They had been horsing around at home when Brando fell over and dislocated his shoulder. He was in a lot of pain when he returned to the set in Paris and had limited movement of his upper body. Result: delay to complete principal photography thanks to slow working.

I pitched up on the set, where Brando was sitting slumped in a chair looking grumpy. Bertolucci took me to meet him and explained he needed Brando in a shower scene, which involving vigorous washing. Brando's doctor had confirmed this was out of the question for several days, supported by our local doctor, a man called Zucherelli. Bertolucci said he could work around his star but he anticipated an extra day's shooting as result. Having been shown all the back-up documents, this did not seem unreasonable and I was not in any position to challenge the director's artistic license, so I duly reported and the claim was paid. When I went to see the film in Rome several months later I discovered that what Bertolucci had not told me was that rather than washing himself, Brando was vigorously washing the girl.

She was a bit of an oddball was Maria Schneider. She acquired celebrity status as result of *Last Tango* but she must have been very unhappy and sought solace in sex, drugs and booze. While making a film for Carlo Ponti in Rome a year or two later, she fell in love with a girl who was committed to a psychiatric hospital and Maria elected to have herself also committed so that she could be with her. In comes a claim for delay on basis she was nuts, and when I told Ponti she was just playing up so nothing doing, he produced medical evidence to the contrary. Frank Silvestri's consultant backed Ponti's man, so we were scuppered. Money probably passed, but this was Italy. Some you win, some you don't.

There's a postscript to this story later.

CHAPTER 11

Settling down

Three days before the year was out I found myself on my knees at Annabelle's feet for some reason or another during a cosy supper à deux in the Chesham Street flat, and moments later she accept a proposal of marriage before I even had time to actually make it – well, that's my story. I called my prospective father-in-law the next morning to ask for his daughter's hand and cunningly booked an appointment in his office for midday in the sure and certain hope lunch would be involved. Not a bit of it, I ticked the box and we went our separate ways. At a New Year's Eve party some rather exotic Swedish lady came up to me and asked huskily "your fiancée, she is so beautiful. Is she Swedish?"

The actress Romy Schneider was lucky enough to look a bit like Annabelle, but she was Austrian.

About Annabelle

Annabelle was born on April 6, 1949 (the first day of the new tax year) in Sussex, the third and youngest child of Donald Methven, a lawyer and Pam, née Sidebottom. If she had been born a day earlier her parents would have had a whole year's child tax allowance and Donald was most upset, or said he was. Annabelle had an elder sister, Susie, who walked on water, and a brother in the middle, Colin, who was quite the opposite and always in trouble. When Annabelle was about 13 the family moved from Sussex to a row of converted cottages in Russells Water, a village about five miles north west of Henley-on-Thames, and she went to a convent near High Wycombe which has since closed.

At sixteen she was sent off to learn Italian in Rome, working for some aristocratic household where she attracted the (allegedly) unwanted attention of the Marchese and she was returned to London by the Marchese. She was then sent to Montpellier University to learn French and fell in with a *pied noir* stallion, whose parents were French but lived in Algeria.

Having learnt not much French, let alone Italian, she went to a secretarial college in London called Queens where she learnt to type and – well, be a secretary. That's what girls did in those days. After graduating she took several jobs ending up working for the Corporation of London, by which time I had met her. She was and still is pretty much perfect, lovely and loving as well as round and squidgy in all the right places: the ideal companion for life as well as being a wonderful cook and mother, housewife and best friend.

All her immediate family were quite charming and very good-looking too. Her father went to Wellington and on to Magdalen College, Oxford, where he had his wicked way with the ladies left and right if the rampant rumours were to be believed. He trained as a barrister, volunteered for the army when war broke out, was taken ill in West Africa and spent the rest of the war at a staff liaison job in London. He was often in daily communication with Winston Churchill, who would ring him up asking for news on this or that issue of the day. It was Donald's job to find out and report back.

During this time he met and married Pam Sidebottom, who worked in nearby offices and had been warned to steer well clear of the dashing major, which warnings she elected to ignore. Pam was very beautiful, blonde in her youth with high cheekbones and a clear rosy complexion. Her mother was an Anglo-Argentinian whose first language was Spanish and her father built railways, as one did. Part of her charm was that she was shy and tended to keep herself in the background, but she had a considered and sensible opinion on the important matters of the day almost until she died, aged 96.

Susie and Colin were both unusually good looking. Annabelle thinks she's the runt of the litter. Would I marry the runt of a litter, when I'm so good looking myself? I've already said Romy Schneider looked a bit like her but not as good, and it doesn't get better than that. Susie was drop dead gorgeous too, and still is. She was born in 1942. She has her mother's high cheekbones and good skin, fair hair and neat figure. More importantly, she is bright and articulate. She had strings of admirers, just like my own sister Georgina, and all worshipped her, which must be quite boring. In the end she married Ian Pasley-Tyler, a banker whose parents owned a pile in Northamptonshire. They were married in 1968 and Nigel Barttelot (Nigel the Rival from my Verbier holiday in 1968) was Best Man.

Colin was born in 1946 and was a bit of a con man by all accounts. He used to take the bus to school having been given the correct fare by his mother. The conductor would come along and ask for the money and Colin would look sad, tell the conductor his parents could not afford the fare and hope the old bat sitting next to him would ante up, which they usually did. This was clearly good grounding for the successful insurance broker he was to become.

He followed his father to Wellington and then the army, where he joined the Green Jackets as a private soldier. However he did not care for walking and transferred to the Enniskillen Dragoon Guards, otherwise known as the Skins, where he rode around in a ferret car, when he wasn't riding around with the local damsels. After a short service commission he signed off and went to work for Willis Faber & Dumas, a pre-eminent Lloyd's broker, for the rest of his business life. He was one of the few members of Lloyd's who came away with his fortune intact. Funny that.

Marriage

Annabelle and I were married in the late afternoon of Wednesday, March 8, 1972 at the Guards Chapel in London during one of many miners' strikes, when there was limited electricity so you had to choose your moment. I don't think the Household Brigade was best pleased with us wanting to use their chapel, but I had sung in the choir there when at

Eagle House, I went there most Sundays and Dad was Chaplain-General as well as an honorary Grenadier, so they went along.

Dad married us and Robert Stopford, the Bishop of London, blessed us. He had his chaplain in attendance, and Freddie White, chaplain to the Household Division, was there too, so there were four clerics in on the act. We have lived happily ever after – well, as much as one can with all the slings and arrows life tends to throw, and there were plenty to come in our direction.

My sister Georgina, Annabelle's cousin Sally Morris and her best friend Sarah Bull were the elder bridesmaids. The young attendants consisted of Robin Hillyard's son Dominic and daughter Lucy, cousin Jane Hopkins' son Charlie, and Emma Dixey, whose father Peter I had worked with in my days at the Royal Exchange Assurance. My Best Man was Mike Dewar and the ushers were my flatmate Christopher Seddon, Derek Plunkett, a J&B Rare whisky salesman, Roger Ker, a soldier to whom I would be Best Man later that year, Anthony Palmer, late of the flat in Drayton Gardens, and my two soon to be brothers-in-law Colin Methven and Ian Pasley-Tyler.

We had our reception at Grocers' Hall in the City, the guests being taken to and fro in London Routemaster buses hired for the occasion, as indeed they were again 37+ years later at our daughter Arabella's wedding to take her guests from St Peter's Italian Church in Clerkenwell Road to Grocers' Hall. However our reception was considerably shorter than Arabella's. No sooner had we arrived and Tom Hustler had done his stuff (Tom was default photographer on such occasions although the press, well all right the

Portman Press, were also in attendance), there were the speeches and we were off in a gold Rolls Royce (oh dear) to the Skyline Hotel near Heathrow for the night. I think we were only at our reception for an hour and a half.

The Skyline was brand new and had a swimming pool in the lobby: cool or what? All right - I agree, totally naff. The room was even naffer, with an orange en suite bathroom and no means of opening the window for some fresh air as the air conditioning was not working, this being England in March. Mr Brunger, the Beadle (general manager) at Grocers' Hall, had thoughtfully put a bottle of champagne in our luggage which we polished off in short order, Annabelle on an empty stomach and me not much better. I had been in the office all morning, skipped lunch and had a few eats at the reception. In any event we went down to the coffee shop. I wolfed down a steak and a couple of beers. Annabelle pushed an omelette round her plate and we retired back to our room, where she was sick most of the night. Some first night.

Honeymoon, and morning sickness

The next morning we flew to Antigua on a BOAC (now BA) VC10. Well, we were on a Speedbird package: flight, hotel and half board. Annabelle, still looking green, sat by the window, me in the middle and a small but plump Peruvian businessman on the aisle. It was rather cramped and he did not smell that fresh. On arrival the heat was a pleasant shock after the drab early spring back home and we were collected in an ancient American gas-guzzler, which took us to the Hawksbill Beach Hotel. It's still there but much bigger and modernised. Our room overlooked the beach and my bride was off there in a shot to soak up the rays, which she did all day every day, and was badly burnt in consequence, to the extent that she could hardly walk by day three and was generally off colour. She couldn't eat any of the breakfast or dinner, all excellent, all included and was only hungry at lunch, which was extra. So the $200 cash (say $1,200 today) which I had thought would be more than enough to cover out of pocket expenses was soon history.

One day I took Annabelle sailing in a Topper, which was about twice the size of a surfboard. The combined weight of us on board plus the absence of any breeze meant we ended up stranded on a coral reef. It was a long time before I heard the end of that one. Now I come to think about it, I remember - it's still current. Another day we rented a Mini-Moke, a Mini Minor chassis with a Jeep body, in which we toured the island, very pleased with ourselves until some schoolchildren started throwing stones at us. It was a very pretty island, but we have never had any desire to return.

Back in London after the excitement of the wedding and honeymoon, life was a bit of a letdown, particularly as there was nothing exotic going on in the office although we were busy. However that was to change, and sooner than intended. I came home from the office one evening towards the end of August and noticed that Annabelle was looking a bit off colour. I asked her if she was feeling OK. She said she was, but she had been to the doctor. I asked why if she was feeling OK, and she said why do you think? It took a few moments for the penny to drop, then it dawned on me that school fees would be along shortly.

On the move again

A couple of days later I had business in Rome and we had arranged to meet in Paris and spend a long weekend in the Loire. We decided to stick to the plan, even if there was a strong chance Annabelle would be feeling queasy. That was another holiday on the edge, especially when we enter our hotel dining room on the first night and encountered some chap to whom Annabelle had taken exception at a dinner party a few weeks earlier. I was also told during that trip that we needed larger accommodation and anyway she didn't care much any longer for all the skeletons in the cupboards at Chesham Street, even if they were few and far between.

Annabelle was working for John D Wood, the estate agents, who had an office off Chelsea Green, and she was told that the up and coming area to live in London was Fulham, which she thought was somewhere on the way to Sandown Races. I did not fancy moving to the sticks, having lived close to one end of Pont Street or the other for the best part of the last dozen or so years.

Anyway I agreed to take a look and we went off to inspect a four-bedroom house in Perrymead Street, London SW6, which had been lived in by a tax inspector and his family since the thirties. He told us he had bought it for £900 and would we care to part with £36,000 if we wanted it, despite no central heating and one ancient bathroom. We agreed that it didn't really matter where you were living once you had closed the front door. The commute wasn't great but I could manage, so we did a deal there and then.

We then drove back to civilisation and went to a cocktail party, where I ran into a friend and told him what we were doing. He said that if we wanted to buy in Fulham, the house should have a lion on it. I asked what he meant and he said he had no idea, but that was what he had been told. Well I can tell you we were out of that party and back to Perrymead Street SW6 without looking back. When we arrived we stood on the other side of the street and saw four lion statues on each corner of the parapet above the second floor bay window. So that's all right then. All houses on this, the Peterborough Estate, came to be known, years after we had moved on, as "The Lion Houses" and commanded a premium, thanks to their design and build quality.

We moved in at the end of September 1972, having sold Chesham St to a barrister called Mills-Owen from Hong Kong, whose father was a judge. He gave us about £30,000 for the flat and Richard Hartley, one of our neighbours who was still renting on the second floor, nearly blew a gasket. Six months before I bought our maisonette for £9,000, Richard had been offered the lease on his much nicer flat for £5,000, which he had rejected as being too expensive. He was an eminent libel QC, and he is still there.

Perrymead needed a new kitchen and two new bathrooms as well as central heating, redecorating and new carpets throughout, not to mention some furniture. We hired a jobbing builder called Mr Whitford and we agreed that he would work exclusively for us for as long as it took. We were therefore very cross when from the car we saw him fully kitted up beetling into another house in nearby Waterford Road, where clearly he had another job. I was so incensed I rang the doorbell and asked the chap who responded if I could talk to Whitford. Obviously Whitford had warned him and he said, "No you can't. Now f*** off". His name was David Selby. Annabelle recognised him when he answered the door and had hidden herself while I took the flak. Evidently Selby had taken her out at some stage. Selby is still on the radar. So is Mrs Selby.

Shih Tzus

That first Christmas I wanted Annabelle to wake up and find a Paddington Bear toy (they had just hit the shops thanks to the efforts of Jeremy Clarkson's mother, yes – the TV petrolhead) peeping at her from the top of her Christmas stocking, but could I find one? Harrods, Hamleys, Peter Jones et al were fresh out of them. In fact I don't think there were that many made then, just a few for Christmas to see if they caught on, and clearly they had. Anyway that was that and on the Saturday before Christmas we parked our new Fiat 128 estate car opposite The Carlton Tower Hotel in Sloane Street and walked down Hans Crescent to shop in Harrods, as one did in those days. It was a pretty good store. Its cable address was 'Everything London'.

A few yards down Hans Crescent there was a pet shop called Town and Country Dogs. In the window there were three what looked like miniature English Sheep Dog puppies and most attractive they were, so for fun in we went. We mollycoddled all three and to say we were rather taken would be something of an understatement. They were Shih Tzus; we had vaguely heard of them because Elizabeth Taylor had one.

When I asked the price and was told forty guineas (£42)

quite a sum then, we handed the dogs back and left. But two hours later we walked back to the car past the pet shop and there was only one puppy in the window. His name was Sam Sam and he was the first in a line of Shih Tzus we have had with us continuously to this day. Lovely Dogs! The girl who sold us Sam Sam was called Loraine Melville and we see her from time to time as she lives nearby.

No 1 Son

The first few months of the New Year 1973 were spent building up to the arrival of our first-born. I was made to attend a Father's Class run by Betty Parsons, whose son is Nicholas Parsons, the 'host' of the game show *Just a Minute*. All Annabelle's pregnant friends' husbands went, so there was no escape. The only thing I can remember learning was to help her breathe during the contractions, whatever they were. The baby was due on Friday April 13, but happily there was no action until the following evening when we having supper with my old flatmate Ant Palmer and his lovely then wife Nicki at their house in Wilkinson St, Lambeth.

Just before we sat down to eat, Annabelle's waters broke and we rushed off to the Westminster Hospital, thinking an arrival was imminent. No such luck. Annabelle spent the entire night and all the following morning lying on a hard delivery table while I tried to sleep on a clapped-out sofa in a corridor nearby, but like an idiot I had dosed myself up with coffee laced with brandy and didn't sleep a wink.

Christian Mark Methven Youens arrived at 2.14pm on Palm Sunday, April 15, 1972, and his proud and rather tearful father went off to give thanks at Evensong in Westminster Abbey. I'm ashamed to say I'd never been to the Abbey before and I've never been since. Annabelle was expected to remain in hospital for at least a week and I was expected to dance attendance at every available opportunity. As luck would have it Pier Paolo Pasolini went sick while directing *Arabian Nights* in Isfahan, Iran and filming had ground to a halt. There was no such thing as paternity leave then. Annabelle went ballistic, but business was business and I had to go, so I arranged for Harrods to deliver a fresh rose every morning - talk about fingers down the throat. Off I went to Rome to collect Frank Silvestri and on to Tehran. And Isfahan. I left on Wednesday and was back at lunchtime on Saturday, but there was still hell to pay, roses or no roses. I did investigate buying Christian a rug in the Isfahan Grand Bazaar, but as they were about half the price in Harrods I kept my wallet in my pocket. The poor chap never did get a Persian rug.

CHAPTER 12

Georgina

Two months after Christian arrived we had another reason to celebrate - my sister Georgina married her beau, Piers Weld-Forester. Well, he wasn't so much beau as completely wild. He had been a Greenjacket and had gatecrashed my friend Mike Dewar's stag night back in July 1968, which I had organised in the Café Royal. Not long afterwards, thanks to a different kind of gatecrashing, Pier's Commanding Officer suggested he might want to think about another career. Piers had a low-slung Ferrari, which he was adept at driving under the barrier and past the sentries at his barracks in Germany. He did it one too many times.

Piers took the hint and went into long-distance motor racing, as one does. The next time I met him, a year or so after the stag do, was on the Central Line, covered in oil, bleary eyed and unshaven: Piers, not me. He was in the middle of some motor marathon in Brazil and had taken time out to fly back to London, collect some spare parts from somewhere in the East End and fly back. He was on his way in from Heathrow and his return flight left that afternoon.

By the time he met Georgina, who was a model and had had no shortage of boyfriends, he had his own long-distance road haulage business, Frostie Trucking (Frostie having been Piers' nickname at Harrow). He specialised in hauling 40ft refrigerated containers out to Tehran, charging his UK client for the return trip empty and then usually finding cargo anyway. He was due to inherit an estate in Ireland, complete with a title. One time coming back from a weekend in Ireland, in the early hours of the morning, he and Georgina managed to drive the Ferrari from the Severn Bridge to Fulham, a distance of around 120 miles, in 58 minutes.

They were married by Dad in June 1973, like us at the Guards Chapel, and after their reception at the Senior, Dad's club in Pall Mall, now the Institute of Directors, they went away in one of Piers' tractors, complete with a loaded container. At Georgina's insistence Piers had given up motor racing and contented himself riding around town on high-speed motor cycles with her on the back.

On Sunday March 3, 1974 my parents were up at Brodsworth, where Dad consecrated the burial of his mother's ashes - she had died a few months before Christmas - and drove back to Woking after lunch. Annabelle and I had been staying the weekend with our newly-married friends Roger and Rosie Ker. En route we had stopped off at a garden centre near Andover and bought a cotoneaster, which I had just planted in the garden at

Perrymead when the telephone rang. It was my father, clearly distraught, to say that Georgina was on a flight home from Paris which had crashed. It was feared there were no survivors. She was only 22.

Georgina was a photographic model and was always in the gossip columns because she was attractive, well-connected and part of 'Swinging London'. She was often referred to as 'the daughter of the Queen's chaplain' (somewhat stretching the envelope - Dad was one of fifty Queen's Honorary Chaplains) and Piers had taken out Princess Anne several times. She made the front-page headlines next morning in all the papers. She had been on an assignment in southern Spain over the weekend, together with three other models and a film crew. They had been due to fly back by BEA direct to London but the cabin crews went on strike, so they all flew Iberia to Orly Airport outside Paris and waited for a connection.

There were many people trying to get back to London from all over Europe and Orly was as good as any place to head for. There must have been hundreds stranded, waiting for spare seats. Georgina's party was allocated a Turkish Airlines DC10 on its way to Heathrow from Istanbul. Unfortunately a Moroccan baggage handler did not shut one of the cargo doors properly. There was no ground engineer on duty and the flight engineer, who should have checked the external condition of the aircraft before departure, failed to do so. As result the door blew open and damaged both the controls to the rear elevators and No 2 engine, so the pilot was unable to control the aircraft.

The final moments of the passengers and crew simply do not bear thinking about. The aircraft nose-dived into

Ermenonville Forest, north of Paris. Nothing of Georgina was ever recovered. She was wearing a ring, which was a Weld-Forester heirloom, never to be seen again. People are still finding bits of wreckage in the forest, which they leave on the walls of a dreary memorial built at the point of impact.

My parents never recovered from the shock. Dad had just retired and had nothing to distract him, and both of them resorted to alcohol to deaden the misery. Annabelle and I went to see them the day after the accident at their new house opposite Woking Golf Course. We took Christian, who was not yet one, with us, against Mum's advice, as she thought he would be affected by the atmosphere. Good advice, which we decided to ignore. I think she was right and it did affect him and has done ever since, particularly in view of what was to come.

Piers was beside himself with grief, which he did his best to hide. They had a house in Waterford Road not far from us and he moved in with us for several weeks. Annabelle took over his laundry and thought he had been cleaning his motorbikes with most of his underwear. He was besieged by many well-meaning friends including his Best Man, Brian Alexander, who was the son of the late Field Marshal and had just married a banana heiress (Fyffe); Patrick Lichfield, the society photographer and cousin of the Queen; and Gavin McKecken, who was a charismatic businessman and still is. Annabelle and I were somewhat in awe of this bunch of glitterati but we weren't too impressed when one rather attractive woman pitched and offered Piers comfort of a physical nature. She was given short shrift. Somehow everyone kept going. I was lucky enough to have the business to occupy my attention. Annabelle had Christian.

At the end of March the French Authorities held a Memorial Service near the site of the crash and BEA provided an aircraft for close relatives of the victims to attend. I went with Mum and Dad. The aeroplane was a Court Lines chartered Tristar. The name on the fuselage was 'Halcyon Days'. Dad arranged for an Embassy car to collect us at Le Bourget and take us to the service, which avoided us having to sit in a coach with all the other unhappy people. Piers had business in Spain and made his own arrangements to join us. He arrived late and looked as if he had not been to bed for a week. His only baggage was a battered brief case stuffed with Spanish pesetas.

As the victims came from all over the world and were Christian, Jewish, Muslim and other faiths, the service was a mishmash with one man chanting in painful fashion. Dad said 'he sounds like I feel' which set us off giggling, much to the disgust of our neighbours. A memorial service for Georgina was held at the Guards Chapel a month after her death. Dad took it. How he managed to cope I don't know. Mum wanted to run for home immediately afterwards but was prevailed upon to stay and greet the mourners. The chapel was packed.

I never really knew my sister. She was born nearly nine years after me, when I was at prep school. My place in my parents' affection seemed to have been displaced by her, which I resented but learned to live with, even though she sensed this and played up to it. School was an escape. We went our separate ways and were never close, although

Annabelle, who was less than three years older than her, was able to close the gap a bit.

In the circumstances I am ashamed to admit I did not feel Georgina's loss as much as I should have done, since she never really featured in my life except as an irritant. Later on I began to appreciate how much I missed her. The age gap would have shrunk over the years and we would have become much closer, and we would have been united in helping to cope with our ageing parents quite apart from anything else.

Whether Georgina's marriage to Piers would have stood the tests of time is anyone's guess. My mother was convinced to the contrary. Piers was a highly unlikely suitor. He would have become the Marquis of Ormonde, an Irish title, through his mother. Maybe that would have provided a bond. I fear they both would have found a lot to distract them.

There are still people out there in love with Georgina's memory. I sat next to Patsy Seddon, the dress designer, at a lunch not long ago. She told me her friend and partner Peter Urquhart was still in love with Georgina 40 years after her death. Jonathan Hubbard-Ford's wife Carolyn once admitted wistfully that Jonathan (he who introduced Annabelle to me) was also of the same mind.

For all of us Georgina is still 22. Not for her to be wearied by age or condemned by the years. Sometimes I meet people she knew and then, and only then, do I receive a sharp reminder of the passing of the years since that dreadful time.

Sadly more tragedy was to come, a great deal more.

CHAPTER 13

Hot spots and hotshots

My parents went on holiday to Cyprus in May 1974 and took a serviced flat in Kyrenia with a pool overlooking the Mediterranean. They came back feeling a lot better and recommended the place highly, so we decided to try it ourselves that July. At the time I was doing quite a bit of work overseas for overseas clients. In those innocent days you could get away with billing offshore, and the UK tax authorities were none the wiser so long as work carried out in the UK was billed from the UK. This enabled me to be paid offshore in lovely Swiss francs. Zürich office arranged for me to have an account with Julius Baer, a small private bank, from where I collected the folding stuff in large bills, which I brought back to the UK in a sock. The trip to Kyrenia was paid for thus.

We rented a Mini-Moke and had a lot of fun driving

about my old haunts from holidays there in the fifties, until the beginning of the second week. We were driving through Kyrenia town when Annabelle thought she heard the sound of machine gun fire. I pooh poohed her (because I know everything) and said it was a pneumatic drill. When we got back to our block of serviced flats, the staff were running around like headless chickens because there was a revolution going on.

Cyprus had been a melting pot for centuries, principally between Greeks and Turks. It had been a British Protectorate after the war and more recently a sovereign republic, which was acceptable to the Turks, but the Greek Junta wanted to annex the island. So while we were there they decided to take control, and in heavy-handed fashion. Kyrenia and the northern part of the island was mainly Turkish, but Greeks lived there too and heretofore they had all seemed to suffer each other in relative silence. The Junta appointed a villain called Sampson as President, which was all too much for the Turkish government, and on July 20 they invaded Kyrenia.

In the meantime we were confined to barracks, ie the compound in which our flat was located, and were not even allowed to go shopping for the first couple of days until things calmed down. There was a troupe of the Kirov ballet in town, which had been due to move on the day of the coup, and they took over several empty flats in our block. They exercised in the parking area for hours every day and then went swimming in the pool without bothering to shower first. As result the salt water in the pool turned cloudy and grey. It had to be emptied overnight and refilled, which was a long process and we all complained. Eventually the dancers were prevailed upon to wash before swimming and everyone was happy.

By the Thursday we were allowed to resume normal travel and drove to Famagusta to collect some bespoke shoes I had ordered. We saw only a few other vehicles on the road and Famagusta was a ghost town. Luckily I had a radio, which all our fellow residents would listen to for news around the pool. The German Government was sending aeroplanes to collect their citizens from Nicosia airport, which was open for charter traffic, but the Foreign Office was telling all Brits to carry on as normal and evacuation was not necessary. We were booked to return on a scheduled Cyprus Airways flight on Friday July 19 and, on the day before, Sampson announced that everything was back to normal including Cyprus Airways flights.

Our taxi duly collected us on the Friday morning and took us to Nicosia, where we were astonished to see six or seven German charter aircraft loading passengers and other German aircraft arriving as we checked in. We were told our flight had been delayed and in the end had to wait about eight hours, during which time German and other chartered flights came and went. No sign of any British. When we eventually took off, the airport was completely empty save one small aircraft, which took off after us. Our aeroplane was completely packed, with people in the jump seats in the cockpit as well as any spare crew seats. There was no fuel at Nicosia and we had to refuel in Brussels, as we did not have enough to reach Heathrow.

We were the lucky ones. The next morning the Turks invaded and we have no idea what happened to the people we had made friends, with including a charming Greek who had taken a great fancy to my bride. Poor chap. The aircraft which had brought us home flew back and was blown up by Turkish jets the next morning. Nicosia airport was closed indefinitely. HMS *Hermes*, the aircraft carrier, was sent to evacuate British citizens from Northern Cyprus offshore Kyrenia about a week later and ferry them round to RAF Larnaca on the south, which was unaffected by the turmoil. From there they were flown home, the Foreign Office charging an extortionate fee for the privilege. As I say, we were the lucky ones.

1974 was otherwise a fairly quiet year, apart from Annabelle finding herself pregnant again and deciding that our four-bedroom house in Fulham was not big enough for two children and a nanny. We put Perrymead on the market in the autumn, even though it was a terrible time to sell. We asked what we had paid and spent on the place and were given £42,000 in early January 1975, having not looked for the next place until the sale was guaranteed. The economic climate was dire and houses were not selling. My friend Robin Hillyard had been caught between two stools, buying one house before he sold the first, and the cost of the bridging loan almost bankrupted him.

Madras and Bombay

I did have one interesting job in December 1974, which involved a trip to Madras (now known as Chennai for some reason), where Carole Andre was sick while making a popular Italian TV mini-series called *Sandokan*. She was a lovely French actress who had made a bit of a name for herself in *Death in Venice*. I arranged to meet Frank

Silvestri in Bombay (now known as Mumbai for some reason), and together we flew on to Madras, arriving in the morning unannounced, because there was a rumour that production was using Carole's illness as a pretext for a claim, never thinking anyone would check them out.

We knew the unit was staying at the Taj Coromandel hotel so we took a taxi there. Frank ran into someone in the hotel lobby he knew who wanted to know why we were there. When we told him, he rubbished us and said Carole was working on the set. Yes, she had been unwell but had never stopped production.

He took us out to the location and sure enough there she was, acting away. The production manager, Mario del Papa, whom I knew quite well, was surprised and rather embarrassed to see us and complained that we should have alerted him to our arrival. I told him he couldn't have received our telex, email equivalent in those days (ha ha). Carole thought the whole thing would have been quite funny except that her father had been shot and badly wounded in New York. She was anxious to complete her role and go home. Even so she took us both out to dinner at the Madras Club, a splendid reminder of the Raj: colonial facade, huge rooms, waiters in white uniforms, with white gloves too, hovering discreetly.

The next morning we were preparing to leave when del Papa reported that the male Indian lead, Kebir Bedi, who had been injured in a sword fight on another film (Indian actors often worked on several productions simultaneously, they still do for all I know), was now not coming back to *Sandakan* when scheduled and there might be a claim. I said we'd go and see Kebir and learnt that he was at home in Bombay somewhere near the Sun N Sand Hotel on Juhu beach, but no one knew quite where. His agent was out of contact. Kebir had no known telephone and del Papa did his best to put us off.

Well, that was not to be. We flew to Bombay and took a cab to the hotel. Indian cabs were based on the Morris Oxford, called an Ambassador. They were pretty primitive and this one stank of digested curry built up over years. I don't suppose much has changed. Only one door lock worked and there were holes in the floor, so our feet got wet as we went through puddles, of which there were plenty. Their main claim to fame is that every other car on the road was an Ambassador, so there was plenty of help available in the event of a breakdown.

On arrival at the Sun N Sand hotel we asked at reception if anyone knew where Kebir lived. He was one of India's leading actors and just about everyone claimed to know where to find him. He had a flat overlooking the beach about five minutes' walk away, so off we set. We had only gone a few yards when, much to our surprise, a fellow pedestrian yards ahead of us stopped, squatted down and moved his bowels, as Matron would say, right in front of us. No one else showed any interest, so we pressed on.

We found the block, identified the flat and rang the doorbell, which was answered by the man himself. We explained our business and he invited us in. Yes, he had been slightly injured in a sword fight and held up a hand to show us a finger with a small bandage. He was still working on the other film and would be back in Madras to meet his call in two days' time in accordance with his contract. We made our excuses and left. Kebir subsequently found fame as Louis Jordan's leading henchman in the James Bond film *Octopussy*.

Frank and I had dinner back at the hotel, made our way by cab back to the airport and caught an Air India jumbo to Rome departing at 1am. Even in First Class the smell of curry was all-pervading. I was very relieved to change planes for the last leg to London on BEA, where Annabelle met me and took me for Sunday lunch at Thatchers, her parents' place near Henley.

The next morning I called the brokers in Rome to brief them that there would be no claim. They were not best pleased that Frank and I had gone on a wild goose chase for nothing, but if we hadn't gone the insurers would have been at Production's mercy. As it was, when I was next in Rome a week later, I had to go and see the producer and tell him nothing doing. He was an evil-looking villain of whom the brokers were nervous and so was I. He was called Elio Scardimaglia, which did not help. OK, he wasn't Scaramanga, the *Man with the Golden Gun,* but it seemed a close call.

Olivia Harriet

All the while Annabelle was growing greater and greater with child, and on Monday January 13, 1975 at 3.20pm, after the best part of a twenty-hour wait, Olivia Harriet arrived safe and sound. She and her mother stayed on at the Westminster Hospital for another week and I managed to stay in the country all this time, which won a few brownie points. We had moved out of Perrymead a few weeks before Olivia's arrival and made camp in Piers' place on Waterford

Road a few hundred yards away. He was in New Zealand, having discovered the joys of Grand Prix 750cc motorcycle racing with his new best friend Barry Sheene, who had won the World Championship two years before.

Needless to say we were busily trying to find somewhere to live, as Piers was due back mid-February. Annabelle had found a mansion in Wandsworth which she liked, but it was still being renovated and the price of £52,000 was more than we wanted to pay. The owner was desperate to sell, his secondary bank had gone belly up and he was fresh out of funds. Before Olivia was born he invited me to make an offer, so I did - £41,000. He told me where I could put it and that was that, or so I thought. Very soon after Olivia arrived he called me again and asked if my offer was still on the table. I told him it was and we dealt.

On Friday February 14, 1975, sister Georgina's 23rd birthday, or would have been, we moved into 4 Patten Road, Wandsworth SW18. It had seven bedrooms, three bathrooms and a huge kitchen with family area overlooking a large garden as well as a big drawing room and dining room, not to mention a basement laundry and wine cellar. Not sure we really wanted all this, but it was too good a deal to refuse. We had a bedroom, bathroom and dressing room suite the like of which we have never had since.

Olivia, who had a bit of a cold, slept in our room in her cot and was still asleep when we got up the next morning. We decided to leave her sleeping while we dressed and started breakfast. When we went to get her up, she was dead. Out of the blue.

We were completely stunned and momentarily paralysed, and called the doctor. Meantime the Portuguese au pair packed her bags and left. This was a Saturday morning, but Dr Middleton came round immediately and took Olivia away, where to we had no idea and didn't want to. We simply could not think straight. The police may have turned up and made some enquiries before leaving us in peace. I suppose they might have initially thought her death might not have been an accident.

We rang Annabelle's parents, but they were out and I knew Dad was christening the daughter of Georgina's best friend from Downe House. The friend was called Penny née Yeoman and her daughter was to be christened Georgina at the family church somewhere near Bath. If we managed to get hold of my parents that would completely ruin the christening, so we did our best to stay calm and carry on unpacking. Peter Jones arrived mid-morning and delivered a kitchen table and chairs. I busied myself putting the table together so we had something to eat off. Not that any of us felt like eating. Poor Christian - how he coped I've no idea, but he was very brave.

The in-laws returned from wherever they had been some time after lunch, so we could offload on them, and as we did not feel like staying in Patten Road, we drove down to stay with them for the night in time for a stiff drink. In the meantime I left a message with the staff at the Yeomans asking my parents to ring me at the in-laws once the christening party was over. They did. We told them and they came straight to Henley. How we got through the rest of the weekend I can't remember, but I think I went back to work on Monday, feeling pretty fragile. My poor darling wife was in great discomfort with no one to suckle. Dr Middleton gave her pills to calm things down, but the pain was a constant reminder. There was no such thing as compassionate leave, let alone paternity leave, in 1975.

Olivia was cremated at Putney Vale on Thursday February 20, aged five and half weeks. Dad took the service. She was never christened but her would-be godparents came to support us. It was a dreadfully sad occasion, and seeing her small white coffin in the cold chapel affected everyone present. How Dad coped I have no idea, but cope he did. Lovely man.

Patten Road never took off after that. We finished doing the place up and it was a splendid house, but it was unloved and unwanted. We rattled around in it and were miserable, but we had no alternative but to keep going for Christian.

Olivia's was a cot death. She was the victim of Sudden Death in Infancy Syndrome, a phenomenon which has never been explained conclusively by medical science and theories abound as to the cause. She had a bit of a runny nose. She was well wrapped up in her shawl. She was lying on her tummy. The bedroom windows were open, so there was plenty of fresh air. It was mid-February but not particularly cold. Maybe it was a combination of these factors or something else. She was loved, but we were busy and I have always regretted that I did not pay her anything like as much attention as I should have done.

Hopefully one day we will meet again and I will try to make amends. We only ever had one photograph of her, a grainy black and white shot, slightly out of focus, of her in her cot. If she wasn't in her cot she spent much of her life in a carrycot on the ping-pong table at Waterford Road. To Annabelle and me, she is always with us.

Sachertorte and Père Bise

Towards the end of March we had a cast claim in Vienna. It must have been an emergency because I left on a Sunday with Ronnie Wilkinson, our doctor, as well as Robin Hillyard, the broker. We had meetings with the producer in the lobby of some large hotel and Omar Sharif came over and sat with us. Why, I have no idea. He may have been there for a bridge tournament. He may have been on the film. I can tell you he was utterly charming and fun to be with, although why I thought he was utterly charming and fun to be with I have no idea either. At Ronnie's insistence we dined at the Sacher Hotel, famous for Tafelspitz, a delicious boiled beef, and Sachertorte, a rich chocolate cake like no other. I thought I'd just mention that.

By the end of April Annabelle thought she had sufficiently recovered from Olivia's birth to cope with a break and we decided to try skiing, which we had never done together. We flew to Geneva, rented a Renault 4 and drove to Val Claret in the French Alps. The weather was kind and we enjoyed some gentle skiing, as she was not up anything too energetic. On the way back we treated ourselves to dinner and the night in a Michelin three-star restaurant called Père Bise on the Lac d'Annecy at Talloire. Bernard Levin, the late columnist from *The Times*, was always singing its praises, so we thought we'd give it a go.

Well, arriving in a Renault 4 didn't exactly set the doorman's heart racing, but we were shown to a comfortable suite in a converted barn on the lakeshore. I thought the dining room would be quite small, gingham tablecloths and simple but good food, albeit expensive. Not a bit of it. The dining room was enormous and packed. The tables were large, covered with thick white linen. The staff were all in tails, well the waiters were and so was the sommelière, yes a woman, who looked as if she could go at least three rounds with Cassius Clay – all right Mohammed Ali to you. She plonked the wine list down and left it open at the expensive end where the starting prices were in the thousands - of pounds. I thought we were in for a dry meal until I eventually found some local wines at reasonable prices, well, reasonable for a three-star place.

The menu was equally frightening. The Michelin Guide recommended the Table d'Hôte, so we went for that with lamb as mains, but not before starters and fish and followed by pudding and cheese or vice versa. Madame la Sommelière reappeared and I order a half bottle of white and some claret with the main course. She said "don't you sink zee claret iz a leettle light viz zee lamb?" I was cross.

Breakfast by the lac *en plein air* was magnificent but the bill was a bit of a shocker - FFr 700, which was the equivalent of £70. I think the previous week's skiing cost £200 all in, max.

The Youens family at Brodsworth Vicarage in 1938. From L to R David, Stephen, Dorothy (Granny to me), Margaret, Peter, John (Dad) and Rosemary, with dogs unknown.

Dad with his mother & father at Brodsworth circa 1939.

My parents at their wedding in Buxton, October 1940, with Best Man Noel Agazarian and Bridesmaid Rosemary Youens.

The author aged 18 months with Grandfather Alfred Chandler, at Priestcliffe, Derbyshire in 1945.

At an Officers' Mess party in Occupied Germany in late 1946.
L to R: my parents John & Pam, Granny Youens,
Marie & Stephen Youens – newly married.

The author on the running board of a commandeered Mercedes staff car, Bad Rothenfelde 1947.

The author and Mother at Berne Airport 1951. Waiting to board a Swissair flight back to London and Prep School.

The author about to be dropped off for his first term at Eagle House, September 1951.

The author 11 years later in the summer of 1962 working as a waiter at the Hotel Victoria in Wengen, Switzerland.

The author and his bride, Annabelle, about to leave their wedding reception at Grocers' Hall in the City on Wednesday March 8, 1972.

The bride and groom's parents earlier the same day on the steps of the Guards Chapel: from L to R - John & Pam Youens and Pam & Donald Methven.

Piers & Georgina Weld-Forester (the author's sister), also on the steps of the Guards Chapel after their wedding in June 1973.

Christian Youens in the garden of 4 Patten Road, Wandsworth, South London, in the summer of 1975.

The author in June 1976 near Pagsanjan Falls in the Philippines, on the set of Apocalypse Now

Arabella Youens aged 18 months in the garden of 158 Mount Pleasant Road, Singapore, in 1979.

Adam Youens with the author, also at 158 Mount Pleasant Road in November 1981.

West Soley Farmhouse, near Hungerford.

The author's immediate family, by Ursie Burnand in 1990.

The author skiing in Idaho with Adrian & Bill Norris in 1993.

The Methven family at Donald & Pam's Golden Wedding lunch at home in Salisbury 1991: from L to R Colin and Cathy Methven, Susie Pasley-Tyler, Charlie Methven, Imo Pasley-Tyler, Arabella Youens, the author, Annabelle, Donald Methven, Sarah Methven, Pam Methven, Ian & Guy Pasley-Tyler. (In absentia Alexandra Pasley-Tyler and Christian Youens.)

The author with Christian near Noosa in Queensland, Australia, in 1994.

At the Swilcan Bridge on the eighteenth fairway, St Andrew's Old Course May 2007: from front L to bottom R, Peter Crofton-Atkins, the author, David Roberts and Nick Blackwell.

Robin Hillyard and the author, circa 2008.

Arabella and Luca d'Avanzo at their wedding reception in Grocers' Hall December 11, 2009. From R to L – Christian, Oliver, Anna & Flora Youens, the bride and groom, Annabelle, Thomas Youens and the author.

The author and his bride of 44 summers and counting.

CHAPTER 14

Globetrotting

It was around this time that Graham Miller decided he wanted to cash in his chips and retire. He was approached by Jacob Rothschild, acting on behalf of the owners of a Cyprus copper mine called Esperanza with spare cash to invest, and was made a serious offer for the business. Neither Jock Sutherland nor Jimmy Guild had the funds to compete and we junior and salaried partners certainly did not, so he sold. Esperanza had been a profitable copper business, which had been in the process of wrapping up, having, so the directors thought, mined all there was to mine. However before they closed, their geologists discovered a new rich seam still within their original mining rights and so they sold these rights to others, packed their bags and asked Rothschild for investment advice. Esperanza became a holding company not only for Graham

Miller but also Caleb Brett and Gellatly Hankey, who were marine surveyors.

Graham stayed on for several years as a consultant, sitting in Esperanza's offices, and in the early years our new shareholders kept hands off, leaving us to manage ourselves as much as possible. The MD was a man named Robert Loder, a Rothschild acolyte; a patrician and very able. His finance director was Oliver Stocken, who was in the same mould. He went on to join a new merchant bank, BZW, which became Barclays Capital. Oliver ended up as Finance Director of Barclays plc and chairman of the Marylebone Cricket Club. While the relationship was fine in the early days, loss adjusting is not a corporate business and should be owned and managed by loss adjusters, and so the relationship inevitably soured.

The rest of 1975 from a business perspective was more of the same. I used to go and run errands for Zürich office, including writing up reports based on notes in files and sometimes going to visit claimants. One day I took the train to Locarno, had a delicious lunch en route as only Swiss Rail know how, did whatever had to be done and then took a train to Geneva, changing at Bellinzona and Domodossola en route. All very romantic but no restaurant car and I arrived in Geneva with my stomach flapping against my ribs. After completing business in Geneva I flew to Zürich, beavered away in the office for a couple of days and flew home.

Other times I did much the same in Rome. By then we had an office in EUR run by an extremely talented man called Bill Bolton, to whom I had handed over much of my film business portfolio. He had a rather tricky wife called Valerie, and one time I went to meet him at their flat, which doubled as an office. Bill did not show up when he was expected and I occupied myself with the cases on his desk while dodging Valerie's attentions. Eventually she left me alone and Bill came back, but he did not bother to go and greet his wife, rather he joined me in the office, where we talked shop. After a while Valerie appeared, not realising Bill had returned and not seeing him, wearing a T-shirt which left nothing to the imagination and not much else. Bill gave me a funny look, but thank God he was there to save me from a fate worse than death.

Annabelle once came with me to stay at the flat in EUR when the Boltons were away on holiday. I worked and she went off to visit her old haunts. The flat had a weird alarm system with laser beams all over the place. You had to leopard crawl from the front door about 10 feet to the alarm box and switch it off, keeping your head down to avoid summoning the Carabinieri.

We also had a happy time in the evenings dining at the restaurants I had been going to for years but on business. One such favourite was Bolognese on Piazza del Popolo. Marcello Mastroianni, probably the most celebrated Italian actor then and now, even though he is no longer with us, was entertaining some lovely at the next-door table. Annabelle was fascinated and tried to ignore him. He on the other hand was eyeing my little wifey throughout the meal and trying to attract her attention, much to the irritation of his companion.

Tehran and Multiple Choice

In the early part of 1975 the firm was invited to set up shop in Tehran to deal with claims on the huge infrastructure programme initiated by the Shah to try and keep the natives happy. It involved building roads, dams, generating stations, barracks - whatever was considered necessary to bring Iran into the back end of the Twentieth Century. Sedgwicks and Willis Faber placed the insurance in London and the German insurer Allianz took an active interest. The project was fronted locally by Bimeh (Farsi for reinsurance) Tehran owned by Mahmoud Zand, a member of the 'Thousand Families', who held all the aces in the country and no one else got much of a look in. Mahmoud's client was Bimeh Markazi, the Government monopoly. It was a very cosy arrangement.

We hired an insurance jack-of-all-trades called Dennis Shepherd to represent us, because he knew the local market and had good contacts. We've been here before. Shepherd was not all bad - he could investigate the circumstances of a claim, decide on coverage and agree quantum - but he could not write a report to save his life. People used to go out from London to do a stint helping him in the office and I went out after Christmas 1975 for 10 days and had a lot of fun. The working week in that part of the world was Saturday morning through Thursday lunchtime. Long hours too.

The outstanding memory of that visit was lunch at Leone's, a restaurant downtown, which only served top of the line caviar and ice-cold vodka. The caviar arrived in bowls one would normally eat cereal at breakfast from, accompanied by a pile of blinis and chopped egg, sour cream etc., one bowl per person. The Russian vodka arrived in quarter bottles, each wrapped in its cocoon of ice, one per person. We went there on Thursdays to celebrate the end of the working week and wonder briefly what the poor people were doing.

Before I left London on this trip Graham Miller had suggested I might want a change of scenery and spend some time abroad. He offered me the chance to open a new office in Paris, take over from Bill Bolton in Rome, work with Sheppard in Tehran or take over the office in Singapore. However the last option was remote at this stage.

When I went back to London in early January 1976, I said I was interested in Tehran because I got on well with Zand, who was very keen for me to come, but thought I would not be able to work with Sheppard, unless he reported to me, which understandably he was not prepared to do. The move was put on hold. Paris and Rome were more of the same, so not very attractive, but Singapore was coming unravelled thanks to the incumbent manager. By mid-February Singapore was firmly on the cards and I arranged to go out to familiarise myself with the place at the end of March with Graham Miller, who would be there for a local area managers' meeting.

At the beginning of March Annabelle and I went skiing in some new resort called Isola 2000 in the southern French Alps, purpose-built by the British entrepreneur Bernard Sunley. We booked ourselves for a fortnight and by lunchtime the second day we had done almost every run in the resort. I had chosen the place because it was all easy skiing, which I thought Annabelle could cope with. However she had fully recovered her strength and fitness, not to mention her confidence, and was a far better skier than me.

One evening we were sitting in a restaurant and fell in with a French couple at the next table. They were gents and probably spoke perfectly good English but they let us prattle away in our rudimentary French, which I speak but don't always understand, whereas Annabelle is the opposite. In fact she is good at picking up what's being said, not only in French but in Italian and Spanish as well. Most annoying - but useful.

Anyway we got around to discussing what we did and I told the story about Marlon Brando washing Maria Schneider in the shower. The French couple did not say anything, but by this time I was in full flight and told them about Maria committing herself to an asylum. "Yes", said the man, "she was a difficult child as well. I should know because she's my sister". I wanted the ground to open up and swallow me, but luckily he didn't seem to be to upset and we laughed about my faux pas. I can be quite good at them sometimes.

We were committed to two weeks at Isola and did not know what to do with ourselves after the first few days, but luckily my parents' best friends the Mainwaring-Burtons came out the second week with their three boys, who were younger than us but a good time was had by all. Long lunches boosted by Tony MB's flask with something lethal and different every day to give us Dutch courage.

Singapore sampling

A week after our return I set off for Singapore. By then it was as good as a done deal that we would be posted there and the current manager, a rather dour Glaswegian chartered surveyor called George Scott, agreed to move on, but he was not going to make it easy for me and told the local insurance market that I was OK but all I knew was movies. He was not entirely wrong, but it was hardly necessary to tie one hand behind my back when he was leaving and anyway he didn't know me.

In any event the firm held a cocktail party at the Tanglin Club to say goodbye to George and introduce me. He had a lovely time introducing me to Chinese insurers without warning me that the first name is the surname, and waiting for me to make a fool of myself. He introduced me for instance to Mr Chew Loy Kiat and I said "Hello Mr Kiat", when I should have said hello Mr Chew. In the event Chew became a firm friend and I'm sure couldn't have cared less.

The Singapore market was a polyglot crew. There were plenty of local Singaporean companies, including a Government-backed firm, whose boss was the aforementioned Mr Chew. There were several Japanese there to underwrite the massive Japanese investment in the Republic. There were Red Chinese, Malays, Indians, Australians, New Zealanders, Americans and of course most of the UK insurance offices. The standard of their staff was way ahead of the Brits I was used to dealing with at home, and that came as a shock. I had to keep my wits about me at all times, which did me no harm, but it was a bit of a wake up.

I spent most of the week I was there learning as much as I could from my future colleague Keith Fisher, who ran the office in Kuala Lumpur, which he had opened the year before after a stint in Lagos. Like George Scott, who was the first UK adjuster into Singapore in 1971, Keith was the first in Malaysia. The only other office we had at that time in the Far East was Hong Kong, which Tony Davis, an ex-policeman from Rhodesia, had opened in 1964 and he was the first Brit there too. Keith knew everyone in Singapore and I decided to stick to him like a limpet until I got the hang of things.

On the social side I knew no one, but I did have an introduction to a couple called Bryant. Peter worked for Guinness Mahon, a small merchant bank, whose chairman Harry Kissin was also chairman of Esperanza, so my ultimate boss. Kissin, who was ennobled by Harold Wilson along with several shady characters, had connections to the security services, as did some of the Rothschild family.

Peter Bryant's wife Christine was a cousin of Fiona Lamplough, a great girlfriend of Annabelle's, so we had connections both sides. Peter invited me to drinks at home one evening and his chauffeur drove us to an estate called Adam Park, off Bukit Timah Road, consisting of elegant black and white colonial mansions standing in their own compounds, many with pools and grass tennis courts. My heart sank. Oh dear, I thought to myself, Madam won't be happy unless she has one of these. We entered the house via a large hall with a drawing room and dining room off and views over the lawns to the skyscrapers on Downtown in the distance.

Peter poured me a drink and apologised that they could not asked me to stay for supper but they were going out to dinner. 'Do you go out a lot?' I asked. Well, they preferred to be in on Sundays if ever possible. At that moment there was a click clack on the wooden stairs and a blonde vision of loveliness, long legs, neat figure, perfectly manicured, wafting some exotic scent, appeared all dressed up and ready to party. I was agog. This was Mrs Peter Bryant and a long call from Wandsworth SW18.

The house, and all the others on the estate, had been built for the British between the wars and now belonged to the Singapore Government. I made a note to call the Ministry of Finance in the morning to find out about renting one, only to be told I had to have a work and resident's permit first.

We decided to rent out Patten Road while we were away and Annabelle went to see a girlfriend who worked in a new estate agent in Fulham called Stead & Glyn, two chaps from her last stamping ground at John D Wood in Chelsea. The purpose of the visit was to compare notes on a new diet. George Stead appeared from his office and asked what we were going to do with the house. Annabelle said we planned to rent. Stead said no one would want to rent a big house in Wandsworth but he might find someone to take it off her hands.

In those days squatters could take possession of empty houses and it was the devil's own job to get them evicted at great cost, by which time, and they had plenty of it, they would have trashed the place, stolen anything worthwhile and lived rent free. Such was life under the Labour Government of Harold Wilson. With these concerns in mind and the fact that we didn't like the place anyway we decided to sell. The house was quickly bought by Johnnie Mackenzie, who sold Black & White whisky in the Far East. Annabelle met him 20 years later. He had sold Patton Road and bought an estate in Scotland.

At the end of April we went to a drinks party and out to dinner afterwards at the Belgian Brasserie in the Old Brompton Road. I had been to Paris earlier in the day and probably had a good lunch followed by cocktails and wine with dinner. So I was feeling no pain as we went home on my Yamaha 650cc motorbike, Annabelle riding pillion in a fur coat, when we were stopped by the police not far from the house. I was invited to blow into a bag, which lit the street bright green, and I was promptly arrested. Annabelle walked home.

After giving blood etc I asked why they had stopped me in particular and was told that I had overtaken a panda car, whose driver thought my rear wheel was iffy. This was confirmed by the officer who drove the bike back to Wandsworth nick and I, who was stone cold sober by this time, was forbidden to drive it home. I was quite cross about this as I had thought there was a problem with the rear wheel and had taken the bike into Gambier Reeks, the bike shop on New Kings Road (long gone), to have it checked and was told it was OK.

As it happens one of their mechanics, Dennis, who was a friend, was also a motorcycle cop in his spare time, or maybe vice versa, and I complained that his colleagues had done me over the night before because of the wonky wheel. He asked for details and I never heard another word about the offence. Good man. Was I lucky?

A year or so earlier I had been in the office early one Saturday morning to supervise the removal of an enormous photocopier from the top floor by crane in the street. On the way back I had a straight run along the Embankment and up Gloucester Place with all the lights green. I shot across Trafalgar Square and under Admiralty Arch at about 70mph, when I glanced in my rear view mirror and saw a motorcycle policeman sheltering from the rain under the Arch. Damn. I let go the throttle but sure enough he came up behind me and I pulled over waiting for the inevitable, when a voice came from under his helmet "going a bit quick there, weren't we, Rich?" Yes, it was good old Dennis and I got away with it. I've found it always pays to keep in with the law.

On one of my last trips to Rome that month, George Scott showed up on the basis he might take over that office from Bill Bolton and I was asked to show him the ropes as Bill was expected to be out of town. In the event he wasn't, but it seemed a good idea for him to meet the local players. I only mention this because one evening we had dinner at Taverna Flavia, a movie hangout, with Frank Silvestri. Ava Gardner, who was dining at a nearby table, came over and sat with us for a while. She was past her prime but quite charming. I thought that would be my last exposure to the glitterati, as I was off to the Far East, but I was wrong.

CHAPTER 15

Singapore

Annabelle, Christian and I set off for Singapore on May 15, 1976 by Singapore Airlines, which had only been going for about four years but had established a first class reputation and was very popular. BA and Qantas also flew there from London, but we thought as we were going to live there we might as well fly local. No complaints about the flight service but we landed at Frankfurt, Rome, Bahrain and Bangkok before arriving after a 20-hour journey, completely exhausted. There was a large party to greet us, including Jock Sutherland, one of the London partners, who had been holding the fort for me, Arnold Mannering, a friend of Harry Kissin and our local Mr Fixit, and Phil Rivers, an old Singapore hand who worked out of our office on marine business.

We piled into two cars and were driven to the Goodwood

Park Hotel, where I had stayed in March, the best Singapore had to offer. They had a block of flats at the back for long-term residents. With some difficulty I managed to shovel the greeters off and we collapsed, only to be woken at 9am by Jock, complaining because I was not at my desk.

The first week or so was spent sorting out permits and licences, meeting the Market and getting my head round the files. I also joined the Cricket Club, which was within walking distance of our office in Malayan Bank Chambers overlooking the Singapore River - then a smelly creek. Members were allowed to park there all day for a fee, much cheaper than using a public car park. It also had the advantage of Sammy, one of the parking attendants, who for about the equivalent of £8 a month washed the office car as many times a day as was necessary. Sammy was a lovely Indian who lived at the club and slept under the building. He was born in Singapore and had never even been to Woodlands, the town by the Causeway, let alone Malaysia.

One of our big supporters was the South British, a New Zealand insurer whose local management consisted of Peter Rackley and Ian MacAndrew, and we became good friends. While we were getting our feet on the ground, the Rackleys took us out for Teppanyaki, which was a first for us: Japanese-style fish and meat cooked right in front of us on a hot plate, washed down with flasks of saki. Quite delicious.

As it happened Jock Sutherland had already booked to give Peter and Ian lunch the next day in the Gordon Grill, which was the Goodwood's main restaurant, and whose speciality was rib of beef. I was still full from the night before but both guests managed to eat half a cow. I had heard about New Zealanders with big appetites, but this was new territory.

We were also swept up by the café society, and on our first Sunday we were invited to a large lunch party by the Barnetts. Geoffrey had recently opened the ill-fated Singapore office of Barings and Fiona was pregnant. Little did we know that Annabelle was too, with Arabella. Tom and Bernadette Rendall were there. Tom was fighting a rearguard action with the Singapore Government over alleged malpractice at Haw Par, a local trader built on the back of Tiger Balm ointment. This business was eventually closed and the Rendalls had to depart in haste. He had a really torrid time to come.

Apocalypse Now

One of the reasons I was keen to go to Singapore was because I wanted to get some overseas experience as a general adjuster and escape the mad world of film business. That didn't happen. Ten days after we arrived Typhoon Pamela, the equivalent of a hurricane in this part of the world, blew through the Philippines and caused massive damage. Francis Ford Coppola was in the jungle directing a Vietnam War movie called *Apocalypse Now* and most of his sets were washed away. This film was to become a cause celebre as far as insurance was concerned, as well as the best Vietnam War film ever made, according to the critics, if not the public.

Friday May 28, 1976 was the first day people could get out and about after the storm and I arranged to fly to Manila that morning all togged up in a suit and tie, Gucci moccasins, briefcase and a freebie overnight bag from Singapore Airlines. George Scott had been a Commercially Important Passenger and I had inherited his mantle. A beautiful Chinese PR girl called Faith met me at Singapore's Peya Lebar airport. She was one of the best-looking Chinese girls I have ever seen, before or since. She whisked me through Immigration and Customs and showed me to my seat in the aircraft. This time I was in First Class in a Boeing 707. The steward's name as Raj, and somehow he remembered everyone's names because he went through the cabin introducing himself without checking any crib. Caviar and champagne were offered and by the time we landed after a three-hour flight I was quite relaxed.

Production met me at the airport terminal and drove me to another part of the airfield, which had been built by the Americans and was a joint military and civil operation. There I met Mona Skager, the Associate Producer, as well as the construction manager, and we were flown by helicopter to inspect the damage. This was a first for me. I was briefed on the way that Marlon Brando played Kurtz, a renegade American officer who was fighting his own battles in Cambodia, and Martin Sheen is sent to terminate his command 'with extreme prejudice'. The storyline was based on Joseph Conrad's *Heart of Darkness*. Many of the sets, including Kurtz's base, were feared to have been destroyed.

By the time I had digested the significance of all this, we were over Pagsanjan, a village in the jungle about fifty miles south east of Manila, where the unit had been on location before 'Pamela' arrived. The pilot landed to get his bearings and the rest of us went for some refreshments. Locals told him that the rivers in the area had risen by anything up to thirty feet and many buildings had been swept away. We were given vague directions where we should be looking and took off again. After searching around for half an hour we found the remains of a series of sets and when it became clear that filming here would not be resumed for weeks, we flew back to Manila as we were running short of fuel.

I was sitting beside the pilot and saw that there was a traffic jam between the airport and Makati where the unit was based. Clearly it would take Mona and the others forever to reach their hotel, if they had to take me back to the airport hotel, where I was staying and then drive all the way back past the helicopter base and on. So I suggested to the pilot that we should drop them off, and then he flew me to the hotel. Everyone thought that was a good plan, so the pilot asked the Tower for permission. They thought about it for a bit, said it had not been done before, then gave us the all clear.

As we came in to land on a lawn in front of the reception area I realised we were the object of the attention of crowds of tourists returning from their first day out after the typhoon, all gaping and wondering who was this bigwig arriving. The pilot turned to me and asked if I minded if he hovered a couple of feet above the lawn because it might be wet and he didn't want to risk the aircraft getting stuck. Well, I thought, a bit late to back out now, so I gathered my things and stepped out into a bog about two feet deep. There was no alternative but to wade across to the hard standing about twenty feet away. When I emerged I was covered in mud up to my knees, much to everyone's amusement, and sloshed my way into the hotel.

I only had a clean shirt and underwear, so I handed my trousers to a maid and asked her to do what she could and I cleaned up my Guccis as best I could, before setting about reading all the paperwork Mona had provided, including the script. It was soon clear that this was a serious loss, worth a good fee, but the script had no dénouement. That's always a worry and maybe this catastrophe was the solution to everyone's problems. Dump the clunker on the insurers and walk away.

Eventually I had had enough reading and went down to the dining room in my damp trousers and shoes. There was only one diner, me, and I had the undivided attention of about a dozen waiters. Feeling more than a little self-conscious, I ordered a large vodka tonic and a Caesar salad. A trolley arrived with all the salad ingredients and three chefs set about preparing it in time to a five-piece band playing European melodies Filipino style immediately behind them. When the salad eventually was placed in front of me it was completely knackered. I never went anywhere again without spare shoes and trousers.

I have no idea what the rest of the meal consisted of but I know I went to bed feeling quite happy. The next morning we were off again in the helicopter back to Pagsanjan, where by this time most of the construction crew and set dressers had arrived to start assessing the damage, which would take several days. There was nothing more I could do, so I was flown back to the airport and took the next flight home.

No sooner was I back when Keith Fisher called from Kuala Lumpur and asked for my help in dealing with a fire claim in Kota Kinabalu (known locally as KK), the main town of Sabah, a Malaysian state in North Borneo. KK, which used to be called Jesselton, was a one-horse town and port, where the Commercial Union was the main expat insurer, and one of their clients owned a textile shop, which had been destroyed. Bill Seath, the branch manager, was worried because the fire looked suspicious, the owner was the mistress of the local head minister and we were talking cowboy country here. Thanks, Keith.

The point of the story is that the mistress, who was quite attractive in a Malaysian sort of way, was acutely aware of her insurer's suspicions because the fire brigade had been reported in the local press as finding more than one seat of fire. At about midnight I heard a knock on my hotel room door and there she was, apparently ready to persuade me her claim was kosher by any means possible. Happily I did not find her hard to refuse and duly reported the encounter to Bill Seath next morning. In the end I think we did a deal, otherwise the boyfriend was going to make life complicated for the CU. Business in the East.

I was up and down to Manila a couple of times during the next two weeks. In the meantime shooting was suspended and the US cast and crew were sent home. By now we had a good idea of how long it would be before shooting could resume and the likely cost of the suspension to insurers. It was somewhere in the area of $4m, a very significant sum. Soon after this had been conveyed to the Fireman's Fund, I received a call at about 4am from Ed Hamby, the underwriter, asking me how quickly I could make myself available to attend a meeting in Los Angeles. I explained I would have to let him know once the travel agent opened in the morning and would send him a telex.

There were no direct flights to LA. You had to change in

Tokyo. There was only one direct flight to Tokyo, which had already departed, so I ended up flying to Hong Kong, staying overnight, flying to Tokyo and picking up a Pan Am flight to LA. Even this was a palaver, because I had missed the only direct Hong Kong flight and had to go via Bangkok. Still, there was a bonus in that the Cathay Pacific pilot invited me to sit behind him for the landing at Hong Kong's Kai Tak airport. This was very exciting because the flight path was over Kowloon where blocks of flats stand right up to the airport boundary and passengers can almost tell whether the residents are having cornflakes or Rice Krispies for breakfast.

The aircraft from Tokyo was a brand new Boeing 747SP, which Pan Am had only recently taken into service, and this one had just travelled round the world with one refuelling stop at Delhi, according to the stewardess. SP stood for Special Performance and this aircraft, which was a regular jumbo but without the rear section of the fuselage, held the record for the fastest circumnavigation by a commercial aircraft. It flew higher than other jumbos, so the flight was smoother. The upper deck was a bar and eating area for us lucky First Class passengers.

We picked up a day crossing the date line and arrived in LA before we left Tokyo. Don Cass picked me up at LAX. This was my first ever trip to the US. He took me straight to his offices in Beverly Hills, just off Wilshire Boulevard, where Ed Hamby of the Fund and Scott Milne, Don's boss and head of the brokers Albert G Ruben, were waiting for me along with Gunther Sachs, the production company's attorney, Mona Skager and others from Production. The plan was to come up with a deal in principle to limit the suspension period to a fixed number of weeks, agree what costs would be included and what would not. Quite complicated guesswork on both sides.

The meeting started at about 1pm and by 5pm we were not going anywhere as no one could agree with anyone else, no matter whose side they were on. I went out for a pee and as I was standing in the stall Scott joined me. As we were both responding to the call of nature he came up with a compromise, which he asked if I could live with, ie broke to the Fund, and I said I could. At that moment Gunther arrived and as he was at the stalls Scott put his proposal to him. Gunther liked it and the three of us went back to the meeting. By this time, it has to be said everyone was getting tired and they all grabbed at an opportunity to settle. An hour later we were done and dusted and Scott, Ed and Don took me off for dinner.

I can't remember what happened the rest of the evening but I did not get to bed at the Beverly Hilton until after 4am. I was so tired I could not sleep, and watched TV until it was time for breakfast. When the shops opened at 10am I went round to Robinsons, a department store nearby, to buy some presents, but they did not take American Express or Diners Club - my only two credit cards - and I only had Singapore dollars, which they rejected too, so I went home empty-handed.

The trip home was the reverse of the trip out. I left LA at lunch time, 24 hours after I had arrived, settled into my seat, the Pan Am stewardess took my meal order and the next thing I knew we were landing back in Tokyo, where I changed planes for Hong Kong. I was too late for any connections for Singapore until next morning, so I was put up at a hotel and caught a direct flight first thing. It was a long trip. I had left on Friday at 1pm and arrived back on Monday at 2pm. Away only three days, but it seemed like a month. At least the wife was pleased to see me and I did not have time to feel any jet lag.

Settling In

Things calmed down after that. We stayed at the Goodwood Park for the best part of three months before we found somewhere acceptable to live. In the meantime Annabelle made friends with an American couple, Jim and Margot Butler, who were also staying at the Goodwood with their three children. They were from Greenwich, Connecticut, and Jim worked for what is now Citibank.

She also met a girl called Liz Liverton, who had a boy called Charlie about the same age as Christian. Her husband, Tony, worked for Jardine Matheson, a big Hong Kong trading house, and they invited us to go one Sunday at the end of June for a picnic at Jason's Beach on the east coast of Peninsular Malaysia, a couple of hours drive from the causeway connecting the island of Singapore to the mainland. Some other friends of the Livertons, Mike and Rachel Jamieson-Till, came with us. Mike worked for Clive Discount, a city firm of discount brokers - now long gone with Big Bang - and they had no children at this stage.

We set off in convoy, Mike driving a clapped-out Mercedes and us in a Toyota I had inherited from George Scott. We stopped off at a coffee shop like no other in Kota Tinggi for refreshments en route. Well, I can tell you we were as far away as it gets from downtown Singapore, let

IT'S ALWAYS FRIDAY

alone Beverly Hills. The coffee shop was a dirty-looking shack on the side of a dusty road to nowhere, but by the time we arrived the others were ensconced and drinking Coca Cola or whatever in bags of ice through a straw. Liz was drinking tea from a battered aluminium pot out of a china mug. All thoroughly unhygienic, we thought.

We ploughed on for another hour or so down a bumpy track full of potholes, across which Mike drove as fast as he could. Eventually we pitched up at a manky beach where we made camp and had our picnic in the sweltering heat and humidity. Afterwards we went for a swim in the murky waters of the South China Sea. Sounds exotic, but not at all. When we returned to our things someone had nicked money and jewellery from Rachel and Liz, but I think the Youens got away scot free. That was the only time we went to Jason's Beach. Now it boasts at least one socking great resort hotel.

Finding somewhere to live was proving very difficult. We had set our hearts on a colonial house like the ones in Adam Park where the Bryants lived, but nothing was available. As luck would have it the Lettings Department of the Ministry of Finance, which was responsible for these houses, had its offices in Malayan Bank Chambers, the same building as our office. It was no hardship for me to go and pester Mr Leong, the officer in charge, on a regular basis, and eventually he offered us 27 Mount Pleasant Drive. This had been a police mess and then lived in by the Swedish architect of the Shangri-La hotel, a modern high-rise and the first of the legendary chain.

This poor man and his family had been turfed out about two years before when the Government planned to turn the area into a car park for motorists who would otherwise be charged to enter downtown Singapore, known as the Central Business District (CBD). It was assumed most people would leave their cars outside the CBD and take public transport. However in the event most opted to pay (S$8, equivalent to £2, per day or S$30 per month, by the time we arrived in 1976), and Mount Pleasant, once abandoned as human habitation, had been quickly reclaimed by the jungle. However Mr Leong was good enough to offer the place to us on the understanding that if we wanted it, the Government would make it habitable again at their expense.

We went to see it. It was enormous and Christian always referred to it as 'Normus House'. The footprint was similar to two tennis courts parallel to each other but separated by a third court in the middle – i.e. in the shape of an E without the middle bar. I may be exaggerating, but not by much. Marble covered the ground floor throughout and the upstairs flooring was wood. Due to the ceiling height each of the four bedrooms, which had their own facilities, was the shape and size of a self-respecting three-bedroom two-storey house back home. There was a huge landing where you could have a ball if you so desired. In addition there were two sets of servants' quarters. We were crazy but we took it because apart from anything else the rent was the same as George Scott's nasty little suburban villa, to which Jock Sutherland had taken exception and let go when Scott left town.

Mr Leong was as good as his word and did the place up to our specification as well as reclaim the compound (garden) from the jungle, which was otherwise almost all around us. We had to provide white goods, including air conditioners, which was rather expensive but we thought - what the hell, we're here to work hard and play hard so let's enjoy ourselves. Mr Chan in Dauby Gaut, an area on the way in to downtown Singapore, made us rattan beds, chairs, tables, sofas and the like for a pittance. The quality was superb and some are still in service with us to this day.

Pictures, lamps, ornaments, cutlery, crockery, kitchen utensils and what have you arrived from home, including Sam Sam the shih tzu, who had been languishing in kennels, and we moved in in August 1976 after three months camping at the Goodwood. We also installed an above-ground swimming pool - bliss. If we had installed an in-ground pool, we would have improved the property and therefore the rent would have been increased: Singapore logic for you.

Soon after we moved in, one Saturday afternoon a stray dog, so we thought, of indeterminate parentage walked rather grandly into the house and set Sam Sam off barking like a loony. It was his territory, damn it. I was about to shoo the interloper out when in walked her mistress, a gorgeous Californian blonde, who introduced herself as our nearest neighbour. Lucky us. She was called Adrian Buchanan and her husband John was also in insurance. We became firm friends and were forever in each other's pockets from that day to this, although Adrian had some hiccups along the way and sadly John died a few years ago. She had two children by her first husband and then Adam by John, who was a year or so older than Christian. They got along fine, mainly because they played together but never said anything to each other.

I was starting to get to know the local insurance market and managed to keep most of our supporters on board, despite George Scott's best efforts to the contrary. Apart from the South British, the New Zealand Insurance Co stayed loyal and their man Don Wyber became a good friend even if he had a fine time giving me a hard one on account of my accent. The Commercial Union and the General Accident (all four companies are now AVIVA), along with some of the local insurers, including Overseas, Asia, Insurance Corporation of Singapore, as well as the Japanese carriers including Tokyo Marine and the Taisho all supported us, some to the exclusion of our competition. Soon after we had set up shop four years earlier, other UK adjusters, including our old friends Toplis & Harding as well as McLaren Dick and Thomas Howell, all decided to open local offices. So we had plenty of competition, which was good.

I was also extremely lucky with my right hand man Chan Hwee Seng, who was first class and without him I would never have survived. Chan was an auxiliary fireman in his spare time, and once rang me in the middle of the night from a payphone with a dead man on his back to say there had been a disastrous explosion on a ship and I should alert the Insurers. He was held in high regard by the Market and is still to this day. The third member of our little team was Denny Sim, hard-working and practical but terribly slow to issue reports.

Everyone else whom Scott had recruited had jumped ship before I arrived. His secretary however stayed on. She was Carol Ambrose and, by extraordinary coincidence, her father had been secretary to Annabelle's uncle, Nigel

Morris, when he had been Singapore's Commissioner of Police in the fifties. The other typist was Rajam, an Indian girl with a ginormous bust, who ran with the expats. She had a long on/off relationship with a creepy insurance broker called Denzel Townsend, who kept blowing hot and cold over her for as long as he could get away with it. Our bookkeeper was Tan Ker Leng, a rather sad Chinese woman, who lived for the job and worked all hours including weekends. I think she did other work besides us but she looked after the books fastidiously, so I wasn't bothered. She was scrupulously honest.

The only other people in the office were Phil Rivers and his secretary. Phil was a blow back from the past. He was a marine surveyor with a Master Mariner's Certificate and his main job was to certify the seaworthiness of cargo ships for insurance purposes. He dressed like a planter in a jungle jacket and matching trousers and always wore a red handkerchief around his neck. He had married a Malay woman and had gone native including taking her Muslim religion, except refusing alcohol. He liked his beer and whisky and during Ramadan he was always travelling because the fasting rules of Islam did not apply to travellers.

As far as I was concerned he was forever poking his nose into my side of the business and stirring up trouble, not only for me but also for our two associated companies, also owned by Esperanza: Caleb Brett and Gellatly Hankey, which was embarrassing. By mid-November Esperanza decided to let him go. Graham Miller volunteered to come out, deal with him and check up on me. He was most impressed with the house, let Rivers go without implicating me and departed.

The *Apocalypse Now* saga dragged on, but eventually it

reached a point in September 1976 when quantum could be assessed and the Fund sent a Public Accountant out from LA called Bob Kendall to audit the claim. I thought that was throwing good money after bad, but it was none of my business. I went up to Manila to hold his hand and the only memorable part of the trip was that we were invited to play golf with the local Filipino film producer at Manila Golf, which was quite magnificent. We had two caddies each, one to carry our bag and one to hold an umbrella over each of us at all times to protect us from the elements, wet or fine. In addition there was a caddy master to make sure they all delivered. Finally the claim was sorted and that was that, or so I thought.

Both lots of parents came out see us at the end of the year, mine at the beginning of December and Annabelle's over Christmas, which we celebrated in some style including a dinner party for the High Commissioner, Peter Tripp, and his wife, who was a bit batty. I think our house was bigger than theirs. Ant and Nicky Palmer came to stay in early January on the way to see her family in New Zealand.

Later that month we were invited to lunch with the Sultan of Johor at his palace outside Johor Bahru just over the Causeway. He was about 80 and very pro Britain. His palace was full of a mix of Oriental treasure and tat. He did have a magnificent collection of cars including several Rolls Royces, Bentleys, E-types and so on in an enormous garage. Annabelle was expecting Arabella any moment and found the visit quite an ordeal.

Arabella Clare Methven Youens arrived at 2pm on Saturday February 5, 1977 at Gleneagles Hospital, where Annabelle had a private room, a far cry from the public wards at the Westminster. Delivery was supervised by a long-term expat doctor called Willie Waddle, who arrived late and slightly the worse for drink, but all went well. Arabella started to yell moments after she first drew breath and has never really looked back. When she came home she was constantly attended by our amahs, a mother and daughter, Muna and Jamilla, who carried her everywhere, and when she started to scream they immediately picked her up and walked round patting her on the back. Woe betide them if they stopped.

Apocalypse Now Part II

Almost a year after the typhoon claim on *Apocalypse Now*, the film was still on location in the Philippines when Martin Sheen suffered a heart attack. To make matters worse the script still had no dénouement. He wasn't required on set and Production initially thought he would recover in time to meet his call some two weeks away. However this was not to be and a claim for delay due to his ongoing incapacity was expected. He was in the Makati Medical Centre, a hospital built for the express purpose of taking care of President Marcos' heart problems, but I wasn't convinced Sheen was receiving the best medical treatment and arranged for a cardiologist to come down from Hong Kong for a second opinion.

At about 6am one morning I was asleep in my Manila hotel room when the phone rang and it was Sheen in a right royal state, cursing me for interfering with his treatment. Rather bleary-eyed I explained that everything was being done in his best interests and I'd come and see him after breakfast. He seemed to be a bit mollified and by the time I arrived he had calmed down. I, for my part, was rather nervous to say the least. I did not know Sheen from a hole in the ground but I did know he was essential if the film was to be finished. All the big set piece action sequences had been filmed and all that remained was dialogue scenes to tie it all together. No Sheen, no story, no movie.

He was sitting up in bed wearing a tee shirt with the legend "Apocalypse When?" a reference to his frustration at the length of time the film was taking to make. His wife, Janet Templeton, was with him and she couldn't resist having a go at me and saying that she had sent a message to Francis Coppola that morning to the effect that as soon as Sheen was fit to travel she was taking him home. I didn't need to hear that and tried to appeal to her better nature, if she had one. I reminded her that without her husband there could be no film and everyone's efforts over the last year or more would be wasted. I said that insurers would be willing to pay for a dedicated team of cardiac paramedics to be on hand all the time once her husband was discharged and that I had already lined up the personnel - white lie. By the time we finished it was agreed he would stay put and finish his role barring further illness or accident.

I was slightly shaking when I left. There was a production driver waiting outside and I said I needed to see Francis Coppola, the director, immediately. I also needed to talk to Lee Katz, who had come over from LA to oversee completion of Principal Photography on behalf of all the investors including United Artists, Paramount and Zoetrope, Francis' own company, which was mortgaged to the banks.

After a few minutes' drive we arrived in front of a twenty-storey block of flats and the driver said to take the lift to the top floor where someone would meet me. When I exited the lift there was a quite gorgeous, but come to think of it a bit obvious, blonde waiting for me. It turned out she was a Playboy bunny, who had appeared in the action and decided to stay on Manila for whatever reasons. She said arrangements were being made to take me to the location and would I like a drink while I waited.

After a few minutes she reappeared and said my transport was ready. She led me up onto the roof of the building, where a Huey helicopter in US Military livery was all revved up and off we went. Quite alarming taking off from the top of a small twenty-storey building, believe me. We landed about half an hour later in the grounds of one of President Marcos' palaces and I was driven down to a river, where a boat was waiting with my fellow passenger, a lady reporter from *Newsweek* magazine, who was due to interview Francis.

We eventually fetched up at a houseboat in the middle of a lake, where I found Lee and the great director discussing the merits of growing Merlot and Cabinet Sauvignon grapes in the Napa Valley as opposed to Bordeaux. Evidently Francis had started a vineyard in California with vines imported from the Gironde and we were all invited to give our verdict on the finished product from both terroirs.

This was all a bit of a letdown. Here was I arriving with news that Sheen would stay and finish the picture, and the main man couldn't be less interested. Perhaps he was a little disappointed that he had lost another opportunity to abandon the film to insurers. Anyway a good time was had by all and the film was finished a couple of months later with Sheen killing Marlon Brando with an axe, but that scene had been filmed a year or so earlier. Brando only worked twelve weeks.

First home leave

1977 was the Queen's Silver Jubilee year and we went home on our first leave by British Airways, whose slogan was 'Join the Jubilee', one stop in Bahrain this time. However when we arrived at Peya Lebar airport for a 10pm departure the aircraft was still in Melbourne, so we went back to Mount Pleasant for some sleep and were recalled at 5am.

We were allocated the middle seats at the front of steerage, immediately behind First Class - there were only two classes then - and Arabella had a carrycot attached to the bulkhead. Soon after take-off, at I suppose at about 7.30am, the Captain apologised for the delay and said all drinks were on the house. When a steward appeared with a bar cart she apologised for being about to serve dinner, because that's what had been ordered for the night before. I asked a Bloody Mary and Annabelle followed suit. By the time the bar cart left our section of the aircraft it was out of tomato juice.

The Queen's Jubilee was celebrated in style with street parties and HM did several walkabouts, including one in the City attended by Christian and me. She wore a bright pink outfit and looked very happy as she and Prince Philip mingled with the great unwashed. In fact she walked right by us and Christian had a fine view of her, first from the top of a pillar-box and then on top of my head. A passing policeman observed that I was wearing a funny looking hat, sir.

We decided it was time Sam Sam the Shih Tzu had a friend and we went back to Christopher Grieveson and the pet shop boys in Hans Crescent to see who was on offer and met Zoo Loo, who flew out to join us in Singapore. She was another black and white well, - grey and white - and she was to have puppies and travel the world, keeping us company not only in Singapore, but also New York and Hong Kong before coming back to the UK nearly ten years later. Despite two lots of six months' quarantine, one in Hong Kong and one in the UK, she lived the longest of all our Shih Tzus to date and was by far the most loyal. Her only bad mark was that she took years to house-train, but that was more down to the life she led than bad behaviour on her part.

Concorde

I had planned to leave the family at home for a couple of weeks and go back to Singapore to catch up, as no one was standing in for me. Reports on cases needing my approval were piling up. However towards the end of the first week back in the office I was summoned to attend a meeting in LA to agree the Martin Sheen claim, so I decided to go on from LA to London, finish my allotted vacation and take everyone back to Singapore. The cost of a First Class return fare Singapore/LA was the same-ish as a round the world ticket, so I opted economy LA to Washington, then Concorde, which had gone into service about a year before, from Washington DC to London and economy back to Singapore.

Business done in LA, I flew United in Coach, which was extremely good, to Dulles Washington and then had to overnight at the Capitol Hilton, before Concorde to London next morning. The Capitol Hilton was just down the road from the White House. The area was, much to my surprise, a tip. The hotel room door was armed with more locks than a bank vault. The restaurant was closed by the time I arrived so I went in search of a hamburger at a McDonalds, somewhere I'd only heard of but never seen, a hundred yards up the street. En route I was accosted by a lady of evidently very easy virtue who called out to me from behind a tree: "want a f***, honey?" American ladies of the night are clearly not known for their style, even within spitting distance of the White House. However I made my excuses and hurried on.

The bus which took us out to Concorde looked like any old coach, but when we arrived at this stunningly elegant aeroplane, hydraulics lifted the passenger section up to the door and in we marched, me following a couple eating hamburgers out of polythene boxes, which I thought was a bit insulting to BA fare.

I sat in Row 1 next to an English businessman who turned out to be Hector Laing, the Chairman of United Biscuits. He knew my father-in-law, Donald, who by this time had left the law and was Vice Chairman of Cadbury Schweppes. Laing was very affable and I piqued his interest by telling him what great biscuit eaters the Malays were. Did UB have any interests in that part of the world? No, he said, but about six months later I read that they had bought a controlling interest in one of the big manufacturers in KL. Rupert Murdoch was two rows back, but I managed to avoid him.

With the advantage of hindsight, Concorde was a monumental waste of taxpayers' money to save businessmen and celebs a few hours crossing the Atlantic. However when it was conceived in the fifties British and French aviation was in its ascendancy and both the US and Russia were also trying to develop supersonic transport. No one had any concept of the technical hurdles ahead. While all the major airlines initially showed serious interest in the project, by the time they had to commit themselves fuel costs had escalated, and there were environmental questions.

When Concorde was ready to fly the takers were down to BA and Air France. Only twelve commercial aircraft were ever built. It carried a hundred passengers in cramped seats with tiny portholes, but it was a great way to fly and definitely something to brag about. There was no sensation of speed, but the clouds below whizzed by two and a half times as fast as in a conventional jet.

Back to Earth

Soon after we returned to Singapore I was sitting next to a woman at a dinner party who had recently arrived and she was complaining that her colonial house wasn't big enough. It turned out that she and her husband had moved into 158 Mount Pleasant Road, just around the corner from us. It was one of the houses we had been pipped on the post to rent when we were camping at the Goodwood. I offered to swap and in August we moved.

The couple we swapped with were called Kerry and Judith St Johnston. Kerry was an Old Etonian, 11th

Hussar, who had studied law at Oxford and then been successful in the shipping world before coming to Singapore as Chief Executive of Private Investment Company of Asia, taking stakes in emerging local businesses. They took a fancy not only to our house but also our Shih Tzus, and promptly ordered two dogs from Grieveson et al at Town & Country Dogs, who must have thought Christmas had come early. Sadly their marriage came unstuck a year or two later and we were asked to take on the dogs, Fred and Bertie. However we could not cope with four Shih Tzus and after several months decided to give theirs away. Several years later Bertie came to live a few miles from us on Long Island. It's a small world, even with Shih Tzus.

South China Sea Islands

There is a group of islands in the South China Sea off the east coast of Peninsular Malaysia, the largest of which is Pulau Tioman (pulau meaning 'island' in Malay), about an hour by launch from the port of Mersing. Tioman was the base for the film unit making *South Pacific* in 1957 and the location of 'Bali Hai' in the film was Pulau Tinggi, about ten miles away. Tioman was still unspoilt. There was one hotel, the Merlin, which was a long single-storey building with fairly basic accommodation overlooking a magical beach with no one on it except hotel guests and the place was never remotely busy. Pulau Tulai, about half a mile offshore, was something out of a Bounty advert: white beaches, swaying coconut palms and crystal clear blue sea. We had many happy long weekends at this idyll, the first in September 1977.

One time we did however come seriously unstuck. We rented a rather clapped-out fishing boat in Mersing with Tony Martin, a timber grower, his girlfriend Christine Bryant (late of Adam Park - she had split with her husband Peter) and Mike Elphick, who was head of the local office of Sime Darby, a multinational trader. We spent the day cruising around the islands near Tioman, one of which was called Rawa and had a very basic hotel. After an early start from Singapore and an uncomfortable three-hour drive we set off in the boat fortified by Bloody Marys followed by fishing and a long lunch. That evening we decided to moor off Rawa and have a picnic supper on the beach, which we assumed was in the public domain. Never assume anything in Malaysia, least of all the State of Johor, as we later discovered.

We tied up at the hotel's pier and disembarked. No one objected and we set up camp, lit a bonfire and took refreshments while preparing supper. After an hour or so we had the uneasy feeling we weren't alone and discovered we were surrounded by about 30 angry-looking natives armed with knives, rolling pins and other assorted weapons. Their leader, who was probably the manager of the hotel, told us in no uncertain terms we were on private property and should leave immediately. Fortified with industrial quantities of Dutch courage we elected to dispute his authority and the situation became quite alarming even to us, so we decided to beat a retreat to the boat. In a kind of rearguard action, we made our way back to the jetty, where Annabelle decided to make a stand, climbed onto the trunk of a convenient tree and berated our would-be assailants in language which today would have been considered highly racist. After this she felt a lot better, but we still had to drag her protesting loudly back to the boat.

The following day we eventually sailed back to Mersing, where we were promptly arrested by several police officers while trying to disembark. Mike Elphick, who was bringing up the rear, had an attack of diarrhoea, so he made a dash for the boat's primitive facilities. Immediately the police drew their weapons, ran after him and stood over him while he attended to his needs.

We were taken to the local nick and told that we had been accused of insulting the Malay nation in general and the Sultan of Johor in particular. I said that simply was not true. We had only had lunch a couple of months earlier with the Sultan, whom we very much admired – all right, a bit of an exaggeration, but they weren't to know.

It transpired that Rawa was owned by the Sultan's brother, whose name was Tunku Mohammed Archibald, and his son had witnessed the events of the evening before. We apologised and said we thought the beach was public and had been very upset with the way in which we had been treated. I was also able to tell our captors that I was friendly with the Chief of Police for Johor and able to name both him and his assistant, with whom by good fortune I had had dealings a week or two before. This seemed to mollify them and the senior officer went off to have interminable conversations in Malay on the telephone.

After an hour we were told to drive to Kota Tinggi, home of Liz Liverton's battered aluminium teapot, telephone the Tunku from the local hotel, there being no means of telephoning directly from Mersing, and apologise. We decided discretion was the better part of valour and agreed to do this. So we set off in convoy followed by the Tunku's wretched grandson, who was not best pleased we had got off so lightly.

Mike made the call from Kota Tinggi and the boy's mother answered. Much to Mike's astonishment, and ours, the woman turned out to be broad Yorkshire, and told him we were lucky not to be detained at her husband's pleasure in the Johor Bahru Hilton. Since there wasn't one we decided she must have been referring to the local prison. We all breathed a sigh of relief when we had crossed the Causeway back into home territory and were somewhat apprehensive the next time we went to Malaysia, but we never did hear anything more.

Ang Pows

Later in September 1977 there was a devastating fire in a huge plywood factory in Sandakan, on the north coast of Sabah, a Malaysian state in Borneo. All the machinery was completely destroyed, along with the finished stock and most of the raw materials. The owner of this business, Sandakan Plywood & Veneer, was a local bigwig who had not bought Business Interruption insurance and was underinsured anyway. The Japanese were enjoying a construction boom and buying all the plywood they could lay their hands on for concrete shuttering, so he needed to sort himself out quickly to get back in business, and I asked what I could do to help. We did a deal which I thought was highly favourable to both him and the South British Insurance. The claim was paid and that was that.

However come the following Chinese New Year I was

presented with a magnificent Ang Pow (gift): a large hamper full of goodies, including two bottles each of Dom Perignon champagne and Chivas Regal Royal Salute whisky, the latter in velvet bags. There were cakes, biscuits, tins of foie gras and heaven knows what else. Well, this was very embarrassing. Accepting gifts like this was very much done in Chinese circles but strictly taboo as far as English loss adjusters were concerned.

Sending it back would be the height of bad manners and loss of face all round, so I called Peter Rackley at the South British, told him what had happened and offered to send the hamper round to him. He said he always knew we'd paid too much and told me to keep it. Thanks, Peter. No one else in the office drank alcohol, luckily, so I kept the booze and everything else was shared out between the others. A similar Ang Pow arrived at Chinese New Year for several years afterwards and was accepted gratefully.

Brunei

The tiny sultanate of Brunei, on the west coast of Borneo, was a frequent source of business. Its ruler was and still is one of the richest men in the world and a benevolent one at that. Well, he was then, but more recently he has embraced Shariah Law and sanctioned its medieval punishment regime. His wealth was derived from oil and no local paid any income tax. Brunei was known as the 'Shellfare State'. Shell had the monopoly and generated massive revenues for the Sultan, not to mention significant profits for the company. Life for the locals was pretty basic and apart from the capital, Bandar Seri Begawan to the northwest, there were only two other towns, Seria and Kuala Belait, in the main oil-producing area to the southwest. Every now and again a street or two of shop houses burnt down.

Chan and I would fly over, usually on Brunei Airlines, which was managed by Singapore Airlines, and just as good. They had three Boeing 737s, which could be converted quickly into a private jet for the Sultan, so the loos in First Class were twice as big as normal and the taps were gold plated.

Having surveyed the damage, the losses were usually total; we would set up shop in one of the hotels and meet the individual traders, who were family businesses, to agree their claims. This meant there were usually four or five families waiting to see us in the corridor outside our rooms at any one time. This was accepted by management during the day, but was not very popular at night, so we would usually pack up at 8pm and go in search of dinner and a drink. Brunei was dry, being a strict Muslim state, but booze could be had, at a price, to be delivered to one's table in a teapot to be drunk from a china cup. A whisky and soda definitely tastes better out of a glass, preferably crystal.

Farewell to Piers

My widower brother-in-law, Piers Weld-Forester, disappeared off the radar when we went off to Singapore and we hardly ever saw him again. I think his trucking business went downhill while he was busy racing his motorcycle with his mate Barry Sheene. It was on one such occasion at Brands Hatch at the end of October 1977 that Piers ran out of road. He sustained fatal internal injuries and died near the track. He was 31 years old.

My old flatmate Nick Hallings-Pott once commentated that when you were with Piers, you knew you were alive, and that could not be a better epitaph. He filled every minute with sixty seconds worth of distance run, but took enormous risks without forethought and may have had a subconscious death wish. We had little in common, but I do wish I'd taken the trouble to know him better. By coincidence he was going out with one of Annabelle's former flatmates, a devastatingly attractive barrister called Peta Binding, when he was killed.

Hong Kong

Christmas 1977 was spent in Hong Kong, where Annabelle's brother Colin had recently opened an office for the eminent Lloyd's broker Willis Faber & Dumas and kindly had us all to stay, including sister Susie and husband Ian Pasley-Tyler, who were touring Asia. Our neighbours from Mount Pleasant Drive, the Buchanans, had by this time moved to Hong Kong as well and a regiment of Greenjackets was based at Stanley Fort, including Peter and Marion (née Burns) Chamberlin and Roger (I was his Best Man) and Rosie Ker, so we partied with a passion from the moment we landed. Happily everyone had staff springing in all directions so the young were well cared for.

Bangkok

Business continued to boom and I was under some pressure from the Commercial Union and others to open an office in Bangkok, so in early March 1978 Annabelle and I went up for a look see with our friends Anvar and Baroona Peerbhoy. We stayed at the Oriental, probably one of the best hotels on the planet then, and I met the local Market, thanks to introductions from Anglo-Thai, a local Inchcape company with whom we had ties, no pun intended. Annabelle and Baroona had a fine time retailing and we all met up in the evenings.

One such evening we four were invited to a Thai dancing restaurant by an English insurance broker who had gone native called Leighton Fowles, whom Annabelle immediately christened Leighton Buzzard. When I mentioned this engagement to the Anglo-Thai expat manager, David Sims, he said we could not possibly do that and insisted we went out with him.

We gave him dinner at the Normandie Grill, which was on the roof of the Oriental, with splendid views over night time Bangkok and then he took us out for, well - splendid views of night time Bangkok. We ended up in some shed off one of the main drags to watch a show, where the cabaret artistes did mind-boggling tricks with bananas, candles, chopsticks and I can't remember what else. Even if I can, it's not for publication in a family memoir. We returned to Singapore with sore heads and a plan to open a rep office.

HMS *Tiger* arrived the following week on a goodwill visit and some of us had been asked to provide entertainment for the sailors. In 1966 the *Tiger* had been the platform for meetings between the then UK Prime Minister Harold Wilson (my pet bogeyman) and Ian Smith, the Prime Minister of Rhodesia, now Zimbabwe, who had unilaterally declared independence from Britain on account of HMG's insistence that white minority rule be ended. Wilson had a secretary called Marcia Falkender, a hideous old bat referred to in *Private Eye* as Lady Forkbender, with whom many were convinced he was having an affair. We had been taken round the ship and there was plenty of scope for hanky-panky, given the proximity of their living arrangements.

I asked Rajam to round up some of her friends and we gave a barbecue at home for about twenty of the crew, officers and men. Rajam did them proud. She produced about eight Singapore Airlines hostesses, all glamorous – well, they had to be to work there in the first place - as well as several of her girlfriends, who were equally lovely and exotic. From somewhere she also produced a complete (but English) dog. Guess who had all the sailors' attention.

April saw us back in London for four weeks leave including a week skiing in Val d'Isère. We had fun, but we learnt that the UK housing market had taken off in the past year and the house we had sold in Wandsworth had at least doubled in value whereas our funds in the stock market had barely moved. Panic stations. We spent a lot of time looking at possible purchases but always pulled back because the letting market was dead and we would still have had the problem of squatters. I even went down to Cornwall to look at a potential holiday home but walked away. In the end we remained bricks and mortarless until we moved to Long Island four years later.

Arabella had been born with a lazy eye, which was operated on by an ophthalmic surgeon called Keith Lyle, who was 74 at the time and considered the best in the profession for dealing with Arabella's condition. She was operated on in May but could not fly until July, which meant

Annabelle staying put in England while I went back with Christian.

Sam Sam and Zoo Loo slept in our bedroom and one night I awoke to hear a lot of scuffling. Switching on the light I saw them joined together back to back. Whatever's going on? Surely not? Surely. Later in the year Zoo Loo became the proud mother of five beautiful Shih Tzu puppies.

One evening I was invited to dinner by David and Helen Shorrock, David represented the Sun Alliance Insurance Co locally and their agent was Guthrie Trading. They wanted me to meet Guthrie's new Finance Director to whom David would be reporting. I think they must have thought I'd smooth the path. His name was Roger Wood and I don't know about smoothing Shorrock's path but we took off, Roger and me. We ate and drank the Shorrocks out of house and home and have never looked back since.

Annabelle and Arabella reappeared in mid-July, Arabella wearing a patch over the eye Mr Lyle had operated on, which she had to wear all the time for the next several years: a big ask for someone so small, and it was removed by the wearer at every opportunity. Furthermore Mr Lyle had said that he would need to operate again the following year. Really bad luck.

All the delicious food in the Orient was having an effect on my waistline and Nigel Melville, the local Barings manager, had found an Indian lady doctor called Leila Sen who specialised in helping people like us. So I trooped off to see her with another friend, Robert Tatlow, whose girth was even greater than mine by some margin. Leila gave us diuretic pills and vitamins as well as appetite suppressants and told us to come back in a week. She also told us we had to reduce our alcohol intake to one drink a day. Robert promptly went out and bought two what looked like Waterford cut glass vases. When we went round for dinner that night we had one drink each and felt no pain at all.

The first week I stuck to her regime and went back to see Leila feeling rather weak but otherwise OK, so she gave me a Vitamin B12 injection, which she referred to as a Harley Street Cocktail. After about ten minutes I felt ready to rule the world, especially after she had completed her physical examination, which had an unexpected charm. After a month of this I was a shadow of my former self and felt I should call it a day. I have never been keen on pills. Needless to say my weight went back up but I have learnt the only effective diet is to eat less – not that I'm one to practise what I preach, mind.

Emily Findlater

At the beginning of December we were invited to a reception at one of the hotels on Tanglin Road where David Mun, a celebrated dealer in Chinese antiques, was having a promotion. It was an early Saturday evening and we took the children. After an hour, and the acquisition of a rather fine glass fronted chest, we decided to head for home and came out of the hotel to find we were in the middle of a major tropical storm.

We made it to the car but the traffic had seized up and after waiting for half an hour we decided to abandon the car and try a taxi - along with everyone else. In the end we opted to walk. Derek Plunkett, one of the ushers at our wedding, was staying at the Shangri-La on Orange Grove Road, which was along our route home and he was supposed to be coming to us for dinner. We found him on the lobby steps and suggested he stayed put, while we carried on.

By the time we reached Bukit Timah Road the central culvert had overflowed and we were up to our waists in water. Arabella was on my shoulders and Christian was part walking, part swimming with his mother, but eventually we made it home. The Mount Pleasant area was completely cut off by the floodwaters, so the dinner party was cancelled. The next morning we were still isolated and as we had masses of food we rounded up some neighbours and invited them to lunch. A new couple called Patrick and Rosie Findlater, who had just arrived, came too along with their children Alexander and Emily.

By Monday the flood had receded and we were able to resume life as we knew it. However Emily Findlater, who was playing at her kindergarten, was killed when the branch of a tree, sodden from the storm, broke away and fell on top of her. She was three. Her poor parents were devastated and never really recovered. Happily Alexander and his wife have since presented them with four grandchildren who provide great consolation.

As 1978 drew to its close, Roger & Tammy Wood invited us to spend Christmas with them at Fraser's Hill, a resort in the mountains, well sort of mountains, north of Kuala Lumpur, where Roger's employers had a bungalow called Whittingtons. We played golf and I played Father Christmas all togged up complete with a beard sitting on the back of a Volvo estate car going "Ho ho ho" and dishing out sweets to the local children, who must have thought we were all barking. The service on Christmas Day was in the local pub. We had great fun and have spent almost every Christmas ever since with the Woods, either at their place or ours - mostly theirs come to think of it.

Ceylon that was

At the end of January 1979 John and Adrian Buchanan arrived with Adam and we went for 10 days to Ceylon, now for some daft reason called Sri Lanka. We had not seen them for months, so the night they arrived we must have celebrated with a vengeance because when I put the empty bottles out the next morning there were four champagne and several white and red as well as brandy. We were not feeling too bright when we boarded the Singapore Airlines Boeing 707 to Colombo but as John and I stood in the galley making very hot Bloody Marys, we consoled ourselves that we didn't have far to go on arrival because the hotel was very near the airport.

Fat chance. I hadn't realised that there was a new airport north of town and our hotel, Mount Lavinia, was south, not that far but two hours in traffic in a clapped-out VW mini bus with no aircon driven by a wild local called Umpalli. I wasn't popular. Most of the vehicles, commercial or private, were Singapore cast-offs. All vehicles in Singapore had to be taken off the road after ten years and sold as scrap to the Government, who had a nice little line selling them off to dealers in Sri Lanka for a tidy profit.

Mount Lavinia Hotel was a complete dump. The beds hadn't been made. The rooms were dirty and the Buchanans overlooked a railway line. I was even less popular. Somehow we coped and the next day while the wives swam John and

IT'S ALWAYS FRIDAY

I went to see the head honcho at the Government-owned Insurance Corporation of Sri Lanka, the main game in town, so we could justify part of the trip on expenses. My friend Anvar Pheerboy had also given us introductions to the Lloyd's Agent, a charming man called Basil Jesudiason, who invited us to his home for dinner.

The Jesudiasons lived in great style in the smart part of town. Mrs J was Goanese and one of the most beautiful women I'd ever met. She produced a banquet for us of local goodies, some of which she said might be too spicy for us, but we tried them all. Everything was quite delicious, including Hoppers, a new one on us, fried eggs in a spicy pancake: to die for, and we almost did. Everything was so hot with a serious after burn and we were in all kinds of trouble the next day.

Umpalli took us on safari around the north of the island over the next week. He had a disconcerting habit of driving quite slowly on the open road, while as soon as we came to a village he would put his foot on the accelerator and drive at any unsuspecting native until they jumped out of his way. He thought that was great sport. We were not impressed, but no amount of cursing from us put him off.

We started off with the leopards of Wilpattu Game Park, only there weren't any, but we did see a dead mongoose and the rangers' Land Rover broke down. Our hero John managed to get it started by blowing into the petrol tank: old Vietnam War trick. We saw all the sights including Sigiriya, Sri Lanka's answer to Ayers Rock, which Adrian insisted she could climb in her high-heeled sandals but had to admit defeat half way.

The highlight of the trip was a night at the Hill Club in

Nuwara Eliya, a hill station 5,000 feet up and blissfully cool. It was still a proper club in those days and we stayed courtesy of our clubs in Singapore and Hong Kong. We were almost the only people staying. There were wood fires in our bedrooms and all the public rooms. The bar had about a hundred different brands of malt whisky and the latest *Country Life* was circa 1948. The waiters all wore white gloves and the starter at dinner was Brown Windsor soup.

After dinner we went and sat in the main lounge, which we thought we had to ourselves. Adrian by this time had lost the plot and tried to flick her knickers at one of the chandeliers but missed and they landed on a sofa. She went to retrieve them and found them sitting on the head of a hotel servant who was not supposed to be there and was petrified.

The next day we borrowed some golf clubs and played a round on the club course, where we were the only customers and probably the only ones for weeks. Adrian insisted on playing in her high-heeled sandals and was all over the place. The rest of us weren't much better. The locals had to move their livestock in order to let us through. We kept losing balls and having to buy them back from the boys following us around. We loved our stay at the Hill Club and suspect it hasn't changed much since our visit.

The last few days were spent at the Coral Garden Hotel on the beach at Hikkaduwa. It was a pit and the next beach was a resort for American draft dodgers, bare-breasted Caucasians with children, none of whom had seen a bath in weeks, milling in all directions. Most of the accommodation was unmemorable, but we kept finding bottles of champagne and other refreshments in our luggage, which we didn't know we had, and that kept us happy.

What Christian and Adam made of it they never let on, but they were good enough not to complain. Adam was on a dinosaur project, which kept him and his mother occupied much of the time. Their highlight was probably riding on an elephant we met with his mahout in the middle of nowhere. We rounded a corner and there was this wonderful animal and his master. The mahout spoke perfect English and like all his fellow countrymen and women was friendly, helpful and kind with a great sense of humour. The elephant lifted the boys onto his head with his trunk but declined the adults. All in all we had a happy time, certainly a memorable one.

In March 1979 we were instructed by Lloyd's to investigate an aviation hull claim. It was only a single-engine Cessna, but there was a report format Lloyd's required, which luckily a marine colleague in the office knew about. The loss was in the jungles of Sarawak, but the damaged aircraft was back in Kuching. It turned out that the pilot was the local Jehovah's Witness and he gave me a book about a couple of inches thick all about his sect for me to read in the comfort of my home, or so I thought. I had to stay overnight and when he collected me from the hotel next morning he was most put out that I hadn't read it.

CHAPTER 16

Third parties, fire and theft

Back in London, our management structure was changing. Graham Miller had retired. Jimmy Guild had taken seriously to the bottle. Jock Sutherland was not interested and Esperanza was grasping around for suitable candidates to assume the mantle. One such was Bob Bishop, an ex CID man, who had been successful with a small adjusting business and built up a reputation in Lloyd's for quality investigations of dubious losses. Bob, who was fun but totally unsuitable for the job, was hired and we all had a new boss.

One notorious case soon after Bob joined us was to become known as the Savonita Affair. The *Savonita* was a cargo ship which caught fire in the Adriatic and a large number of new Fiats and other cars were allegedly damaged beyond repair. When the reinsurance claim was presented in London, underwriters had been tipped off the claim was suspicious and Bob discovered that while there had indeed been a fire, contrary to information provided in Italy, many of the vehicles had survived intact. One of his men purchased an Audi in Italy, paying two cheques - one for the amount Lloyd's had been asked to pay in the claim less the scrap value and a second for the amount of the scrap, so Bob was able to prove fraud.

However considerable pressure was placed on the Lead Underwriter, Roy Hill, to pay the claim for commercial reasons by the reinsurance broker, Willis Faber. The placing broker was Malcolm Pearson, later Lord Pearson of UKIP, who took grave exception to underwriters being pressured and raised questions in the House of Commons. Willis received a rap on the knuckles for 'robust broking', but the claim was still paid despite the evidence and most unfairly Willis blacklisted us.

Another underwriter, named Tim Sasse, was later to come a cropper having improperly given his underwriting authority, his 'pen', to an agent in New York. The agent wrote duff business in the South Bronx and other low-life areas in the US. Many dubious fires followed. Bob Bishop was retained as Sasse's lead reinsurer, in Brazil of all places, and found evidence of fraud, but not strong enough to stand up in court. Sasse's reinsurers refused to pay and Sasse was hung out to dry. In Lloyd's, certainly in those days, you had to keep your wits about you at all times, and I don't suppose it's that much different today.

Another of Bob's high profile cases involved a very large crude carrier (VLCC) sinking in the middle of the Atlantic several hundred miles off the coast of West Africa with a full cargo of oil. Bob was able to prove the vessel had in fact discharged its cargo in South Africa, where there was a sanction against supplying oil because of the country's apartheid policy. There was also evidence the tanks of the VLCC had then been filled with seawater and it was this which had been lost.

He was good, was Bob, but not up to running an international business and he wasn't really interested anyway. There was a bit of an interregnum before Esperanza appointed a man called Vic Lewis for Johannesburg to run the company but that didn't work out either. Meantime I kept my head down and beavered away in the Orient.

Bash on regardless

The Fireman's Fund sent me a job in Tokyo in March 1979. It was my first visit of many, but first impressions stick. It was a totally alien environment for a Westerner on a brief visit. Francis Coppola's daughter Sofia made a film called *Lost in Translation*, which starred Bill Murray and Scarlett Johannson, and reflects to a T the atmosphere of the place. Of course, anyone familiar with the people, customs and the language will see things differently. Me, it was my least favourite destination.

That month Annabelle discovered she was pregnant and this time round we decided to ship out a nanny for the first three months following the birth. Her mother suggested we advertise in *The Lady*. We had ninety-seven applicants, which my mother-in-law filtered down to a dozen or so and eventually said there were three girls any of whom would do. For some weird reason my bride said I could choose, so I chose the blonde and arranged to interview her at the in-laws' flat near Marble Arch when I was back in London for a dinner in October.

The dinner was late and Robin Hillyard stayed the night. At 9am the next morning the doorbell rang. Who the hell could this be? I opened the door to be confronted by this stunningly lovely creature with a magnificent figure complete with jeans painted on her endless legs. For one moment I could not think what she was doing there. The next she was hired.

We arranged that Sarah the Bearer, for that was how she became known in Singapore, should come out a few days before the birth to acclimatise and I collected her from the airport in my brand new, well all right the office's brand new, BMW 520i. She climbed aboard, took one look at the dashboard and announced that hers had an analogue clock whereas mine was digital. That put me in my place. It transpired she was independently wealthy thanks to a rich godfather – well, that was her story. It also transpired over the next three months that she was a scalp hunter of married men and attracted an army of admirers. Whatever else, she was a cracking good nanny. When she departed at the end of her visa, that was the last we ever saw or heard of her.

In the meantime Adam James Methven Youens arrived safe and sound on the morning of Friday November 30, about half an hour after Annabelle was admitted to hospital. The boozalier doctor Waddle who delivered, or should have delivered Arabella but was otherwise detained, had retired and Annabelle had a Chinese gynaecologist, with whom she was madly in love. Everything went really well and they came home five days later.

Possible arson

A month earlier there had been a massive fire involving several large warehouses in Nelson Road belonging to the Port of Singapore Authority. One of the largest tenants was two Indian brothers called Thrakral. They had had huge quantities of textiles destroyed or badly damaged and our experts concluded that the material salvaged was of considerably inferior quality to that described on the bills of lading. In addition the brothers were suspected of insurance fraud involving losses at sea.

Ince & Co, a London solicitor, was investigating on behalf of many insurers and had set up a team of experts who called themselves FERIT or Far East Regional Investigation Team. Well, they must have thought it was funny. The leader was an Ince partner, Richard Sayer, who was an old friend, along with their local self-styled guru and our old friend, Phil Rivers, and a man called Richard Sherriff who saw himself as a maritime version of Sherlock Holmes. They had the Thrakrals in their sights and since the textiles in my claim came from Bombay everyone thought it would be a good idea if I went and checked provenance.

Bombay was still the same dump I had visited with Frank Silvestri five or six years earlier, as was the Sheraton Hotel at the Fort. I arrived at about 3am local and not only was the bed not made but the lavatory had not been flushed. My enquiries were a bit of a waste of time and money, but I did have an opportunity to look up some Singapore friends called Mick and Sally Finlay. Mike was Cadbury Schweppes India and I was invited to dinner with them at their house.

Mick collected me in a chauffeur-driven, rather clapped-out limo and when we arrived at the entrance to their drive, which was in the centre of downtown, a bit like driving in off Piccadilly Circus or Times Square, the driver had to stop and pull some sleeping bodies out of the way. Well, I thought they were sleeping. Mike said some of them were probably dead. We had to go through the same performance on the way back. The poverty in India is unimaginable. Babies are maimed so they can beg more effectively, even ones appearing to be no more than Adam's age, and he wasn't six weeks. I was glad to leave, although Mick said you become inured to it.

In February things were coming to a head in London with the firm's management becoming unravelled and I was called back for consultations, which sounds rather grander than it was. Singapore Airlines had been flying Concorde in collaboration with BA between Singapore and London intermittently because of spurious complaints from chippy Malaysia about interfering with the environment, fishing etc. They just wanted to be difficult and then the Indians got in the act, as result the service was eventually cancelled.

Anyway Concorde was flying and one side of the aircraft was painted in the BA livery and the other in SIA. Crews alternated so one lot did Singapore/Bahrain and the other Bahrain/London. I thought if everything was about to come apart I'd go in style. I went in to the office for a couple of hours. Annabelle took me to the airport via the market, where I bought a large pomello for my mother. We took off at 11.30am and landed at Heathrow at 1.10pm. Mum had the pomello after lunch and I played golf with Dad, all in the same day. Concorde on a trip like that was worthwhile to a busy captain of industry, not that I fell into that category.

The flight to Bahrain took about three hours as opposed to nearly seven. We were served drinks, canapés, starters and mainers. The refuelling stop was about half an hour because everyone was pulling the stops out. We had pudding and cheese on the sector to London and arrived feeling no pain at all after another three hours, but the last hour was subsonic over Europe, where there were noise abatement rules. Heaven knows what happened with the 'consultations'. I think we agreed to let Vic Lewis go back to Johannesburg and appoint our two most senior men, Peter Simpson and Bill Bolton, to run the business from Brussels where they were based. This worked quite well for a time. I went home two days later, this time on Qantas at the back of the bus.

Grist to the mill

Philips of Eindhoven, the electrical manufacturers, were a big client. They self-insured with a big excess of loss cover, which meant if their claims in any one year exceeded a certain figure, many millions of guilder - this was long before the dreaded Euro - insurers picked up the rest and we audited all claims to make sure they weren't being exaggerated. Philips also had a big charitable giving programme and had donated an expensive cancer treatment machine to the main public hospital in Madras, now

Chennai (why?) The machine was destroyed in a fire and I went to assess the loss. I travelled overnight and went straight to site.

The hospital had built a special treatment centre dedicated to this equipment and everything had been wrecked. However there was no obvious cause of the fire. A patient was being treated at the time and everything was working normally when all of a sudden flames started escaping from the machine and everyone was evacuated.

I was shown all the installation documents and operating guides and as luck would have it I noticed that the equipment could only be operated within certain ambient temperatures, maybe 60-75f or whatever, and low humidity. Daytime temperatures in this part of the world are between 75-90f and humid, we are talking tropical here. I asked to see where the air-conditioning equipment was and was told there were only fans. Since the machine was operating in conditions contrary to safe practice, the fire was the inevitable consequence and there was no coverage.

I went back to Philips' local office and sent a long telex to London. It was hot and humid. There was no aircon and the building was so old it shook and shuddered during the five or so minutes during which the telex was being sent. All done and dusted, I decided best to beat a retreat and caught the next flight home to Singapore feeling rather embarrassed and sorry for the hospital staff. I was later told there were red faces everywhere and Philips supplied a replacement machine free of charge.

Total Indonesia had a big refinery at Balikpapan on the arse end of Borneo and some incident there required an adjuster, so off I set one morning after breakfast. The only way in was by private aircraft and Total found me a seat on one of their Beechcraft flying out of Seletar, a former RAF base to the north of Singapore. When I arrived at Seletar I was told there was a delay and sat down to wait with a cup of coffee, then another. Eventually we took off on a 2½-hour flight.

My fellow passengers were several expat oilfield engineers on their way back after some R&R in Bangkok and were sleeping off the effects of their experiences. The pilot was an unshaven Dutchman of doubtful sobriety, who offered me a coffee from a flask about half an hour after take-off as we bounced around in the thermals. An hour later I realized I was in trouble. The effects of the coffees and the bouncing were taking their toll and I needed to ease the pressure. However there were no obvious facilities, so eventually I decided to mention my condition, which was by now acute, to the captain, who airily pointed to the rear and said something about what sounded like a 'relief tube'.

I climbed over the sleeping oilmen, pushed some bags around and eventually located the wretched device, which didn't look too clean and not that easy to manipulate. Anyway, without going into details I was in such a state I could not relax sufficiently to perform and resumed my seat not knowing where to put myself with another half an hour to land. When we eventually did so, I staggered in great discomfort to the immigration shack, pushed everyone aside and headed for the filthy loos. By this time I was past caring and if they shot me that was fine too, but I lived to tell the tale: the moral of which is don't drink anything before a long flight in a small aircraft with limited facilities, least of all coffee.

Union Carbide had a big plant in Singapore making dry cell batteries for export all over the world. Their stores were badly damaged in a fire and the claim proved to be a nightmare. Union Carbide wanted to declare a total loss, which was their right according to the policy, but there was no evidence the damage was anything like as extensive as they were suggesting. Once I had gathered as much technical information as possible I decided in November to go and see the insurers in New Jersey and agree tactics.

In order to make the trip worthwhile I timed it to coincide with our professional institute's annual dinner in London, the same dinner where the year before Sarah the Bearer had shown up the following morning. Jimmy Guild was President and managed to make an excellent speech despite being totally smashed. His friend John Dark, a film and TV producer, replied on behalf of the guests. Oh dear, and there were ladies present.

On the Wednesday I flew to New York for the first time and arrived a day before the Presidential Election, when Ronald Reagan was attempting to unseat Jimmy Carter. I stayed at the Plaza Hotel on the corner of Fifth and 59th and was completely overawed by all them tall buildings.

The next morning I was collected by my corresponding US adjuster on the case and driven to Summit, New Jersey, home of AFIA Insurance, my illustrious client. After the meeting I said I would take the train back to the city and caught something called the Irralackawanna Railroad, which was something else. The seats were rock hard and the carriages still had holes in the sides made by Indians' arrows, or so I told myself.

Somehow I made it to Hoboken, Frank Sinatra's

birthplace as everyone kept telling me, and took the PATH to 33rd Street not far from the Empire State Building. It was raining and misty, but I stood a block away transfixed. The top floors were lit in red, white and blue. It was after all Election Day. I walked back up Fifth Avenue to the hotel, showered, changed and went to dinner with our Singapore friends the Colbys. John's father, William, had been Director of the CIA, and John was very well connected. So much so he had had lunch that day with President Eisenhower's son and told his guests that in Washington circles everyone was convinced Reagan was a shoo-in.

The next morning the Americans had a new President and I bought Annabelle an Apple necklace as a souvenir from Tiffany, as one does, before flying to Houston to meet our associated company Matthews Daniel. They were oil adjusters and we worked with them in Singapore. Not a bad crowd, but very pleased with themselves, if difficult to understand at times. After that I spent a couple of nights in LA seeing Ruben and the Fund before heading home.

At the end of November we had a products liability claim for British Insulated Callenders Cables (BICC, my grandfather's old firm). They had a scrap metal business in Israel and someone had inadvertently – well, maybe - managed to include some unexploded ordnance in a consignment of scrap, which had been sold to Marubeni in Japan. When it was thrown in their smelter, two technicians were killed in the resulting explosion and the smelter extensively damaged.

It took me an hour in a high-speed train to reach the plant from Tokyo Station and I never left Tokyo. That night I was invited to dinner by BICC's agent, a very urbane man named de Conte, half Japanese, half French at his apartment overlooking the Royal Palace grounds. He poured whisky from a decanter and it was delicious. Evidently he had perfected a blend of Johnny Walker Black Label, a brand I've never cared much for, and Chivas Regal. His charming Japanese wife produced the most delicious meal, both beautifully prepared and presented.

We were instructed to deal with a fire claim in a motor cycle showroom early in 1981 and after the claim had been settled I had a mad rush of blood to the head and asked the owner if I could try out one of his big machines with a view to buying. He gave me a free run and I chose a water-cooled 1200cc Kawasaki. I bought Annabelle and me a couple of helmets and we rode this beast out to a dinner party that evening. We walked in carrying our helmets, but no one took us seriously until I rode the bike into the dining room. Our host, Mike Elphick, demanded a ride and off we set. How we survived I don't care to think about. He had Annabelle's helmet perched on his head and both of us were well refreshed. I managed to drop the bike at the end of their drive and had the greatest difficulty getting it upright. Once on the open road, but still in the 40mph limit, I opened up the throttle. Well, the acceleration was in direct correlation with the speedometer, even with us great hulks on board. In three or four seconds we were doing over 100mph, a steady as a rock and we were Masters of the Universe. Luckily we came to our senses before we were caught by the police, and made it back to the party in one piece.

However it was a salutary experience and I took the bike back next morning. Mr Chan, the owner, insisted I tried something else and this time I came home with a 500cc

Honda, a lot more sedate. However as I was going along Mount Pleasant Road on a sortie that evening, unbeknown to me a cat was one side of the road watching a snake on the other and just as I was passing the cat pounced across the road into the bike. I lost my balance and slid down the road in a pair of shorts and a tee shirt with scratches everywhere. The cat did not survive to tell the tale and the snake had a good laugh. That was the last time I rode a motorbike. The wife has banned me ever since.

Certainly life was very busy and we burnt the candle at both ends on a regular basis. Quite frightening really. Looking at the diary at the end of June we were either entertained or entertaining twelve nights on the trot, including giving a dinner party ourselves for nineteen on a Tuesday night. What were we thinking about? I was usually in the office by 7.30am six days a week. Well, we are still here, hale and healthy, so it didn't do us any harm - or did it? Someone else can make that judgement.

The fake statues

When I was in London, which I was fairly frequently, in July 1981 I was summoned to a meeting in Lloyd's to discuss the insurance of a container load of Khmer stone and other carvings, the risk of which a marine syndicate had accepted for transit from Singapore to Amsterdam. However the declared value was US$35 million and at the last minute underwriters were starting to get cold feet. Evidently someone had telephoned the brokers, CT Bowring (now part of Marsh), suggesting the cargo was made up of fakes.

Would I please have some expert check the validity of the carvings against their description in the manifest?

Well for starters I didn't know what Khmer meant in artistic terms, but I had heard of the Khmer Rouge, which I had assumed was just some nickname for the Cambodian regime, so I didn't know where to start. I called the office and asked Denny Sim to call David Mun, my antique dealer friend, and see if he could point us in the right direction. I also asked Denny to have the insured, a Brit called Knight, meet us as soon as I was back 'on station' 24 hours later.

The consignment was due to be shipped to Amsterdam the day after I arrived back, so speed was of the essence. Denny had spoken to David Mun, who could not help us but knew a man who might, and this chap was reluctantly press-ganged into coming with us to inspect the statues in one of the dockside warehouses, accompanied by a very cross Mr Knight and his Thai wife/girlfriend.

There must have been over fifty statues of various Oriental deities including a substantial number of images of Buddha in different poses. Most of them dated from seven or eight hundred years ago, according to the manifest, and had probably been looted from temples in Thailand, Cambodia and Laos, the latter two being lawless countries at that time and Thailand not far behind once you were outside the main cities. Our expert was very dubious that there could be so many pieces and offered the view that they were likely to be 17C or 18C replicas, still valuable but not US$35m.

According to Knight he had stockpiled the collection in Bangkok over several years, visiting remote parts of Indo China before shipping them en bloc to Singapore. There he had attracted the interest of many potential buyers and an Arab syndicate was poised to buy the lot once they arrived in Amsterdam for the fabled US$35m. While this was all going on Maersk Line, on whose container ship the cargo was about to be loaded, were asking why the delay. They were informed there was a problem over the valuation. What valuation? When told US$35m, they refused to accept the container, stating it was allegedly worth more than their ship and its entire cargo combined.

We duly reported back to underwriters, who decided to come off risk immediately. Knight had already paid the premium and was furious. He insisted underwriters had to provide cover and threatened to sue if his sale was jeopardised. Back in the office I was calling everyone I could think of around the Far East to see if anyone could give me sound valuation advice. One such was Gerald Godfrey, probably the leading dealer in Oriental antiques, who had a splendid shop in Ocean Terminal in Hong Kong full of all sorts of goodies of the highest quality. However he could not help me with Mr Knight's collection, which was outside his area of expertise. He was however able to give me some confidence that all was not as Knight was contending.

He asked me to read out the list and stopped me when I got to 7 Sukhothai stone images of a running Buddha dating from the 1200s. He said that he knew there was one such believed to be 13C statue in a museum in Paris, which the Thai Government had been trying to persuade the French to return for years without success - and we had seven?

I don't think Knight was setting up an insurance scam. It was more likely he wanted to use the Lloyd's policy as evidence of value when negotiating a sale. Whoever tipped off Bowrings may have been a disgruntled rival or staff member.

The local agent in Singapore of another Lloyd's broker, Hogg Robinson, had introduced the business to Bowrings and he asked me to come and support him when he attempted to persuade Knight to accept the premium back. He was a long term Far East hand called Barnet Deakin, whose daughter Gail was married to my friend Tatlow, he of the Leila Sen diet fame. We met in the Mandarin Hotel lobby so that we were in the public gaze and after a heated session, Knight accepted the cheque and that was that, or so I thought.

About three years later, by which time we had moved to New York, I received a call from an attorney there who had been appointed by AIU, the big American insurer, to deal with a suspicious marine claim. It seemed that Knight's container with the statues had been lost at sea. It had allegedly been deck cargo on a small bulk urea carrier which had sprung a leak and sunk in deep water somewhere not far from the Gulf of Suez.

AIU were not really risk bearing insurers but underwriting agents, who had huge clout which allowed them to write whatever came through their door without a great deal of due diligence. Clearly none here, and their leading marine underwriter was the same Lloyd's syndicate that had rejected Knight first time round.

I called the New York attorney several times to find out what was happening with the case, which he refused to disclose. I have an uneasy feeling underwriters did a deal with Knight and cut their losses.

RICHARD YOUENS

The Royal Yacht

While I had been back in London prior to the Knight saga, Annabelle had instructed me to buy her a dress she had seen in some glossy, which she wanted to wear to a party on Wednesday July 29, 1981 to celebrate the Royal Wedding. Patrick and Rosie Findlater were throwing a party for the occasion and my bride of nine summers looked terrific. We were married on a Wednesday too. It was a black tie affair and we arrived wearing Charles and Diana masks, which caused a bit of a furore.

Lee Kuan Yew, the Prime Minister - well, benevolent dictator would be more accurate - refused to allow the wedding to be broadcast on Singapore television. Singapore had been a jewel in the British Empire and he did not want the citizens of his brave new Republic to hark back to days of yore, I suppose. The Malay government were equally hyper. Not so the Thais or the Indonesians. The Hong Kong and Standard Chartered Banks offered to pay for the relayed broadcast, but Lee would not budge. Several Findlater guests arrived late from Bangkok and Jakarta having seen the early stages on local TV (we were seven hours ahead don't forget), and everyone crowded round them wanting to hear how it was going. It was a very happy evening.

Several weeks later I received a call from someone who, according to Carol, my secretary, wanted me to join a yacht club and had rung several times. I wasn't interested but thought I'd better call the number and someone answered "Sembawang Shipyard". Funny, I thought, and asked for the extension I'd been given. Moments later a voice responded

"Royal Yacht Britannia". I wondered if I was having my leg pulled and asked for the name I'd been given, Brian Perowne. He turned out to be the brother-in-law of one of Annabelle's girlfriends, Cordelia O'Brien, who had given him our name as a contact, and would I like to come to a party in the yacht that very evening? I practically bit his hand off. The yacht had dropped Prince Charles and his enchanting bride off in the Middle East at the end of their honeymoon cruise and was sailing on to Australia, where she was providing accommodation for the Monarch during the Commonwealth Prime Ministers' Conference.

Annabelle was back in the UK putting Christian into Ludgrove prep school and I was booked to have dinner with the Elphicks. I called Gilly to say I wouldn't be able to make it etc. She said that was just as well because she was about to ring and cry off as something had come up. I said in Sembawang by chance? We were the only civilians invited by Brian or anyone else. The other guests, and there weren't many, were diplomats or Singapore Government. A contingent of Marines was based in the yacht, with a small band, and they beat the retreat on the quayside while we looked on. After everyone had departed we stayed on for a tour of the yacht. Apart from the royal suites, I was most impressed by the state of the engines, which were immaculate. No oil anywhere, everything shining as if brand new.

We invited Brian to come and have dinner and we took him to the Tanglin Club, along with several other officers including the Admiral, Paul Greening. It emerged during dinner that things were not that rosy between the newly-weds, much to our dismay. They never dined alone. Prince

Charles always insisted that at least two officers dined with them. During the day he was out on deck with the men playing hockey and what have you, while she was frequently up on the bridge, wearing a T-shirt and bikini bottom and that was it. Quite distracting when you're trying to steer a ship. There was even mention of a row about some cufflinks, which it transpired some time later had been a wedding gift from Camilla Parker-Bowles. Naughty woman. If she had left him alone, Princess Diana might well still be alive and at her husband's side.

Peking

The Fireman's Fund had agreed to insure an Italian miniseries about Marco Polo on location in China, provided their adjuster (me) could have instant access to the unit wherever, whenever. This was something quite unheard of. If you wanted to go to China you had to jump through lots of hoops and even then there was no guarantee. Evidently after a lot of toing and froing the Chinese authorities agreed to grant me a multiple entry visa, so production went ahead and I was on standby.

The call came one Saturday in early October 1981. The cameraman was sick and production was suspended. I changed planes in Hong Kong to Peking. The Civil Aviation Authority of China's clapped-out Hawker Siddeley Trident, which had probably been retired by BA twenty years before, was a far cry from the Singapore Airlines 747 I'd travelled on earlier in the day. The seats were not firmly attached to the floor and not everyone had a seat belt. The scary-looking stewardesses were almost as worn as the carpet.

Still, we made it intact and a car collected me at the airport, which was a relief. The hotel was about a mile from the Forbidden City and Tiananmen Square and it was a pretty forbidding place itself, a massive grey five-storey about 500 yards square. My room was equally grim, but there was plenty of hot water and a bathroom down the corridor. The amenity consisted of a permanent supply of piping hot water, some tealeaves and a mug with a lid to keep the beverage warm.

After freshening up, a car collected me and took me up the road towards the now infamous square and deposited me outside the other hotel in Peking, where the production were staying, and in I went to meet the producer, whom I knew a little. He was Franco Cristaldi and had been lucky enough to have been married to the divine Claudia Cardinale, but not for long and he was now married to an Eritrean actress called Zeudi Araya, who was with him in Peking. She was black and very beautiful with Caucasian features, but she was must have had a tough time in China, as the natives don't care for people with skin darker than their own.

It transpired that the cameraman was on the mend and Franco was apologetic that I'd come all that way for nothing. Oh well, the meter was running and I'd head for home in the morning. Fat chance. It was a Sunday and everything was shut down, so the first chance to escape was Monday. Peking was a desolate place in 1981. It was communist to the core. Grim buildings. Frightened looking people scurrying here and there, eyes to the ground. Few cars but lots of bicycles, old iron ones. Most people, men and women, wore Mao suits, green or blue, and matching caps complete with a Red Star. The weather that Sunday was grey, cold and wet - just to add to the place's lack of charm.

I spent the day wandering around the Forbidden City, where the unit had been filming. It was fascinating and I had the place practically to myself. No other Caucasians anyway. The roofs had little statues of animals along them and there were Lion Dogs everywhere - glazed pottery ones, that is. Our Shih Tzus had originally been bred by the Dalai Lamas in Tibet and sent to the Chinese Emperors as tributes. I imagine they ran around the Forbidden City in packs. To be fair that was all quite charming, and I was very fortunate to see it before China opened up to tourism.

I had arranged to meet Franco Cristaldi and his wife for lunch, together with several members of the crew, and we had a jolly party fuelled by Great Wall of China red and white sort-of (rice?) wine. The restaurant had one menu, which was a mix of Chinese and European, so Franco ordered one dish of everything and we shared.

The following morning I went to the Production Office to ask for help with my return flight, only to find they had all gone on strike and no one was talking. Franco said not to worry and organised a car to take me to see a section of the Great Wall itself. We drove for about an hour out of town and there it was, stretching uphill and away in both directions from the road. I went and paid for my ticket and followed the other (Chinese) tourists up some steps, on to the Wall and set off. I was dressed in slacks and a blazer.

Everyone else was in Mao suits, green or blue, and extremely suspicious of a Westerner in their midst. They clearly did not want to be seen with me for fear of retribution. But as we climbed away from the base and up into the hills, the atmosphere cleared and people started talking to me, albeit in Mandarin. I replied in English and suddenly I was among friends. I was wearing my Gucci moccasins and the cobbled surface of the walkway was slippy-slidey, which caused great amusement. When we reached as far as we were allowed to go, I even managed to persuade someone to take my photograph.

Once back in the car I was taken to the Ming Tombs for a late lunch and a tour round, which wasn't quite so interesting, and eventually back to the hotel for dinner with Franco and his entourage. It turned out that Production had managed to get me on a flight to Bombay the following evening. There was nothing back to Hong Kong until the next weekend, so I was grateful for any mercies. Most of Tuesday was spent organising my tickets and getting the right chops on my passport in order to be able to escape.

There was a great deal of toing and froing, one of which involved a trip on a production bus, taking actors to a location. I found myself sitting next to an old Chinese man of aristocratic bearing who turned out to be China's leading Shakespearian actor. It had never occurred to me that Shakespeare was allowed to be read in China, let alone that they had a leading Shakespearian actor. Naturally he spoke perfect English and said the authorities did not approve of what he did, but provided he and his fellow players were discreet they looked the other way.

That evening I boarded a Swissair (good) DC10 (not so good) for the flight to Bombay. I had been given a First Class ticket and had most of that section of the aircraft to myself. As I settled into my seat with a glass of champagne and a two-day-old *Sunday Express*, I felt I was being watched. I looked up and sure enough there was a Red Guard staring at me from the aisle. I looked round and there must have been one Red Guard every five rows all the way back to the tail. I looked at the nearest stewardess, who smiled and shook her head as if to say don't worry.

Eventually they left the aircraft and we were cleared for take-off. It was a relief to be in the air. I stayed in a Bombay airport hotel thanks to Swissair and caught another Swissair flight to Bangkok in the morning and on to Singapore. Bit roundabout, but I was glad to be home and have no desire to go back to Peking ever again.

CHAPTER 17

Another tragedy

Business was brisk and I was in and out of Jakarta, KL and Hong Kong on fleeting trips, then back to London at the end of October to spend time with the new regime at Head Office as well as take Christian out from Ludgrove, where he was apparently settling down, although it must have been a bit miserable when everyone else's parents were close by. I don't think there was anyone else with parents overseas, or at least not as much overseas as we were.

Back in Singapore the Royal Yacht *Britannia* called in on her way home and we went to drinks on board, so Annabelle at least saw the yacht and we had Brian Perowne and some of his fellow crew members back for supper. A couple of days later Annabelle went to London for Christian's first half term and a few days later I went up to

Hong Kong and on to Seoul to meet the Korean market and drum up business.

Seoul was bitterly cold after the tropics and after a day going round meeting people, Nigel Gale, our Hong Kong manager, and I had a look round town before heading back to our hotel. When I went to collect my room key there must have been at least twenty messages from various people in Singapore office, as well as some friends asking me to call back.

With an awful sense of foreboding, the reminder of which will forever send shivers down my spine, I called the office - not without difficulty, calling overseas in the Far East thirty years ago was a stressful business. When I got through Rajam the Indian girl answered and started crying. Then an expat took the receiver and told me that Adam, our youngest, had been found in our swimming pool that morning, pulled out still alive - just - and was in intensive care in Gleneagles Hospital, where he had been born.

I rang the hospital and luckily the Matron, Margot Hurd, who was a friend, was still there. She said he had probably been in the water for up to thirty minutes and was unlikely to survive. I then managed to contact Annabelle with her parents at Thatchers and she was making arrangements to fly back immediately with her father. They hoped to be in Singapore the following afternoon. In the meantime Nigel was trying to book me on any flight back, but the only option was via Hong Kong the following morning.

It was a long sleepless night and I set off for the airport hours early. When we landed in Hong Kong there was a girl from Jardine Matheson waiting at the aircraft door with my name on a placard. Bad news always travels fast. Adam's godmother Caroline Courtauld and husband William, with whom I had stayed on the way to Seoul, were waiting for me in Jardine's VIP suite, with a picnic lunch as I had a three-hour layover. However I could not face the thought of sitting all cooped up in some windowless room and suggested we all go to lunch at Gaddies, a restaurant in the Peninsular Hotel. I can't remember much about the lunch except that I was very grateful to have company and Li Ka Shing, the richest man in Hong Kong, was at a table nearby.

I still had three hours of flying and sat upstairs in a Singapore Airlines 747 drinking rather more brandy that was good for me, which had no effect. I was stone cold sober when we landed. Annabelle and her father, who had arrived a few hours earlier, collected me and we went straight to the hospital. On our way in to see Adam, most of the office staff were waiting outside, which was kind. I suppose they just wanted to be there in case there was something they could do.

Adam was in intensive care with oxygen and unconscious and he remained that way for the next five days. Matron Hurd was on hand and said we would just have to hope and pray he pulled through although after half an hour in the pool this was unlikely.

Over the next days the house was full of people toing and froing all the time. The Findlaters, who had lost Emily two years earlier when the branch of a tree fell on her, moved in. Adrian, Annabelle's Californian girlfriend, had come down from Hong Kong.

We were in and out of the hospital, but there was no sign of improvement and on Monday November 23 we were told by one of the many doctors who were attending him that the only possible hope was to give him a substantial dose of barbiturates. When we asked what could be the best outcome he said that he would live but he would not be able to look after himself, let alone know who we were and react to us. In effect a vegetable. That was no prospect for him or for any of us, so we agreed with Matron Hurd that the best thing would be to let him go. The life support machines were switched off and we were with him when he died just after seven that same evening.

All this time we were puzzled as to how Adam could have gained access to the pool, which was surrounded by a wooden fence with a gate locked with a bolt and hasp. Lourdes, our Filipina maid, lived in and Jahora, our Malay amah, who came every day all day, were looking after him and Arabella. Both of them doted on the children and knew never to leave the pool gate open. Anyway Adam was not that keen on swimming and would not have tried to enter the pool area even if the gate was open.

Jahora had a son called Hamid aged about eight or nine, who may have been jealous of his mother's affection for Adam. Maybe he had something to do with the accident; we'll never know of course. It could just as easily happened when I was at the office downtown and Annabelle was shopping for groceries. He was a week short of his second birthday.

Adam's funeral was at St George's church, Tanglin, on Thursday November 26 in the morning. The saddest sight was his little white coffin, not much bigger than his sister Olivia's six years before, in front of the altar. The church was packed, but Annabelle and I were only vaguely aware of what was happening. Arabella was too young to understand, but was very brave. Poor Christian, when he was told, said, "Well, there's just the two of us again".

Adam's godmother Jane FitzGerald had come from New York in time for the funeral and took Annabelle back with her for a complete change. I stayed put with Arabella until the end of term and then we flew back to London to meet Annabelle at Heathrow, when our flights were due to land at about the same time. However it was bitterly cold in Europe and we were frozen into the aircraft. So was everyone else, and we had to wait on the ground for over three hours for the de-icing equipment and that froze too.

Eventually we all met up and went to see my parents, who had sent a car for us. After lunch we collected Christian from Ludgrove and went to stay the night with Annabelle's family at Thatchers. Adam had been cremated, and we scattered his ashes in the churchyard at Swyncombe, the Methven's local church, where Olivia's ashes had also been scattered.

CHAPTER 18

New York, new friends

While she was in New York Annabelle had met a gold dealer who was married to a Japanese girl, and as they were going to Tokyo for Christmas he offered her the use of his apartment on 85th and York while they were away. She decided to take him up and so we went there on December 21, me armed with the possibility we might be transferred there from Singapore in the New Year, something we were both keen to do. The apartment was part of a brownstone house and came with an Argentinian maid who did not speak any English. However it seems her husband was in hospital, she didn't drive and would we care to have the use of her Cadillac if we didn't mind the invalid controls. We felt it would be churlish to refuse.

New York at Christmas is colourful and lively, which was a distraction. I spent time in the office and Annabelle went off to look at apartments to rent or buy, but the good ones were way out of our reach. The York Avenue apartment was attacked while we were out one day and two blocks away a nun was mugged outside her convent, so we decided that if we did come to New York we would be better off either in Connecticut or Long Island, as we had ex-Singapore friends in both Greenwich and Locust Valley near Oyster Bay on the fabled North Shore of the island.

Greenwich seemed too expensive, so we set off another day for Locust Valley, although our friends the Deers were away in Europe for the holidays. We had hamburgers in a very jolly restaurant called Marbles in LV and then piled in to a real estate agency next door called Douglas Elliman. We were greeted by a tiny woman who told us we looked like "real nice people", in a southern accent, and how could she help us? She showed us several houses but nothing we liked, so we arranged to come back next week and she would show us some more.

At the beginning of the following week Peter Simpson, the Managing Director of Graham Miller, came out from London to see the office and talk to the two American adjusters, who had not been with us very long and looked as if they might be off to pastures new. Unknown to me Esperanza was talking to Continental Insurance, an American company, about buying Graham Miller, and while Peter was in town he got a call to come back to London for a meeting and to bring me with him. It so happened that Esperanza owned a travel agent called Gray Dawes Westray and they had discounted tickets for their directors, one of whom was Peter, and he had Concorde tickets both ways. He invited me to join him.

I called BA to book my seat and a return flight the next evening. No problem - pay with a credit card at check in. I duly presented my Singapore registered Diners Club card, which they could not check because it was a local franchise, but not to worry, if there was a problem they'd let me know in London. We flew back, had our meetings with Continental, whose people I already knew, and I flew back that night First Class. All jolly nice, especially since BA never charged for the flights. I don't know what happened to the Continental deal either, but it never passed go.

We stayed on for another week in New York and on our second trip to Locust Valley, Helen Woodbridge, the southern lady realtor, showed us a brick house with a slate roof in Shu Swamp Road, which suited us to the ground. It was essentially on one floor with three bedrooms and bathrooms to the left of the front door and all the reception rooms and usual offices to the right. It also had two more bedrooms and a bathroom upstairs. Finally there was an enormous basement, complete with a wet bar, party room and workshop.

According to Helen, the vendor was the son of a retired US ambassador called John Portner Humes. The son was called John Portner Humes III and had been married three times before he was thirty. He was now in his forties and an alcoholic, which was much evident from the cases of booze piled high in the basement. He spent most of his time drying out, to little effect, in one expensive clinic after another. The house had not been lived in for some time and he was keen to sell. The place had a good feel to it despite its recent history. Shu Swamp Road ran through wooded countryside about a mile from Locust Valley and the house was set on a hill, in a forest overlooking, if you could see it for the trees, a wooded wetland conservation area, Shu Swamp. It had a two-acre garden, most of which was overgrown, with a small swimming pool full of leaves. The area had been an Indian (we are talking Red here) reservation.

We decided somehow or other we had to buy it, and here Richard Nelson of Esperanza back in London came to our aid with a loan guarantee to our bank, our old friends Standard Chartered, for which we were forever grateful. In mid-January I flew back to Singapore, essentially to clear my desk and hand over to my successor, Mike Patton, who had joined Graham Miller about the same time as me. Annabelle arrived a week later, leaving Arabella with her grandparents, Christian being back at Ludgrove for his second term; a prospect I fear he did not relish much, especially with us still being overseas, but at least in New York, quite a bit nearer.

By mid-February we were wrapped up and ready to leave, having spent the previous four weeks staying with the wonderful, generous and kind Mike and Gilly Elphick - we couldn't face 158 Mount Pleasant Road again. We were sad to leave Singapore in such circumstances. We had had a wonderful time there. We made a lot of friends, most of whom have remained close ever since. The staff were very loyal and I felt I was letting them down, but they understood we wanted a fresh start. Back in London I spent a frantic week going round and meeting all the underwriters, mostly at Lloyd's, who had supported us in New York, before taking up the new job.

We decided to spend a few days in between the old and the new at Lyford Cay at the invitation of Mike Baker

Harber, the husband of Annabelle's cousin and bridesmaid, Sally. Lyford (sometimes referred to as Lifeless on account of the mainly elderly membership) Cay is a gated community for the über rich on New Providence Island in the Bahamas. There is also a clubhouse where we stayed in splendid isolation. As luck would have it Annabelle's uncle and aunt, Nigel and Rosita Morris - Sally's parents, who were very good friends - were also staying on the estate. Annabelle's sister Susie's in-laws, Henry and Haroldine Pasley-Tyler, had a house there and they were in residence too, so we were among friends.

One evening the Pasley-Tylers invited us to dinner at some smart restaurant on the estate. I was told I had to wear a jacket, so I went to the shops and acquired the most garish I could find, a bright turquoise number with a sea green patterned lining, made by Lilly Pulitzer, who was trendy then. In fact she has just come back into fashion again. I have worn it many times since, to gasps - not always admiring. It has even appeared in *Country Life*.

Annabelle warned me the Pasley-Tylers did not drink, so I had a couple of stiff whiskies before we set off. When we arrived at the venue, Henry PT was at the bar with a shaker full of martini; there was white and red wine and brandy with the coffee. I decided I quite like people who don't drink.

The next morning we ran into Henry in the Club lobby looking very po-faced. I assumed he was feeling a bit part-worn from the previous evening, but he was very worried about his wife Haroldine, who had been ill during the night. Food poisoning was feared and she was in a very poor way. We learned later that the fish dish she had eaten the night before was not all it seemed and somehow included stonefish, which is poisonous, very poisonous. Her condition took several months to improve, and she never fully recovered. Annabelle had also had the fish but was unharmed.

After a very happy six-day interlude in the sunny and warm playground of the Lifeless we headed off to winter in New York, where I went back to work on March 8, 1982 - our tenth wedding anniversary. We spent the first couple of days with our friends the FitzGeralds in their palatial UN Plaza apartment overlooking the East River, and I commuted downtown on the subway. The office was located on the 21st floor of 111 John Street, one block from Water St in the thick of the New York insurance ghetto. It was a far cry from the creature comforts of Singapore, small and cramped with clapped-out furniture, no reception, ancient telephones - not a lot going for it really but it was a major change, let alone challenge, and that was what I wanted.

The business was run by an old-fashioned New York "street adjuster" called Steve Bishop, whose very parochial business Bill Bolton had bought on behalf of the company the year before. Steve was perfectly capable but pedestrian and had lost most of his core business soon after he sold to us. Bill had hired two very New York New York adjusters from Toplis & Harding, our main Lloyd's competitor. Lloyd's was permitted by the US authorities to write some classes of business direct in the states of New York, California and Illinois, one of which is Jeweller's Block. This is the insurance of the jewellery industry and 47th New York is the centre of the US diamond trade, which is almost entire monopolised by Hassidic Jews, the chaps with homburg hats, long black coats, long hair and thick beards. There never seem to be less than half a dozen of them on any flight between London and New York.

Our two brave T&H adjusters, John Butler and Jim Donovan, who were gentile to the core, knew most these dealers and everyone seemed to get on. After my experiences in Wengen twenty years before I decided to leave them to it apart from monitoring their reports, which meant translating them into coherent English. The previous office manager before Bishop's acquisition was an aviation specialist and as no one knew what to do with the remains of his account I applied myself to those files and started to sniff around and see what else was going.

In the meantime Annabelle, Arabella and I moved into a serviced apartment at the Beverley Hotel on Lexington Avenue a few blocks up from UN Plaza, so Annabelle could meet up with Jane FitzGerald and make some friends through her while we waited to complete the purchase of Shu Swamp, which was scheduled for the end of the following week. We had ordered a black 3 series BMW, which was delivered at the end of our first week, so Annabelle had transport to go and see schools etc for Arabella.

Part of my role was to keep an eye on a small office we had in Los Angeles, run by a young Brit called Shaun Coyne, who had recently moved there from New York where he had been working with John and Jim on the jewellery business and had picked up some similar accounts in LA.

Residence & Work visas were, and probably still are, hard to come by in the US unless you didn't speak English and were an illegal immigrant with no education, let alone funds. However if you could prove that at least half of the revenue you intended to generate came from outside the US, you could apply for a Treaty Trader visa. Shaun had obtained one of these, albeit after a lot of hassle, and I had been able to obtain one too thanks to his tutelage.

At the end of my first week Shaun called to invite me to attend an insurance brokers' claims seminar and dinner in Los Angeles the following Wednesday. He wanted support because he was to give a paper on Lloyd's. This seemed like a good idea. It would give me the opportunity to meet up with the Ruben and Fireman's Fund people and see if they might like to give Shaun and me some work. We were treated like royalty and had a great time. Wednesday was St Patrick's Day and the Americans go green, the colour - not environmentally, heaven forfend. Green was everywhere, even the beer, and we had a long lunch in the Ruben dining room with Don Cass well away on the piano before going on to the seminar. I was beginning to feel I had arrived.

What Shaun had not told me until we were heading to the venue was that the seminar and dinner was for the lady claims brokers of Los Angeles, and as one might expect they were a right bunch of frumps – middle-aged, overweight, over made-up and looking to party amongst themselves. They were not the slightest interested in us, let alone what Shaun had to say. Quite depressing if one had to deal with them on a day-to-day basis, which thank goodness we didn't. Afterwards Shaun dropped me off at the airport and I took the red eye back to New York. Big mistake. The flight left LA at 10pm and arrived at Kennedy at 5.45am local, 2.45am West Coast time. I went straight to the office and felt like death warmed up for the rest of the day. Still, I learnt one thing, and never took the red eye ever again.

Settling in to Gatsby Country

The next day we completed the purchase of Shu Swamp, and what a circus that was. In England the solicitor sends you the contract ahead of time, you sign it, send it back, on the agreed day pick up the keys from the agent and that's that. In the US it's jobs for the boys. My attorneys, Lord Day & Lord (only the best) provided the venue, a large fancy boardroom with views over the Hudson River, and two attorneys. Portner Humes did the same. There was also a man from the warranty company - que? When you buy property in the US you have to buy warranty insurance to cover you if someone else emerges with a claim on the real estate. He had an assistant. Someone from Standard Chartered Bank, which was lending me most of the purchase price, was there, as well as a secretary to make notes and serve coffee - all on my account. But by the time we were done the Youens were the proud and happy owners of a piece of prime New York real estate, and after being homeless for six years that was a grand feeling

I must have signed several hundred documents before we were finished – well, it seemed that way - and was thankful to make an escape. Annabelle and Arabella were to meet me off a train in Locust Valley, but I hadn't given much thought as to how to get there. It seemed the only way was to take the subway to Jamaica Station on Long Island and change onto the LIRR (Long Island Rail Road) to Oyster Bay. Locust Valley was the penultimate stop. It was a pretty scary trip into the unknown, with some very scary people for company on the subway.

Jamaica Station was in the middle of nowhere – well,

Queens, same thing. The platforms were elevated with no protection from the elements and there was plenty of fresh air about. By the time my train pulled in I just wanted to escape. The locomotive must have been one of the first diesels ever built, with square wheels also on the rolling stock. The seats were rock hard. There was rubbish everywhere and the carriage smelt of the great unwashed. What had I done? Was this to be my daily commute? Surely not. Please God.

There was to be no more welcome sight as we finally pulled into Locust Valley station than my darling wife and daughter waiting to greet me. They had been at the house from lunchtime waiting for the containers with all our effects to arrive once the purchase had been closed. There were two containers, one from Singapore, which had already arrived, and another from London, due next week with everything which had been in store for six years, none of which Arabella had ever seen. Christian, who was due to arrive from Ludgrove next week, had last seen them when he was three.

Christmas came early for all of us and we had a happy time staying with the Deers, unpacking and sorting over the next four days. Annabelle was anxious to have everything organised for Christian's benefit and we finally moved in to sleep on March 23, the day before he arrived. Zoo Loo dog flew in from Singapore at the end of the week and the family was complete again for the first time since Adam had died nearly four months earlier.

I never had to do the Jamaica commute again. Philip Deer used to collect me each morning at about 7.15am in his red Rabbit, aka Golf, as in VW anywhere else in the world, and drive me to Manhasset about 20 minutes away. Here there was a separate branch of the LIRR, which ended in Port Washington on the north shore of the Island where, it was rumoured, the directors of the LIRR all lived. The rolling stock on this track had round wheels, had been built since the last war and provided a more frequent and efficient service into Penn Station, from where we caught the 7th Avenue subway downtown to Fulton Street. We did the same in reverse and I'd meet Phil on the 6.10pm back to Manhasset. This arrangement lasted for about a week until I found a kind couple who lived near Manhasset station and agreed to let me park in their driveway for $40 a month. It was a hurried ten-minute walk to and fro, but that was good for the heart.

The weather was very unpredictable that April, two feet of snow one day then hot sun and barbecues two days later. On Annabelle's birthday, April 6, I went into the City in bright sunshine and by lunchtime we were snowed in. John Hollinrake, who ran the office in Milan, had been in Venezuela and called in on his way home to see clients, none of whom was available because of the weather, so he managed with great difficulty to persuade John Butler and me to join him for lunch. We didn't leave the restaurant until six and I was not too popular when I eventually arrived home slightly worse for wear just before nine with no gift to celebrate her 32nd birthday. The snow was not an acceptable excuse.

Back in the film business

The following week I got my first break from the Fireman's

Fund. Marty Ritter, the legendary film director (*Hud* and *The Spy who came in from the Cold* among many others) had been ill while making *Cross Creek* about Marjorie Kinnan Rawlings, the author of "The Yearling", on location near Ocala in Florida. The Fund's long-term adjuster in New York, (I can't remember his name), who evidently had made a muddle of a claim for Rodney Dangerfield on *Easy Money* and was again in trouble on *Cross Creek*, was asked to withdraw and I took over. There but for the grace of God etc., but I was delighted to have the chance of some action and never looked back the rest of the time we were in New York - very lucky.

The Ocala trip was memorable for two reasons. There was no local airport so I had to fly to Orlando and rent a car. The highway to Ocala was empty, so I decided to get a move on, but within two minutes I ran into a speed trap. A Highway Patrol car was immediately on my tail. I pulled in and started to climb out of the car. Big mistake. The patrolman, quick as a flash, pulled out his gun John Wayne style and I was made to 'assume the position'. I had no idea what he was talking about and put my hands in the air, apologising profusely in the broadest Limey accent I could muster, while being scared witless. The accent must have had the desired effect. He put his gun away, asked for my papers and eventually sent me on my way with a reprimand. First rule for an Englishman driving in the US when stopped by the law - be as English as you can be.

Ocala is a big horse-breeding area, which was why the unit was there, but it is also very swampy and very popular with water moccasins, a particularly aggressive and poisonous snake. On arrival I was handed a pair of knee-high leather boots and told to wear them at all times. Ophidiophobia, the fear of snakes, is one of my foibles, so I was very nervous and keen to make an escape at the earliest opportunity. Despite squelching around in the swamp for a couple of hours I am pleased to report I never actually saw a snake and was mighty thankful. I went again a couple of weeks later and had my first shoeshine at Gainesville airport on the way back. That was exciting. I'd always cleaned my own shoes heretofore.

The following week I was back in Los Angeles because we were talking to some more Toplis & Harding adjusters about coming to join us, which would have involved opening a new office in San Francisco and expanding Shaun's operation in LA, none of which I was very excited about because they were all much older and more experienced than me as well as not keen on reporting to me in New York. Besides the two key players, Don Maxson and Jim Young, were both seriously weird. So much so that Maxson for no apparent reason threw himself out of a high floor room at the Pegasus Hotel in Kingston, Jamaica, a few years later.

Not only were we planning to expand on the West Coast but the boys from Esperanza in London were planning to relocate for tax purposes to New York and sent one of their bean counters David Shepley-Cuthbert, aka at Eton David Shapely-Custard, to sniff out the lie of the land. Within a few months my little territory was not going to be quite what I'd signed up for. At the same time things were said to be becoming unravelled in Singapore. My old friend and ex-colleague Chan Hwee Seng was unhappy with my successor, Mike Paton, who was not pulling his weight and had upset our supporters. Chan was being wooed by the competition and after a week in London going round the market I flew on to Singapore, did what I had to do to calm things down and carried on round the world back home. There's a note in my diary that I had flown 68,000 miles that May in 1982. I don't think Annabelle was best pleased.

Piping Rock Club

Happily June kept me in New York, which was just as well because Philip Deer had proposed me for membership of Piping Rock Club not far from Shu Swamp. Piping was a very old school, preppy establishment - straight up my street really. It had a splendid clubhouse almost entirely surrounded by a wonderful 18-hole golf course, as well as indoor and outdoor tennis courts (all-weather and grass), squash and paddle tennis. The food in the dining rooms was excellent, served by friendly and efficient staff. There was also a summer location at the beach on Long Island Sound, with several swimming pools and a great restaurant. The membership went back generations of old money. My kind of Shangri-La.

The only problem for me, apart from no money let alone old money, was that all prospective members had to meet at least 30 governors, of which there were about 33, and for the most part this meant an interview in their offices. I calculated that I spent a week of office time in the aggregate going round the governors, most of who were very friendly but surprised at the influx of Brits from Singapore applying to join. Apart from the Deers, the FitzGeralds had joined the year before and David Band, who had been in Singapore when we first arrived but had since been in Hong Kong and Paris with JP Morgan bank, was also doing the rounds. He and Olivia moved to Locust Valley the same time as us and had looked at the house in Shu Swamp a few days before we did.

One of these governors had a seat on the NYSE. I assumed he had a book of private clients and was slightly taken aback when he told me he just sold his own business to the Market. He commuted downtown by helicopter from Oyster Bay and offered me a seat, which I somehow declined. Another was Nelson Doubleday the publisher, who was Jackie Kennedy's boss. He was a bit of a rough diamond. After about five minutes' general chitchat, I was still calling him Mr Doubleday and he said "don't give me that Mr Doubleday shit, call me Nelson!" Good man. Evidently he had put Jackie up for membership of Piping but she was turned down because the governors did not want the attention of the press. Happily that was never going to be a problem with me and I joined in July, just in time for Christian's holidays. I did have a problem though, I never had enough money to make as much use of the place as I would have liked.

Allegations of fraud

At the beginning of July our sister company, Gellatly Hankey, found itself in serious trouble in Hong Kong. One of their marine surveyors, Captain Don Brockbank, had received a visit at 3am from the Independent Commission Against Corruption (ICAC). Hong Kong's Government had a lot of rotten apples throughout its various departments, not the least the police, and Governor MacLehose had set up the Commission to clean up their act about eight years earlier.

Having served its initial purpose it was charged with investigating corruption wherever it was suspected, and Brockbank was suspected of taking a bribe to certify the seaworthiness of a cargo ship which had recently sprung a leak and been scuttled outside Colombo harbour.

I knew Brockbank and was instructed to go and find out his side of the story as well as attend the initial hearing in Court. I left New York at lunchtime on Sunday July 11 and flew to Hong Kong via Tokyo, arriving on Monday evening. I spent all Tuesday with Brockbank and our lawyers Johnson Stokes & Masters. Brockbank had surveyed the vessel in Taiwan in January on behalf of underwriters and was satisfied that it was seaworthy for another 12 months. She subsequently sailed for Colombo carrying a full load of bulk cement. On entering the harbour she started to take on water and the harbour master ordered her to be removed immediately. She was towed to deep water, the seacocks were opened and she was left to sink in very short order. Certainly no one from insurers had a chance to inspect her before she was lost.

The authorities took the view that she was unseaworthy when she was surveyed and the certificate could never been issued without some skulduggery on Brockbank's part. I don't think he was in anyway involved and suspected the ship that sank was not the one he originally surveyed, so he had been set up, but with the ship at the bottom of the Indian Ocean the evidence was gone. There were and still are a lot of villains out there. Poor Brockbank never survived the ordeal and died a few years later a broken man. Such a shame. He was an honest sailor with a lovely wife.

I left Hong Kong on the Wednesday evening, flew to London to report on the case the following morning and was back home on Friday evening in time for supper, having gone around the world in five and a half days and worked a full three and a half. What a hero, but it can be done going west to east. No jet lag, there wasn't enough time and I was in Lexington Kentucky three days later. It makes me weak at the thought, as I dread any attempt at long haul flights nowadays, but travelling was a lot more relaxing pre al Qaeda.

The Swiss Cheese Vault

We had a rather weird case in Denver, Colorado at the end of August. An almost brand new privately run safety deposit vault had been broken into and many of the deposit boxes forced open. It appeared that the perpetrators had penetrated the vault by overcoming the quite sophisticated protections and entered only those boxes which had been let, apart from setting off several dummy boxes booby-trapped with tear gas. It was clearly an inside job and the owners looked deeply suspect. The vault traded as the Swiss Security Vaults and was being referred to in the local press the following day as the Swiss Cheese Vaults, wait for it - because it was full of holes. Those Americans and their subtle sense of humour. Mr Seely, the owner, was most put out.

The press and TV were all over John Butler and me during our investigations. The vault windows were blacked out for privacy but the cameras were able to pick us out quite clearly as we went about our business, for the nation to see minutes later. I was also badgered for an interview and came over very plummy but I don't think anyone actually listened to what I was saying - they just loved my accent, oh dear me. Anyway there were no repercussions, so no harm done. We had our lawyer Alan Martin with us and he and I had to go to London and explain ourselves to Lloyd's the following week. As result underwriters denied the claim and Mr Seely closed the business, job done for him I suppose. Pity the poor old depositors.

007 again

At the beginning of November 1982 there was a problem on a James Bond film on location in Nassau called *Never Say Never Again* starring Sean Connery, who had sworn he'd never make another Bond film, hence the title. It was a remake of *Thunderball*, which had originally been written, by Ian Fleming and others including Kevin McClory, as a film script, but the movie initially wasn't made for lack of funds. Fleming turned the script into a novel and our Kevin was most upset because there was nothing in it for him.

Anyway I went down to Nassau and found the Second Unit, the one that had whatever the problem was, filming offshore our happy playground of Lyford Cay. I was taken out to the location, which was a wreck, to be cut with the inevitable shark-chases-our-hero scenes. I think there must have been a camera problem, and while I wasn't planning to witness the retakes I did need to gather all the information. Job done, I was anxious to be on my way, but the only way back was to be dropped off on some rocks at the shore, where my car would be waiting.

Unfortunately for me I was wearing Gucci moccasins (they must have been part of my uniform in those days), and I slipped on said rocks, landing heavily on my left elbow, which sprang a leak. There was blood all over the place and I was in shock. It took a while to get my act together before I was taken to Lyford Cay, where there was a pharmacy and I was patched up. I also had a large brandy in the bar to calm myself down before heading for the airport.

By the time I arrived back at Shu Swamp late that night I was in considerable pain, but foolishly did nothing about it other than drive into the office downtown for the next couple of days to avoid bumping into people on the transit system. By the weekend I was exhausted and took to my bed for a couple of days. I should have gone to see the doctor, as I suffered pains in the arm and shoulder for years afterwards. No James Bond, me.

No souvenir

The week before Christmas, Radio Corporation of America (RCA) had some drama in Sao Paolo, Brazil, and by the time the business was concluded I had missed the last connection home via Rio and had to wait until the following evening. Such a bore having to hang around in Rio for a day, but RCA laid on a car and driver to show me the sights, which was kind of them.

If you haven't climbed Sugar Loaf Mountain, like me you wouldn't know that it is in two sections and you walk from one to the other across a plateau. The moment you approach the plateau, ie the moment you alight from the cable car, you are set upon by photographers and souvenir salesmen and they are pretty cute businessmen, no women that I can remember. On the way back, having been to the top of the second section to admire the splendid view and now retracing my steps across the plateau once more, I was approached by a native carrying mugs, ashtrays, plates and a T-shirt, all with my photograph and the mountain behind me. Well I bought an ashtray, which I took home and proudly displayed on the mantelpiece at a party a couple of nights later. People seemed to enjoy stubbing their cigarettes out on my image and when it came out of the dishwasher afterwards all there was was a cheap white ashtray, no photo, boo hoo.

Blame it on me

I went back to Rio the following May in a roundabout fashion via Lincoln Nebraska, LA and almost Debra Winger in between. Debra was off games for some reason, but more to the point Paramount were worried that their co-production called *Terms of Endearment* was coming off the rails, therefore while Debra was off sick the unit might not be able to film anyway for other reasons. Both Paramount and the Fireman's Fund asked me to dig around and see what was going on. Well, I thought, I may as well somehow ask Debra herself. When I arrived in Lincoln, via St Louis and Omaha, I rented a Pontiac Firebird, with a cunning plan to sweep her off her feet and out for tea.

As I was climbing out of this beast near the production office someone rushed out and said my New York office was looking for me and had called several times. I called back and was told the Fund wanted get hold of me urgently. Their claims manager, Len Lommen, had recently retired and his job had been taken by a very smart woman named Denise Dimin. I called her and she said to forget about Debra and get myself to Rio ASAP. With Production's help we established that the quickest way was via Denver and LA and I headed off back to the airport. I called Denise to let her know what was happening but she was in meetings and I only managed to reach her when I called from Denver. She said the situation had changed but to come on to LA for a briefing.

The next morning I learnt that the first nine days' rushes on *Blame it on Rio* were out of focus due to a camera fault. The camera had been changed but nothing would be reshot until insurers committed themselves to the claim. This was most unusual, but as the producer was a somewhat dubious individual called David Begelman, both the brokers, Albert G Ruben, and United Artists, who were backing the film, were nervous.

Begelman had been an agent for the likes of Judy Garland and Marilyn Monroe before crossing the street and joining Columbia, where he had been successful in turning that studio's fortunes round with *Close Encounters of the Third Kind* and others. However while he was there he was investigated for forging cheques and was fired. At about the time of the present claim a book about Begelman's activities was published called "Indecent Exposure", which brought the case to light, hence everyone's concerns.

I met Begelman in the brokers' offices and learnt that no retakes would be filmed before early the following week and it was agreed I'd meet him and UA's man at the location in three days' time. So I went home and pitched up in Rio as agreed to find that the UA man was Lee Katz, whom I had got to know on *Apocalypse Now*.

The director was the celebrated Stanley Donen, who had made *Singing in the Rain* with Gene Kelly before going on to make *Arabesque* and *Charade*, dated now but magical none the less. The current film starred Michael Caine and a young unknown called Demi Moore.

The first nine days' work was screened and it was all out of focus for sure, but according to the rental company who had supplied the camera there was nothing wrong with it and the focus was nothing to do with the processing laboratory, let alone the condition of the raw film stock, so the only reasonable conclusion was the fault lay with the camera crew. I told Begelman, who had obviously reached the same conclusion but was not prepared to admit it, and he said he would have to fire them. They were all British and did I want that on my conscience? I said I didn't, but that was his call not mine. With that I headed for home; no claim. Paramount weren't best pleased but accepted the inevitable.

As an aside, Stanley Donen and the senior members of the crew stayed a small hotel on Copacabana Beach called L'Ouro Verde, where the rooms were pretty primitive but the food was delicious, served in a dowdy dining room but with white linen tablecloths and napkins. It was here I had my first Caipirinha sitting on a patio at the hotel entrance. It's a local cocktail made from cachaca, Brazillian for poteen, and fresh limes: powerful and delicious.

One night Lee Katz and I walked down the Copacabana to a restaurant someone had recommended and on the way back we were approached by some ladies of rather obviously easy virtue, offering their services. We declined, whereupon they attacked us with their handbags, which had bricks in them, and chased us down the street. We must have looked quite pathetic, but discretion is the better part of valour and all that. We sought sanctuary in the Copacabana Palace Hotel nearby and cabbed it back home. Poor Lee was quite badly bruised.

Glitterati on the fiddle

Our old client and friend the Lloyd's underwriter Flash Gordon used to instruct us whenever he could and he wrote most of the top jewellers in New York, including van Cleef & Arpels and Harry Winston. The broker on these accounts was a charming man called Teddy Denman from JH Minet & Co and he was keen to see me establish a rapport with his clients, so that they were comfortable with me dealing with them and at times with their clients, I suppose. However some of the clients were definitely suspect.

On one occasion Winston's chief salesman, a Swiss named Harry Bochatay, was summoned to Miami to wait upon a wealthy Arab, who was the nephew of the Saudi king. These people keep strange hours and after hanging around nearly a week, at 3am one morning poor Bochatay was woken and instructed to go immediately to the Arab's yacht with his stock of goodies. When he returned to his room several hours later, having made some worthwhile sales, he realised an emerald bracelet was missing from a set consisting also of a choker, necklace, bracelet, ear studs, drop earrings and a socking great ring - all in matching style. Gross or what? Anyway the bracelet was not to be found and in came a claim.

I went to see Ronnie Winston, his father Harry having departed to the great jeweller in the sky, at his shop on Fifth Avenue, to hear the story as well as discuss what to do. I asked to see the rest of the set. Ronnie instructed some menial to remove it from the safe and he tossed it over to me in bubble wrap. "How much?" I asked. It cost $5m and he hoped to sell for well in excess of $10m, said Ronnie. Well that would help pay off my $150k mortgage.

Bochatay had been with the firm for twenty years and was above suspicion, so someone in the Saudi's entourage must have pocketed the bracelet. We agreed that Ronnie would tell his client that he was making a claim and that Lloyd's wanted to interview all witnesses wherever they were, including Saudi Arabia, where we had offices, and take statements. The Miami Police Department would have to be informed etc. A few days later the bracelet mysteriously turned up and was returned.

Ronnie used to lend jewellery to high-profile clients to wear at high-profile events, which encouraged the well-heeled but also-rans to reach for their wallets. One such sort of high profile was an ex-wife of one of the Bunker Hunt brothers, they who tried but failed to corner the world's silver in 1979-80. The ex went to a party in Los Angeles wearing a fine pair of ruby and diamond drop earrings, one of which went missing during the evening, allegedly.

I met her with Ronnie at his Fifth Avenue store and she said she had alerted the event organisers as soon as she realised the loss. The venue was thoroughly searched, staff questioned and so on but the police had not been informed.

It was explained to her that this was essential if Ronnie was successfully to claim off Lloyd's and a few days later the missing earring was recovered. Who are these people? I suppose to some it's a game and on these two occasions they were called. Ronnie seemed to think she was trying to supplement her divorce settlement.

No evidence

In August 1983 I had a job in Huntsville, Alabama, which left my ego bruised. A production company had been filming a show called *What Waits Below* (its shooting title was something else) in which dragons somehow featured, on location in some huge privately-owned subterranean caverns. After the crew had wrapped and departed, the location owner complained that stalactites and stalagmites had been broken, there was graffiti on the walls, rubbish all over the place including human faeces - film crews can be a rough lot.

The producer was a friendly bear of a man called Sandy Howard, who had made *Return of a Man Called Horse*, and I had taken Annabelle and Christian to meet him at Wilton House outside Salisbury in 1975. Christian was two with long page-boy cut hair and dressed in a very smart coat with a velvet collar. Sandy greeted him with "oh gee what a pretty little girl" and his mother was very cross.

Anyway Sandy was in denial about the alleged damage to the caves and thought the owner was trying it on. Denise Dimin, from the insurance company, told me to be sure and take my camera. She wanted plenty of evidence one way or the other. The owner, who was called Jay Gurley and was seriously weird, picked me up at Huntsville airport in a clapped-out Wagoneer smelling of wet dogs and I spent two hours walking about three miles underground photographing everything I could see which could possibly be construed as damage. When I got home late that night I took the film out of the camera so it could be developed - no film. That was embarrassing. I called Denise to confess and she laughed, but she never allowed me to forget it.

More muddle

The following month I had to go and see the production making *The Bostonians* on location in Martha's Vineyard, so I took a flight to Nantucket, as one does. On arrival I got in a cab and asked the driver to take me to Oak Bluffs. He said "that's Martha's Vineyard". I said "that's right" and he said, "You've got the wrong island, Buddy". I had it firmly in my head that Martha's Vineyard was a place on Nantucket. Not very clever. I had never bothered to check. Anyway I went back into the terminal, which was really just a shack, and asked how I might get myself to where I was supposed to be. Within moments a smartly uniformed pilot with four gold rings on his sleeve appeared and agreed to fly me there for $70. I nearly bit his hand off.

When I eventually arrived at the production office, the first person I ran into was the lovely Jessica Tandy, who was the reason why I was there, but I had never heard of her let alone knew who she was, which was a pity. She turned out to be quite delightful and surprisingly shy, but I suppose she may have been putting it on - she was an actress after all. What was wrong with her I can't remember, but her husband rang me at home a couple of days later to say she was worried her condition might affect insurers' willingness to cover her in future, particularly as she was no longer in the first flush of youth. I did my best to reassure him and also alerted the Fund. In any event she went on to make *Driving Miss Daisy* and *Fried Green Tomatoes*.

Back on Martha's Vineyard, business done, I shared a ride back to the airport with Vanessa Redgrave's pretty daughter Joely Richardson, who was 18 at the time and yet to find fame and fortune. On arrival I discovered I'd manage to leave all my travel documents on the producer's desk. No, it wasn't one of my best days and I was flying to Minneapolis at crack of dawn next morning. Luckily someone had already realised what had happened and my papers arrived with my old friend Brian Brockwell, the Production Accountant, who waited on the tarmac to make sure I boarded the right plane back to La Guardia and stood there until we had taken off.

In early October I went off on what can only be described as a wild goose chase after a consignment of gold, which had disappeared in transit from Lima to Caracas via Bogota on a KLM flight. I don't know what I hoped to achieve, but off on the trail I bravely set. All along the way officialdom was unhelpful and unfriendly. In fact in Lima they were downright scary, whereas in Bogota they were pussycats. I had expected the opposite to be true.

When I was leaving Caracas the immigration man demanded to see some piece of paper which I did not have and made a major fuss. He was sitting at a desk in box with sides all around about five feet high and I had to lean over the side in order to converse with him and eventually he started rubbing his thumb on his forefinger - wanting money. I only had a $10 bill so I gave it to him and he waved me through. Such a fuss for not a lot, but I was relieved when American Airlines took to the friendly skies and the island of Aruba was a speck below.

Golf champion for a day

One Saturday morning later that month David Band, who had been with us in Singapore and was now living in Locust Valley, rang up to see if I could step in for his partner, who had dropped out of a members only golf competition at Piping Rock. I protested that my golf was not nearly good enough but David was insistent and Annabelle gave me a pink ticket, so off we set.

Well, for some reason we both played rather well when it mattered and found ourselves the leaders in the clubhouse. Despite a large field still out there, we remained that way and in front of all our fellow competitors (American, old money, remember?) we were presented with a silver bowl each, cash and later had our names engraved on a huge cup, which sits in the pro's shop to this day. The prizes were presented by Nelson Doubleday, Jackie Kennedy's boss, who leant forward as he did so and said in a stage whisper "f*****g Brits". Very satisfactory result, we thought.

Villa Narcissa

In November I was back in Los Angeles, and this time Annabelle came with me because we had been invited to stay with Lee Katz, late of *Apocalypse Now* and *Blame it on*

Rio, and his girlfriend Elin Vanderlipp at her place on Portuguese Bend south of LA. Lee and Elin had been to see us several times in Singapore and were kind enough to return the hospitality, but in spades. Elin's husband, who had long since died, owned the Villa Narcissa on its own estate overlooking the Pacific Ocean. In 1916 or thereabouts his grandfather had purchased about 20,000 acres of an area called Palos Verdes on Portuguese Bend and built his villa on the prime spot, having purchased a Tuscan mansion and shipped it to site.

It wanted for nothing and nor did we. We had our own suite with his and hers dressing rooms and bathrooms. Elin had her own chef, who was Michelin standard, and breakfast was brought up to us by the butler. There was even a Roman style amphitheatre in the grounds above the villa for al fresco entertainment.

The first time we stayed, Annabelle did Beverley Hills and the Getty Museum while I beavered away doing whatever during the day and we lived in great style come the evenings. We were lucky enough to stay several times. Elin and Lee were most generous hosts, but they've both since gone to the Great Hollywood of the Skies. He was one of the doyens of the industry - his first screen credit was as Assistant Director on *Casablanca*.

The only downside to Villa Narcissa was the drive. Palos Verdes is about 40 miles down the 405 and the 110 freeways, but the traffic is always a nightmare. Sepulveda Boulevard and Pacific Coast Highway is the alternative, if you can find it. Still, it was always worth the trouble. No idea who lives there now, but hopefully it's one of the children – maybe Elin's daughter Narcissa.

Australia on a freebie

Soon after we moved to New York, Pan Am introduced Air Miles, the first airline to do so. I managed to run up enough to enable Annabelle and me to fly to Melbourne First Class and we set off at the beginning of December 1983 via LA. However our connection to Sydney was held up in San Francisco due to a bomb scare and we were delayed five hours. By the time we arrived in Melbourne with a stop for immigration in Sydney we had been travelling for thirty hours and had no idea which way was up.

We had to go through Customs in Melbourne, and since the officers had nothing better to do they went through all our luggage in detail. It was only some time later that Annabelle realised some of her jewellery was missing. Great baptism. Thanks Australia.

We stayed with Mike and Gilly Elphick, who had moved there from Singapore two years before, and they had organised a lunch party as soon as we had showered and changed. Well, what to do? And we went for it. As result it took us all of the first week we were in the country to acclimatise. Part of the deal with Pan Am was the supply of a Ford Falcon, a full-sized limo, free of charge, so we drove up the coast to Sydney over two days and stayed in Gilly's parents' flat overlooking Elizabeth Bay before flying home via two nights in Auckland. Apart from a night in Ulladulla on the way to Sydney we stayed with friends everywhere else. All right then, we're cheap.

CHAPTER 19

Back to the Far East

In the second week in January 1984 I received a call from London to say they wanted us to move back to the Far East, based in Hong Kong. Evidently there were problems in Singapore which needed sorting. Since we had bought Shu Swamp with a view to remaining in America, this came as a bit of a shock to the system and the last thing we wanted was to move, but as my application for a Green Card was unlikely to come through for another year or so, there wasn't a lot of choice.

The plan was for me to take over Hong Kong office from Nigel Gale, who had been with me in Seoul when Adam had his accident, and to be the regional manager of the other offices as well. I argued that it would be a lot less expensive for me to remain in New York and visit the Far East once a quarter. Besides Nigel was doing a good job and would not want to leave (the plan was for him to open an office in Stockholm – as far as I could make out, solely because his wife was Swedish). I also had a sneaky feeling that once the problems in Singapore had been sorted, there would be no job for me. Be careful what you wish for.

The only plus side to the move was that Esperanza, our holding company, was in the process of selling itself to Inchcape, a trading conglomerate with substantial interests in the Far East, and I thought it wouldn't do me any harm to be near Inchcape's seat of power. In any event I dragged my heels for as long as I could and in the meantime set off for Singapore on a brief visit to see the lie of the land.

There were a lot of unhappy bunnies in the office, mainly thanks to the inept manager, now departed, a man called Richard Jones. He had been with the competition when we had been based in Singapore and bought his business at the bar of the Cricket Club. My old friend and colleague Chan Hwee Seng was very cross that Jones had been hired in the first place. He had warned London but no one took any notice. There was another expat in the office called Paul May, whom no one liked much either, but at least he was a professional loss adjuster, even if he ate with his mouth open. Then I went up to Hong Kong, where it was quite clear Nigel had no desire to leave, let alone set up shop in Stockholm. I touched base with friends, stayed with the Courtaulds, played golf at Shek O and talked to estate agents about accommodation, should we need it.

I went home via London and convinced the powers that were that Chan should take over Singapore and May would serve as his No 2. I also said that Gale was not willing to be transferred and if pushed would join the competition, which would be a big mistake as he would take all our best people with him. I tried to persuade people that I could look after the region from New York but they weren't having any. I think Maxson and Young, the people on the west coast, had put the knife in.

So I did not really have a choice. I agreed to go to Hong Kong once Arabella had completed her school year at Greenvale, so I set off for home, it must be said, with a very heavy heart. On the plus side we knew and liked Hong Kong, where we had plenty of friends both social and business, and it was more money which was always tight in Locust Valley with Christian at Ludgrove and Greenvale wasn't exactly cheap. The main downsides to moving were that I had a good book of business thanks to the Fireman's Fund and we had a home of our own which we loved. Not only that it was great place to live, but also Piping Rock was, and probably still is, all said and done, the best country club on the planet.

Soon after I got back to New York, Burt Lancaster had an altercation with Margot Kidder, my old friend Philippe de Broca's wife at that time, on the set in Mexico. It was said that she had tried to attack him in line with the script. He thought she was going to hit him in the chest, where he was recovering from a bypass operation, and pushed her away. She tripped over some cables and fell backwards, hitting her head. Nobody thought anything of it, although there was a suggestion neither cared much for the other and Burt may have pushed harder than was necessary. As soon as Burt had finished his role he departed and Margot started complaining of headaches, which was where I came in.

The location was a place called Cuernavaca, about 80km south of Mexico City, and the road passes not far from the impressive and still active 18,000ft volcano Popocatepetl, which is to Mexico City as Mount Fuji is to Tokyo, although Mount Fuji is only 12,000ft. It was a great sight and I was fascinated, having been taught about it at prep school but never expected to see it with my very own eyes.

The other memorable bit about the trip was dining al fresco at a restaurant down the back streets of town. The entrance was quite unprepossessing - just some steps up to an old wooden doorway with no sign or anything to indicate what lay within. We ate in a walled garden with exotic flowers and trees and equally exotic birds wandering around the lawns. The food was 'international cuisine' but jazzed up to appeal to Mexican tastes. As result it was excellent and we drank Mexican wines from the Baja California, which were surprisingly delicious. I was a bit dubious until reassured that the Mexicans had been making wine since the Spanish brought vines over from Europe three hundred years earlier. No, Rioja wasn't offered, thank goodness but thanks for asking.

That Easter we collected Christian from JFK for the holidays and the next day we flew to San Francisco to stay with our friends John and Adrian Buchanan, who had been transferred there from Hong Kong. John was a bit of a rolling stone. When we first met as neighbours in Singapore he had just fallen out with Singapore Reinsurance Co and joined AFIA, an insurance underwriting agency representing a group of American insurers. Next thing he was with a Malaysian joint venture, having had to leave Singapore in a bit of a hurry and under something of a cloud, but we never knew why and didn't want to know. Now he was with Jardine Insurance Brokers in San Francisco.

All the uncertainty of John's career had caught up with them both and much to our dismay we arrived into an unhappy home and a tense atmosphere, of which we had had no inkling. We did our best to make ourselves scarce and went off to view the sights, then went away for a few days with Adrian and Adam to visit Yosemite National Park. We shared a log cabin and Annabelle was convinced she saw a bear looking at her through the window. I thought it was more likely a peeping tom with a black face.

I was pulled over for speeding on the way back to San Francisco. My papers were in the trunk so I got out of the car to find them, whereupon the Highway cop pulled out his gun and told me to assume the position. I should have remembered the Ocala experience and been quicker off the mark. Anyway I did step away from the trunk and with the plummiest Limey accent I could muster explained what I was doing. I said we'd been up in Yosemite, wonderful place blah blah, and it transpired he liked to go hunting there, so we became friends and I was let off with a caution.

One day we drove out to the Napa Valley and had to wait quite a long time to be served lunch at the Domain Chandon winery, sitting in the sun drinking the house fizz, which was very refreshing. As result I managed to lose the car keys, and had to call Hertz to find out what to do. This involved a taxi ride about twenty miles to a Ford dealership to collect a duplicate key. The taxi driver was one of the weirdest people we'd ever met. It was impossible to tell what sex it was, let alone what it was saying to us. We were much relieved when it delivered us back to the car safe and sound. There are some very strange beings in them there Napa hills.

We headed back home with heavy hearts on account of the Buchanans' mutual unhappiness and for the next couple of months one or the other or both of them were on the telephone to Annabelle with the latest upsets. We had two lines at Shu Swamp, but one telephone number. Each telephone receiver had two buttons on the top, which lit up when a call came through. If one line was busy the incoming call automatically was transferred to the other line. We could accept calls on both lines, it was just a matter of depressing the button of the line we wanted to talk on, which put the other on hold. It was a brilliant system thirty years ago but there's still nothing remotely similar available in the UK. Sometimes Annabelle had to juggle between the two Buchanans, one on each line.

By early May we were winding down at Shu Swamp and preparing to move. We had tried to sell the house but there were no serious takers, so we rented it to a couple. He had been CFO of Exxon Corporation and she was his trophy wife as well as a real estate agent. We had a garage sale on my 41st birthday, in the middle of which Mum rang to say Dad had had a stroke and was in hospital. The doctors did not know if he would survive, so I caught the next flight to London. I remember, after she called, going to our bedroom and praying fervently that he would recover. God answered my prayers, to the extent that he survived for another nine years but was unable to speak or write. The stress this induced was too much for my parents and eventually they lived apart.

I went to see Dad in hospital in Aldershot, which was a shock both ways. He was astonished to see me and turned away in his bed to face the wall. I was shaken to see someone so vibrant and full of life change so quickly into a wreck. Very depressing for both of us, it seemed. I think Dad was disappointed he had survived. Georgina was always his favourite and he wanted to see her again. Afterwards I drove over to Ludgrove to see Christian, who had already heard what had happened. I fear he was not having a happy time there with his brother Adam dying, us being so far away and now this, but he put a brave face on it all. Janet Barber, the headmaster's wife, had heard that I'd missed my birthday party and had baked a cake, so we had an impromptu party in her kitchen.

Dad was discharged from hospital two weeks later and went home, but he was very unhappy and frustrated with his inability to communicate. Mum tried to persuade him to have help from a speech therapist but for whatever reason he refused to cooperate, much to her frustration, and they began to take it out on each other. She would nag him to do simple things and he would ignore her, much of the time fortified by strong liquor, Mr Gordon's being his preferred option. Things never got better.

We left New York at the beginning of June, having packed the contents of Shu Swamp into a 40ft container, which was shipped off to Hong Kong. Zooloo the Shih Tzu had already gone ahead and was in quarantine for six months. She was a tough little animal and bravely coped with long distance travel, having made it, so far, from London to Singapore, Singapore to New York and now New York to Hong Kong.

Meanwhile we spent ten days in London, which included a brief business trip to Munich with Bill Bolton to hobnob with Munich Re. After lunch we were asked if we'd ever seen the Englischer Garten (English Garden). No, we said, tell us about it. Better we show you, said our hosts and we set off across the street from their offices and into a public park. After a couple of minutes' walk we rounded a corner and almost immediately realised that we were the only people in the neighbourhood with any clothes on. Our hosts thought the looks of astonishment on our face were well worth the trouble. The Englischer Garten, in case you are interested, is bigger than Central Park and on a par with Richmond, but so far as I know only a small area is set aside for those of a naturist disposition.

A couple of days later Annabelle, Arabella and I set off for Singapore, where we had arranged to stay at Tony and Christine Martin's house with hot and cold running servants for ten days - they were away in South Africa - while I spent time in the office, mostly churning out long overdue reports on files and glad-handing the Market, most of whom were old friends anyway. It was as if we'd never been away. One of Esperanza's number crunchers, David Shepley-Cuthbert, was also there with his wife for a look-see, as they were about to be transferred there, so we gave a party for them. As noted earlier David had been known at Eton as Shapely-Custard and his wife arrived dressed from head to toe in bright yellow.

We finally arrived in Hong Kong at the beginning of July 1984 and set about finding somewhere to live while camping with our friends the Courtaulds and ending up in the Hong Kong Hilton, which was one of the best hotels in the place but a lot cheaper than the likes of the Mandarin or the Peninsular. We found an 18th floor flat in a brand new build called Garden Terrace on Old Peak Road in Mid-Levels with magnificent views over Central and the harbour. This being Hong Kong, the place was decked out with carpets and curtains to Annabelle's choosing at lightning pace and our container from New York was standing by, so that we were all done and dusted before the month was out.

Life's Hell in the East (Part 2)

Living in a rented apartment on the 18th floor of a 38-storey block was quite a change after our own house in two and a half acres of Long Island with Piping Rock just up the road, but we did have one consolation in the form of Shek O country club. Pat Deveson, the Taipan (CEO) of Inchcape, kindly offered to sponsor my application for membership. There was a ten-year waiting list, which I was lucky enough to avoid, and we were members almost immediately.

Shek O was the green lung of Hong Kong, especially for us dwellers in Mid Levels. It consisted of a short 18-hole golf course, several tennis courts, a pool and somewhere to eat - fine dining it wasn't, about 40 minutes' drive from downtown. Shek O village was a dump located at the north-western end of Victoria Island, but the club's commanding position overlooking the main sea lane into Hong Kong harbour was as close to heaven as one could get, with views to die for.

The golf course was tight, with the added excitement of being hit a by a stray ball on the first few holes. There were at least seven par threes, including one that had no fairway to speak of. The tee was on the edge of a precipice overlooking a bay with rollers coming in 100ft below you whatever the tide and the green was 170 yards away, immediately the other side of said bay. The great joy of playing there was being surrounded by friends. There weren't many members and if you didn't know them you soon did. No visitors were allowed unless playing with a member.

There was an unwritten rule that the membership was restricted to the expat community - ie no Chinese. If you were lucky enough to own, or your company rented for you, one of the houses overlooking the course, you were automatically entitled to membership. One wealthy Chinese ship owner called YK Pao bought such a house and had to be admitted, shortly before we joined. He was a 'boy done good' and had been knighted for his charitable efforts. I met up with him and his wife on the course one afternoon and as we walked down one of the fairways overlooking the ocean, he pointed to a huge car transport entering the roads and said it was over 300,000DWT. How did he know? He'd just built it. His wife was a bit of a peasant too, but seemed pleasant enough.

The food at the club was simply terrible and the staff don't come grumpier, but no one cared. Just being there was pleasure enough and we went there as often as we could. It fact it was the making of Hong Kong for us. We probably should have been soaking up the culture, but after a week or two of travelling and being cooped up in an office we just wanted to be away from the crowds and out in the fresh air. This was as good as it gets. I am still a member of Shek O, but haven't been back for years. Evidently the club has been completely renovated. The old staff have been replaced by people who can smile as well as serve good food. I paid an entrance fee of about £600. Now I'm told it's well over £100,000, with a long waiting list. Lucky me, but I'm unlikely to go back – well, not to live.

Hong Kong was fun but nothing like as exciting as New York from a business point of view. I spent a lot of time flitting between Singapore and Bangkok as well as Manila and the odd side trips to places like Guam. Despite the number of people living there, Hong Kong is a village. Everyone knows everyone else's business. On every flight it's a disappointment if there aren't at least two other passengers you know. I was lucky enough almost immediately, thanks to an old Singapore friend called Peter Barnard, to be made a member of Cathay Pacific's frequent flyer club and was regularly upgraded. Service on most of the airlines in the Far East, Garuda Indonesia excepted, was very spoiling, but we all came down to earth with a bump when confronted with the queues at Hong Kong Immigration. Quite often there would be long lines at the desks, which were open, and officials lolling around in the background doing nothing, when they could have been manning the many empty desks.

I was so cross that I wrote a letter to the English daily *South China Morning Post* complaining about the inefficiencies of the service and the bad impression it must give to newly-arriving tourists and business people, usually after a long flight - not difficult, nowhere is near Hong Kong. A few days later I was again held up at Immigration needlessly and complained to the officer in charge. He gave me an evil look and asked, "Did you write the letter?" I am ashamed to say I bottled out and replied "what letter?" It's all right for you to call me a wimp but if I hadn't, I'd have been a marked man for evermore.

Things start to wobble

Early in 1985 our tenants in Shu Swamp offered to buy the house, and once the price and closing had been agreed we needed to decide what to do with the money. At that time the pound was weak and the dollar was strong and in February I went to see my friendly Standard Chartered bank manager, Michael Taylor, who had been so helpful when we bought Shu Swamp and was now in Singapore, for advice. We agreed that I would buy £200,000 at at £1 = $1.13, the rate at the time we met, at some future date to be agreed but no later than July I think. It went down to £1=$1.05 at one stage before firming up to $1.28. Anyway Michael and I did the deal on a handshake and went our separate ways.

Shu Swamp was sold at the end of March and while we were on leave in April we went house hunting in London. Wandsworth was way beyond our reach and we settled for a flat, well more of a pied a terre really, in Maida Vale. It was a garden flat in a refurbished block in Warrington Crescent, with a patio leading on to communal gardens. We were delighted with it until about nine months later the place started to develop rising damp all over the place. The only satisfaction was that the developer, who lived next door, had the same problem. In any event when we completed the pound was $1.84, which was more than helpful and the flat served as a useful base when we were in London.

In October 1985 I was asked to attend a board meeting in New York with all the other senior managers. I still had masses of Pan Am air miles, so Annabelle came with me from Hong Kong and we went First Class for free. However soon after I arrived at the venue for the pre-meeting drinks and dinner, Peter Simpson and Bill Bolton took me to one side and told me my days in Hong Kong were numbered, something I had always feared from the outset. They said there wasn't much else to offer me; I could go to Milan if I liked, but at a considerable drop in salary.

I can remember now the feeling of dread which swept over me. Arabella was due to start at her prep school after Christmas and Christian was due to go to Eton the following September. I had been with the firm nearly 20 years. I didn't want to work for any other adjuster - Graham Miller was a one-off - and besides I wasn't professionally qualified. I said I'd think about it and we headed for home via Los Angeles to catch up with the Fireman's Fund and Ruben as well as stay with Lee and Elin at Villa Narcissa.

After we had checked our bags at LAX for the last leg back to Hong Kong, we went up to Pan Am's Clipper Club lounge to await boarding. The girl in reception gave me a message to call Denise Dimin at the Fund. I duly did so and Denise, who knew I was in some trouble over my future, asked if I would go home via Hawaii, where there was a cast claim on the child actor playing the Karate Kid, who was sick. I explained that we had checked our bags and were waiting to board, but she wasn't put off. Buy what you need in Hawaii and put it on the bill along with the other expenses, she said. We explained our situation to Pan Am, who weren't in the least bothered and said our luggage would be held for us in Hong Kong to collect when we eventually arrived.

The next flight to Honolulu was at midday on United and the crew made sure everyone had a good time, Mai Tais all round. We rented an open Jeep just for the hell of it and set off for the Kahala Hilton as instructed by Denise. On arrival we explained to reception why we had no luggage and they dispatched us to a shopping mall about five minutes' walk away, where Annabelle had a field day and I remember buying some rather smart tennis shoes.

We managed to spin out our stay for three nights and had a good time sight-seeing, including Pearl Harbour and the half-submerged wreck of the USS *Arizona*, which serves as a memorial to that *Day in Infamy* on December 7, 1941 when the Japanese attacked without warning. We were intrigued that there were very few Westerners inspecting the wreck but there were hordes of said Japanese, presumably there to gloat. Jack Lord, 'Steve McGarrett' of *Hawaii-50* fame, lived in the block next to the Kahala. Disappointingly he was nowhere to be seen, but the hotel did have its own zoo. We flew home via Tokyo and sure enough our bags were waiting for us at Kai Tak, as was one cross Arabella, who had expected us home four days earlier.

I went to London at the end of the month to see if there was a better deal going and had lunch with Bill Bolton, during which I learnt that he was not seeing eye to eye with Peter Simpson or the Esperanza management, which had now moved back to the City from New York. He was thinking about starting out on his own and was I interested in coming with him? I said that our best option was to buy Graham Miller out of Inchcape, about which he wasn't at all enthusiastic, because they had only just bought us and were unlikely to sell. I reminded him that we had the whip hand – we, the staff, were the company, all said and done. We went our separate ways agreeing to talk again in the New Year.

Meantime there was no better deal available and I agreed to go to Milan, which put me a lot nearer London to ginger the troops. I also upped my package in Milan, so I set off back to Hong Kong in a more positive frame of mind than the one in which I had arrived. I'd missed all the direct flights and the best option was Swissair (now bust) via Geneva, where I changed planes onto a flight which was also a connection with Lagos, and before I knew it the First Class section was full of very sweaty Nigerians. The chap sitting beside me, soon after take off, opened his briefcase, which was full of wads of $100 bills and started counting them - no, not the notes, the wads. He seemed to know most of the other passengers, who appeared to be doing much the same thing. About half of them left the flight in Bangkok. Can't imagine why.

Early in the new year of 1986 after the Christmas holidays in Hong Kong, we all went back to London, Arabella to start at her prep school in Dorset, Knighton House, Christian to go back to Ludgrove for his penultimate term and Annabelle and me to visit Milan. The girls went on a couple of days ahead. When Christian and I checked in, Cathay upgraded us from the back of the bus to the very front. There was a certain amount of bragging on arrival at Gatwick, which wasn't that well received.

The next afternoon we all took Arabella to Waterloo and put her on the school train, as recommended by her new headmaster Mr Pratt. We were all overwhelmed by the occasion, somewhat. There she was in her grey uniform, matching mac and yellow beret looking pretty much in control, with her father about to lose it on the platform - remembering my first day at Eagle House, 35 years before. The memory of it, even now that she has two daughters of her own, makes me quite weak at the knees. I needn't have worried; she loved the school, made lots of friends and had a happy four years there.

After we took Christian back to Ludgrove, Annabelle and I went to Milan to meet the staff and some of the clients and try and find somewhere to live. Milan is not an attractive city, least of all in the dead of winter, and we decided to look at Como and Varese, both of which had been suggested by a rather gross estate agent who thought she could smell money. We were shown a flat in a mansion which had been converted and with which we were rather taken. The only trouble was all the windows were at floor level, so you had to stand on your head if you wanted the view. In the end we decided to do nothing and flew back to Hong Kong - on Alitalia, big mistake.

I went back to London briefly in the middle of February ostensibly for board meetings, but the key on Arabella's tuck box wasn't working so I rented a car and drove down to Dorset to fix it, hoping to see her but no such luck. I did manage a dinner with Bolton, who was more souped up about a possible management buyout but was still working on his Plan A, which was starting from scratch, and he had appointed the accountants Stoy Hayward to advise.

We finally left Hong Kong on March 7 and I started in Milan on March 9, 1986, a day after our fourteenth wedding anniversary, leaving Annabelle behind in London, for the time being at least. I made my base in the Hotel Select, which it wasn't, and set about the backlog of files in the office as well as chasing clients for payment of fees. Lloyd's, which sent us most of our business, were appallingly bad payers in those days but I'm told have since put their act together. This meant I was back in London at least one day a week, either a Monday or a Friday so I could be home every weekend. I'm not just a pretty face. The family came out for two weeks skiing in Courchevel, after which we carried on looking for somewhere to live, but our hearts weren't in it. Start up or MBO were the preferred options.

Milan, when I was there, was hard graft and anything but exciting. I was usually in the office by 7.30am and apart from a brief panini break at lunch time, I never left much before 9pm to go and have dinner and a few drinks to wind down. Apart from Chernobyl and the fear of nuclear pollution in Northern Italy thanks to the prevailing winds, the only other diversion was a trip to Venice for lunch. We had a man in the office called Sandro Rocco who was a security expert, and his job was to travel all over Italy advising jewellers how best to protect themselves from villains. One of his insurance broker clients was based in Meastre, an industrial town near Venice on the mainland, and Rocco wanted me to meet them.

This meant a three-hour car journey in each direction with him not speaking English and my Italian worse than limited. After a couple of hours of affable struggle, as we were approaching a bend in the road a car came whizzing round on the wrong side. I must have exclaimed something in German, cursing the other driver, and it turned out

Rocco's wife was German, which he spoke well - whereas mine was marginally better than my Italian, but at least we could communicate, much to the amusement of the brokers, when we eventually arrived.

After the meeting we were invited to lunch in Venice with one of the broker's interns, who was a member of an old Venetian family and knew what's what big time. We had lunch in a restaurant allegedly favoured by Princess Margaret and moments after we sat down a waiter arrived with jugs of slightly fizzy dry white wine, which was nectar. We were told it came from the owner's vineyards in the Veneto and the generic name was Prosecco. Laugh if you will, but in 1986 the only fizzy Italian wine generally known outside Italy was Asti Spumante, which was not particularly dry and was considered rather naff.

After an excellent lunch the intern took us up the tower of the Chiesa Santo Stefano, which was opened specially for us, from where we had an exclusive view of this amazing city, which the architect le Corbusier is supposed to have said was a city of the future, not the past. Even if he didn't, he would have had a point – no roads.

By the beginning of June I was spending more time in London than Italy and we were actively recruiting someone to replace me, because John Beynon, who ran the French operation, was to be transferred to London and I was to take his place in Paris, also managing Europe. However when push came to shove John decided to stay put, which was fine by me, and finally I went back to London still with responsibility for Italy. By this time Bolton had come round to the MBO idea and had broached it with Richard Nelson, who was still our ultimate boss although he reported to Inchcape.

Nelson had no objection if we approached Inchcape, although he thought it unlikely they would consider our proposal, but there was a newish man on the block, so - maybe. The newish man was a petrol head called George Turnbull, who had been with British Leyland before setting up a motor manufacturing division of Hyundai Steel and then building cars in Iran. Why he was invited to run Inchcape was anyone's guess but in the two years he was there the pre-tax profit increased from £85m to £185m, so he was an inspired choice.

Bolton and I must have gone to see him shortly before he took early retirement possibly on account of his health, so maybe he was feeling demob happy because he said that if we could find the money he would sell, but he wasn't inclined to say for how much. Needless to say we were over the moon and as soon as we got back to the office we had a visit from Jeff Bowman, one of Esperanza's number crunchers and probably their best, asking if he could join us. Word travels fast. Bowman said he had missed an earlier opportunity to work with a buyout team and was as keen as mustard to help. Bolton and I were suspicious of his motives, but we needed Bowman or someone like him and on basis of the devil you know, we agreed he should join us.

CHAPTER 20

Settling down in the UK

We had a lot of fun trying to put our MBO together, and it proved a lot more difficult than we had anticipated. Clyde & Co, a firm of City solicitors, was appointed to act for us and the partner who dealt with us was a Rhodesian called Werner Southey. His advice was excellent and he was helpful guiding us through the minefield of identifying potential equity partners. Most of them proved to be sharks out for a quick buck, including Peter Goldie of British & Commonwealth, who told us to our great surprise that loss adjusting was 'sexy'. He and his associate John Gunn went bust not long afterwards. In the end we settled for 3i, formerly Investors in Industry, who appeared to take a longer-term view. Our accountants were Spicer & Pegler, now Deloittes.

While all this was going on, Christian was in his last term at Ludgrove and was due to start at Marlborough in September. We had put him down for Eton at birth but Gerald Barber, the headmaster of Ludgrove, had belatedly told us that he did not think Christian would be a happy Etonian. We needed somewhere to live within easy reach of Marlborough so we could be available to watch him play his cricket etc. We had hardly seen anything of him during his five years at prep school and wanted to make amends.

My parents had decided to move from Bulfigs, Hook Heath Road, Woking, Surrey, where they had lived since my sister Georgina had been killed 12 years earlier, to Stedham, a village near Midhurst in West Sussex. This was so Dad could be near his younger sister Rosie, who could help Mum share her burden, which never happened - sharing the burden that is. In the meantime Annabelle's parents decided to sell Thatchers, Russells Water, near Nettlebed in Oxfordshire, where they had lived for nearly 25 years, and move to a villa on the outskirts of Salisbury.

I always liked Thatchers and here was an opportunity to buy it from them, but my bride was having none of it. Her brother had put her off years before by referring to the place as a row of rabbit hutches. Well he did have a point in as much as it was a row of converted farm cottages, which burnt down soon after the new owners had moved in thanks to some rather tired wiring. As result the new owners found themselves with a completely refurbished house a year or so later, thanks no doubt to the generosity of Lloyd's of London.

IT'S ALWAYS FRIDAY

West Soley Farm House

We spent every weekend house hunting that summer of 1986, looking at anything and everything within reasonable commuting distance of the City as well as Heathrow and not far from Marlborough. As usual whenever you're looking for a house there's not a lot on offer and we looked at some pretty terrible places. Annabelle had seen somewhere near Hungerford in *Country Life* magazine which she said was her ideal, but it was way beyond our pockets, what with the MBO and school fees. In the end we decided to look at it anyway so we could write it off in our minds and pitched up in the drive one glorious Saturday in mid-July.

Strutt & Parker, the agents, said that the local farmer would be there to let us in. We had to drive past the side of the house in order to park and we stumbled out of the car to be confronted with the front of an enchantingly perfect, small, red brick Georgian farmhouse - windows on either side of the front door and three windows above not quite in symmetry.

There was no sign of the local farmer but the front door seemed to be ajar, so we pushed it open to be met by three Jacob sheep in the hall. We were as surprised as they were. They turned tail and rushed off into the kitchen and out into the garden, not forgetting to leave calling cards along the way. We all thought this was magically rural, especially when we found that West Soley Farm House, for this was the name of the place according to the brochure, was also home to several Muscovy ducks and half a dozen chickens along with a cockerel, not to mention some cats, of which we are not fond.

After we had examined the place we went off to look at some other houses on offer but none remotely compared with Soley and we went back there with our picnic and had a late lunch on the lawn with Arabella doing cartwheels as if she had already moved in. We concluded that somehow or other we had to have it and went back to London to work out how, which involved a certain amount of begging with good old Standard Chartered Bank.

Alas Michael Taylor, who had been so helpful in New York with Shu Swamp and later in Singapore with the foreign exchange, was there no more and we dealt with a John Winter, who was equally supportive and promised a bridging loan while we sold Warrington Crescent. NatWest Homeloans agreed in principle to a mortgage and our offer was accepted subject to the usual caveats on both sides. Done and dusted as far as we could be we set off for Burgundy, where we had rented a gîte.

However while we were there things started to become unravelled on the bridging loan front and we had to cut short the holiday to do some more grovelling at the bank in Park Lane. This time I took the wife and children in their Sunday bests and between us we must have done the right thing, because a couple of days later Mr Winter was back on side, or rather his superiors were, and the deal went through at the end of August.

We stayed there happily for the next twenty years. Well, overall happily, but the following year was a nightmare because we couldn't sell Warrington Crescent, which developed leaks and the wheels almost came off the MBO. The fact that the Bank Rate was 12% didn't help either. Still we hung in and eventually arrived in the broad sunlit uplands, albeit grey round the gills, having sold Warrington a year after the move.

West Soley Farm House was about four miles west of Hungerford and a mile and a half from the village of Chilton Foliat. The farm had been owned by the Pearce family, whose branches had lived and farmed the area for several generations, but the branch which owned West Soley had come unstuck and sold the place to a Conservative MP called Philip Oppenheim two or three years before we arrived on the scene. His mother, Dame Sally Oppenheim-Barnes, was also an MP and at the time they were both sitting in the House of Commons.

Oppenheim told me that he had bought with the intention of having a weekend retreat and was still doing the place up when, earlier that same year 1986, he received an approach from Peter Palumbo, who wanted to buy the farm. Palumbo was a property developer and sponsor of the arts. Amongst others he was director of the Serpentine Gallery and was with Princess Diana in a much celebrated photograph of her looking drop dead gorgeous in a black dress the night Prince Charles owned up to having an affair with Camilla Parker-Bowles. That was all still to come.

Palumbo told Oppenheim he wanted to buy West Soley because his ex-wife Denia was terminally ill and wanted to die near the Lambourn valley, where she had grown up. Oppenheim was not interested in selling but eventually had his arm twisted, by money undoubtedly, but shortly after the sale was completed Denia died. Palumbo had no use for the farm and put it on the market. Justin Hayward, who was the lead singer of the Moody Blues, owned the stud farm on the other side of the lane and he decided to combine the two estates, creating an equine hospital out of the buildings which made up West Soley Farm. However after he bought from Palumbo this idea was dropped, but he kept the land and the farmhouse and adjacent buildings became our West Soley Farm House.

The place consisted of the pretty farmhouse, which only had three bedrooms and a big attic, as well as a small drawing room, dining room and kitchen leading into a conservatory. Outside there were stables around a walled yard with a cart barn at one end. There was another huge barn, more stables with a tack room and two garages, all of which were in various states of disrepair. There was also a two-acre paddock. All of this was located in the tiny hamlet of Crooked Soley, possibly so named because the lane through it was crooked, whereas the lane through Straight Soley a mile to our east was straight. East Soley Farm was the preserve of another branch of the Pearce family.

We thought we had arrived in heaven when we moved in at the end of August 1986. In addition to the Muscovy ducks, hens and their cockerel and the Jacob sheep, we also inherited about six cats which we were not too happy about, but they were to be looked after by the ex-farm manager's wife, so that was all right.

By this time we had been joined by Shih Tzu Mark III, called Kato after Peter Sellers' manservant in the Pink Panther movies, much loved by Arabella. I am ashamed to say that Kato made short shrift of the livestock and by Christmas he had the place to himself. He managed to kill off one of the Muscovys, leaving its remains outside the front door to be found by Annabelle when she returned from the shops. She has a thing about feathers and could not bring herself to enter the house. None of the neighbours was available and so I had to come home from the City and move said carcass.

A few days after we had moved in, Christian started at Marlborough. He was in Littlefield House, run by Hugh de Sarum, an old Marlburian of Ceylonese descent, who still holds the 100yds college record, and his wife Wanda, all the way from Atlanta, Georgia. They were a far cry from Mickey Walford, my housemaster at Sherborne, who was a bachelor and had never been anywhere. These two were exotic by comparison. Hugh in his youth had driven a coach from London to Moscow.

When we arrived Hugh told us that by coincidence the boy in the next-door bed to Christian was called Tom Youens Worsely and wondered if there was a connection - his mother was my first cousin. Two beds away was a boy called Dominic Del Mar, whose parents we had known and seen quite a bit of before we went to Singapore, but hadn't seen since. Small world and all.

This trend continued when we went to the local church in Chilton Foliat a week or so later. Soon after we had sat down a woman in the pew behind leant forward and announced herself as Wendy Couvres de Murville, a Belgian friend from our Fulham days. It transpired that she was no longer married to French husband Jean Marie, who was languishing in a Dubai jail for alleged fraud. Indeed she was no longer married to her second husband, Barrie Dynan, whose first wife Amanda had been to my 36th birthday party in Singapore a few years before.

What's more (do pay attention in the back) the said Amanda was now married to Gerald Ward, a local farmer of considerable means and royal connections, and both were in the front pew. Wendy had been married for a third time to some villain who had beaten her up on a regular basis and she was now alone. When we were introduced to the Wards after the Service, he had been a cadet when Dad was at Sandhurst and knew my late brother-in-law Piers and his family. He then introduced us to Lady Wills of the tobacco family, also in church, who had been Piers' aunt. Exhausting or what?

Back in the office

On the business front the MBO had been put on hold because our backers wanted to see the year-end results under the new management and they would not be out before May 1987. I spent a lot of time out in the Far East and Germany, where we were having staff problems. I did get my hand on a case or two occasionally and one such involved a claim on a film produced by Arnon Milchan, who had been a successful businessman in Israel as well as an intelligence agent before making movies including *Pretty Woman*, although that was yet to come.

I went to stay with him and his family on their estate outside Paris for the night and despite great wealth they could not have been more welcoming. He had a Mercedes 600 limousine which he had bought from Aristotle Onassis and the chauffeur drove me to and fro. On the way back to the airport I noticed there was a telephone in the car, the first I had seen, and called Annabelle to let her know where I was - as one does.

The New Year brought more of the same in as much as I was spending a lot of time in the air. One trip involved inspecting what business we had in the Caribbean where we had offices in Kingston Jamaica and Barbados. The latter washed its face but Kingston was in a pickle. We kept these offices mainly to deal with hurricanes but there had not been any serious weather in the islands for several years and my brief was to shut Kingston. Two days before I arrived in Jamaica the *Herald of Free Enterprise* capsized and sank outside Zeebrugge harbour. Nearly two hundred people lost their lives. It was the worst peacetime maritime disaster since the loss of the *Titanic* in 1912. Even that far away everyone was affected and the mood was sombre. Mine included.

I was collected at Kingston airport by our manager, Tom Dawson, and taken to the office, which was closed as it was a Sunday. He unlocked the door and there were cockroaches everywhere - all over the floor and the furniture, and the air was full of them. Yuk. Tom did not seem put out, but a bit surprised. Evidently it was the cleaners' job to clear them out first thing every morning. I was all for fulfilling my commission to close this show down. I wouldn't want to work in Kingston, especially when it was losing money, and I didn't want any of our staff working there either. However Tom was not put off. He liked Jamaica and managed to convince me that we should keep the office open until the end of the next hurricane season.

Annabelle joined me the next day and in the evening we were driven across the island to a hotel in Ocho Rios recommended by our local travel agents. It was full of well-nourished Americans of the lower orders gorging themselves with unlimited liquor and gambling on which crab would win the Triple Crown. Not our scene at all really, but we were so tired we went to bed and agreed to decide what to do in the morning.

I rang the agents and said that if this was the best Jamaica had to offer please book us on the next flight home. To be fair they apologised immediately and said there was a place which would suit us not far away called the Sans Souci. They also said they would send a car and deal with the place we were staying. A few minutes later the manager called and wanted to know what we didn't like about her place. I said that it wasn't our style and she tried to put me through the third degree. However our car arrived and we were off.

The Sans Souci was definitely more our style and by this time Tom Dawson was on the case. He told the management that I was a director of the local company, which I was, and therefore my bill should be in Jamaican dollars, whatever the US equivalent amounted to. Evidently it was the local custom. Sounded good to me. Tom came to collect us three days later to show us a bit of the island and drop us off at the airport. I went to pay my bill, which was presented in US dollars, probably about US$1,500: the Sans Souci wasn't cheap, even then. I explained my deal and so did Tom and so did the travel agents, but the hotel insisted I paid in US because I wasn't a resident. In the end we compromised and I paid the room, well it was a suite, in J dollars and the rest in US. In the end I was never charged for the room, only food and beverages. Yes, I am cheap. I thought we had already established that.

IT'S ALWAYS FRIDAY

The drive back round the eastern end of the island included a quick look at Noel Coward's stamping ground, a villa called Firefly with spectacular views along the coast and to the mountains, was an eye opener. Jamaica is quite beautiful but ruined by politics, corruption and ganja - the local equivalent of marihuana. Such a shame. Ian Fleming lived there for years and several sequences in *Dr No* were filmed around Ocho Rios including the chase up a river, Duns River, and part of the villain's base, which was a defunct bauxite dispatching plant.

In August we went summer skiing in France by car. The day before we set off, August 19, I was beavering away at my desk in Shoreditch High Street, where we had our offices. At about 1.45pm Annabelle rang to say she was all right. I asked what she was talking about and she sounded surprised. She thought I must have heard that someone was shooting people in Hungerford High Street. She had been shopping and heard gunshots as she was leaving our local market town and passed police cars with sirens full blast coming in the opposite direction. Several friends had left messages on her answering machine telling her to stay indoors, so she thought someone might have called me.

In fact West Soley is quite remote, as was the likelihood her being in any danger, but she had every right to be worried. I made some calls to find out what was going on, by which time the gunman, Michael Ryan, had taken his own life, though not before killing 16 people including his mother and wounding 15 others. I only knew he was dead and called Annabelle but could not get through. Hungerford is a dead area for communications and the police had commandeered all the available lines.

I worked late and did not arrive at Paddington until gone 9pm. I was expecting to buy a late edition of the *Evening Standard* or whatever, full of the drama, only to find there was nothing about the massacre even in the Stop Press slot. So much for 'Latest - Read All About It' as the papers sellers were wont to shout.

The atmosphere was somehow very spooky when I arrived home at gone 10pm. Can't explain why. Maybe my imagination was working overtime. I went into Hungerford at about 8am the following morning to buy the newspapers and here you could cut the atmosphere up in chunks. Police were everywhere and hardly anyone else was about. We were glad to get away but the incident cast a pall over the holiday, much in the same way as the *Herald of Free Enterprise* did when we had been in Jamaica a few months earlier. Hungerford, which we liked very much and were somehow rather proud of, retained an air of notoriety for years afterwards. The dreadful things people do to one another completely unprovoked.

Don't bother with summer skiing, by the way. Complete waste of time, in Europe anyway. Weather iffy and snow slushy, not to mention people milling everywhere. Try Chile or New Zealand. We came back early, via Paris, and took the children up the Eiffel Tower. Last time we had done something similar was the Empire State Building with the Pasley-Tylers three years earlier, and met several people we knew. As we walked out on to the top platform of the Tower I said facetiously 'I wonder who we will know' and sure enough there were the Muspratt-Williams, friends from Hong Kong.

You may be beginning to wonder what happened to all

the glamour of the film claims. The sad fact was that by this time I was far more involved in management and others including Shaun Coyne, now back from Los Angeles, and his assistant a pretty (very distracting) girl called Alison McHale, were doing most of the business. They were both very competent and I suspect quite a few producers deliberately made claims so Alison could come and adjust them. Often there were long faces if Shaun or I showed up.

A lot of my time was on the road, mostly New York and the Far East. One such involved a flight to Hong Kong on a Wednesday morning arriving Thursday morning. All day in the office and first thing Friday before flying to Singapore for an afternoon session in the office and the night flight home to arrive in time for breakfast on Saturday. History does not relate what was so important but I was 44 and as someone at Grocers' Company had pointed out a few months earlier I was in the prime of my life. Very kind of them but it makes me quite weak now to think about all that travelling.

When I was in London I was out and about promoting new business and keeping existing clients on board. Everyone knew that we were trying to buy the business out of Inchcape, we were nearly there, and there was a lot of goodwill - well most of the time. I was also expected to put out fires and chase slow payers. One such was an underwriter, little known then, called Robert Hiscox. Our office in Marseille had adjusted a large fire claim involving a château the buildings and contents of which had been extensively damaged to the tune of £2m according to the owners. A French insurer was on for the first £500k and Hiscox had the balance, known as the excess of loss. The

French insurer realised they had a total loss and paid up in full, leaving us to adjust the claim, which was eventually settled for about £1.3m (don't ask how).

In France the standard basis for charging fees was a scale based on the adjusted claim before policy limitations such as excesses and under-insurance over which we adjusters have no control. In this case the gross adjustment before policy limits was £1.5m, the scale fee for which was say £25k - a goodly sum you might think and you'd be right, but there was a lot of work involved. Anyway Mr Hiscox in his wisdom refused to pay because his interest was only £1m and he expected us to charge scale based on that, even if we had adjusted the claim in full. I went to see him and explained the Ps & Qs but he wasn't interested and refused to budge. We couldn't very well sue him so we had to accept. I thought he was rather cheap. All adjusters now charge on time spent, so this sort of problem no longer exists.

One of the many benefits 3i, our equity partners in the MBO, brought to the table was their requirement that we appoint a non-executive director to our board, who would act as their representative. They had a register of such people and we chose a charming Old Etonian, ex-soldier, barrister and former managing partner of Thomas R Miller, the leading Protection & Indemnity Club. He was called Bill Birch-Reynardson, and with him we hit gold. He was very enthusiastic about and wholly supportive of what we were doing. He made it his business to get to know everyone and only expressed advice when invited. As result he was hugely popular throughout the firm. However one or two of our promoters, who came from humbler origins, were a bit dubious about his suitability partly, as one, Ron Gent, put it, because of his accent. Don't be silly, Ron, I told him. He hasn't got an accent. Even Ron laughed.

The MBO was completed, by the way, late in the evening on Tuesday December 8 1987 after the lawyers on both sides had worked flat out over the weekend and straight through the previous night. Heaven knows why quite. They were on a fixed fee. I went to bed at about 1am, now with debts in excess of £250k, a healthy sum in 1987 and school fees for two. Not sure I slept much, but it worked out in the end. I think we were all pretty tired and the Christmas break could not have come at a better time.

1988 was devoted to keeping our heads down and making sure the business prospered, and happily it did. The insurance market liked our going alone and most wanted us to succeed. My main activity was beating the drum and keeping everyone involved in what we were doing. We took a John Lewis view with the shareholding and made sure all key staff members, wherever they were in the world, had shares in the UK holding company, even if the promoters had the prime portion. It certainly motivated everyone. I did keep my hand in and dealt with some claims as well as keep an eye on Italy, which was a bit of a nightmare because the replacement manager was pretty useless and, let's face it, Italy is a hostile business environment for Italians, let alone interloping English - was then and more so now.

One job in Spain involved an actor injured on a B movie called *For Better or Worse* which had to suspend shooting for over a week. One of the female leads was Kim Cattrall, not that anyone had heard of her then as this was long before *Sex and the City*. When I called a meeting of the cast and crew and told them as diplomatically as I could that they were not going to be paid, Kim was very cross and told me what she thought of me in quite colourful language.

I was rather embarrassed, especially as I had Alison McHale, Shaun Coyne's assistant, with me. Have I already said she was a bit of a distraction? I have? In fact the producer was convinced that we were having an affair and suggested as much to both of us at breakfast one morning. I didn't know where to look. All right, call me Mr Goody Two Shoes if you like.

When a claim is not

In September Klaus Kinski, the actor father of the very saucy actress Nastassja Kinski, was making an Italian film on location in Zimbabwe when he was taken ill in Harare and was reported to be at death's door. Kinski was a sixty-plus year old eccentric who lived life in the fast lane by all accounts. I was called by Guido the broker in Rome on a Sunday morning and the only means of flying to Harare immediately was via Brussels and Nairobi.

Frank Silvestri, the insurance doctor, met me in Brussels and we arrived in Nairobi the following morning with all day to kill before our connecting flight in the late afternoon, so we decided to take a cab and tour the sights. Well there weren't any. Nairobi was then and probably still is a smelly slum. We had lunch in a hotel, and decided to see the local game reserve, which was full of mangy-looking animals. We weren't impressed with Nairobi, as you may have gathered.

The last leg of the flight was on a Zimbabwean Airways Boeing 737, and while we were booked First Class we were told it was full. All the announcements during the flight were preceded with the greeting "Comrade Minister, Ladies and Gentlemen", which was rather irritating, especially when we discovered the Comrade Minister and his entourage were the only occupants of First Class. We also had to wait in the aeroplane on arrival until he and said entourage disembarked, in no hurry.

After we checked in to the Sheraton in Harare that evening we met the producer, who let slip that Kinski was suffering from fatigue. Is he working too hard, I asked. Well, no said the producer. In fact we are having difficulty making him work. Why is that? Well, he had recently married a twenty-year-old actress called Deborah Caprioglio who was hot to trot and Klaus was struggling to keep up. Fatigue per se is not an insured peril, particularly when self-induced, so Frank told Klaus to lay off the lady and rest. In the meantime I decided I had no choice but to stay and see Klaus recover sufficiently to resume his role, for fear that as soon as we left he would be back to his bride and have a heart attack, in which event we would be back to Square One.

This meant hanging around for a couple of days while Frank kept tabs on Klaus and Production found productive work without him. One afternoon we went to a game park and the next day we flew to Victoria Falls. I felt rather guilty about this because both Frank and I had our meters running and Bill Bolton wanted me in Madrid, where Roy Kinnear had fallen from his horse during the making of the *Return of the Musketeers* and broken his pelvis. Sadly the poor man died the following day, September 20, as a result of a heart attack while in hospital. By the time I made it back to London three days later, Bill was in the thick of the action, with all the complications of trying to complete without Roy, let alone all the ramifications of his death – but that's Bill's story, not mine.

So in the meantime here were Frank and I flying to Vic Falls for a day's sightseeing on September 21, which included a tour round a crocodile farm, a walk along the gorge opposite the Falls from Livingstone's statue through the perma-rain forest to the Zambian border, all of which was a once in a lifetime experience for both of us: quite spectacular from beginning to end. We also took a boat trip up the Zambezi after lunch, which was fun too. There was a rotting jetty on one side of the wide river with a sign attached reading 'Imperial Airways', the forerunner of British Airways. I like to think it was where the flying boats landed and refuelled on the way to and from the Orient, but it was probably left over from a film set.

Our guide for the day was a pretty white Zimbabwean girl, who was knowledgeable, helpful and friendly, so Frank and I adopted her, fed her and generally chatted her up as one does. However towards the end of the day when we told her about the Comrade Minister and the flight down from Nairobi, she clammed up and did her best to avoid being seen with us again. Poor girl, she was obviously scared stiff of the authorities. What a place, and that was nearly 25 years ago. I dread to think what it's like now, let alone what happened to our charming guide. Two days later Klaus had fully recovered and went back to work so there was no claim, and Frank and I made tracks home. This time we went our separate ways, as BA had a direct flight to London.

It's an ill wind

The following week I was back in the Far East on a fortnight's stint going round the offices (it's tough at the top,) when the call came in that Hurricane Gilbert had ripped Jamaica apart from one end of the island to the other. We were the main game in town, thanks to Tom Dawson persuading me to keep the office open, and it was all hands to the decks. I had to drop what I was doing and help set up a nerve centre in the Court Leigh Gardens in Kingston, which was one of the very few hotels still with power and water. This meant going back to London and changing planes as well as airports, not helped by BA losing my luggage en route, but thankfully it turned up 24 hours later.

Jeff Bowman, our Finance Director, came with me and brought with him a 'luggable' computer made by Compaq. It was state of the art: about the size of one of those wheelie bags people use as carry-on luggage. The keyboard fitted in front of the screen. No such thing as a mouse. You pulled the keyboard away from the screen, plugged the thing in and off you went. It meant that we could keep tabs on all the claims coming in and at what stage they were at, as well as print out a spreadsheet with all this information per insurer client and they received a daily update. How exciting was that? In fact the local market was so impressed as were their reinsurers back in London that we received much positive feedback, which made our reputation. Thanks, Gilbert. We were also able to pay our shareholders a juicy dividend the following year, which helped with the school fees, I can tell you.

We did have one wobble in Jamaica. Several members

of our team were summoned to a meeting with the lady Insurance Commissioner to discuss some sensitive cases. David Symons, an old friend and colleague from our days in the Far East, was lead spokesman and inadvertently commented, in his lovely broad Yorkshire, that one insured was the "nigger in the woodpile". Needless to say this was not well received by the lady Commissioner, who was evidently a sensitive soul, so much so that David's temporary work visa was withdrawn and he had to come home. Up to then he had been doing an excellent job and was happy to work in very trying conditions. His departure left a serious gap in our local organisation for a time. However he was redeployed to the Cayman Islands to deal with their power distribution structure, which had been demolished by the hurricane.

The beginning of the end

At the beginning of 1989 a rift occurred between Scott Milne and his broking firm Albert G Ruben and the Fireman's Fund, and suddenly our cosy little arrangement whereby we handled any claims on all the major film productions anywhere in the world started to come unravelled. It all stemmed from Scott setting up home with his secretary Bette Smith, an extremely attractive and very bright black woman with whom I had always got on well. He then married her, which proved to be fatal. Bette decided she had to prove herself by setting up a completion guarantee business.

At this point I need to back up and explain some background to the intricacies of film finance. When a producer puts together a budget for the cost of financing his production and borrows the money from a bank or a major studio, all parties have to be satisfied that the budget, with a 10% contingency for overruns, will be enough to carry the project. However there is always a chance the overruns will be greater than anticipated for uninsured reasons such as weather, the competence of the director, the nature of the principal artistes, sets costing more and taking longer to construct and so on. Therefore the banks/studios will require these additional potential costs to be assumed by a third party in order that completion of the film can be guaranteed.

The main player in this field was then and probably still is an outfit called Film Finances Inc. and Bette wanted to give them a run for their money. In fact we had always been telling Scott that this was a missed opportunity for him long before Bette appeared on the scene and now here she was setting up The Completion Bond Company (good name I always thought), but needed an insurer to lay off her risk. By that I mean if a production went over budget and contingency Bette would pay the first say $500,000 from her own resources and insure the excess.

The Fireman's Fund was not prepared to back her but a rival carrier called Transamerica was, and to cut a long story short, Scott elected to dump the Fund and transfer all his business, including Film Production Insurance, to them, leaving the Fund high and dry after the best part of a very successful thirty-year relationship. Part of the deal was that we should remain the exclusive adjuster but to Transamerica, and dump the Fund. There was a gene in Scott which seemed to work on the principle that if it ain't broke, break it. He had earlier fallen out with his number two, dear old Don Cass, who had, years before, persuaded me to get my act together and marry Annabelle, and Dick Barry, who had been Ed Hamby's successor as Entertainment underwriter at the Fund, and they set a rival broker under the auspices of the Fund. The whole edifice was crumbling.

Bill Bolton and I had only a vague idea of what was going on, but it all became horribly clear during a visit to Los Angeles in February 1989. No sooner had we checked into the Century City Plaza than we found ourselves being pulled in one direction by the Fund and in the opposite by Scott, who wanted us to switch allegiance to Transamerica, which we didn't know from a hole in the wall. In any event, while Bolton seemed to be all for it, I was not. Quite apart from anything else we were lucky enough to have been supported by the Fund for well over twenty years in London and they had supported me for the ten years I had been overseas. They didn't want us to abandon them and I had no intention of doing so, even if I didn't think much of Dick Barry's successors.

In the end it was agreed that we would work for whomever wanted to instruct us, which we hoped would help us win new clients in Lloyd's, who heretofore had seen us as too cosy with the Fund and Ruben. Scott was furious because he could no longer promote Transamerica as simply the Fund's replacement and tell his clients that nothing else had changed. In fact this in some way precipitated the eventual collapse of his control over the bulk of the film insurance business. He blamed me, which was fair enough, but really he had only himself to blame - well, Bette in fact.

Other players appeared and things were never the same again. Pity, but all good things etc.

However from our perspective nothing really changed. We still did all the Transamerica business as well as the Fund's, but we never managed to break into the Lloyd's market until years later.

Down Under

A few weeks later we held a managers' conference at a hotel near Watford called The Edgewarebury. Most the office managers came from all over the world and we had a very jolly time. Some people never went to bed over the three days we were there. We also invited some of our correspondents, including our man in New Zealand called David Denton, whom none of us had met. It transpired that he was in the process of setting up a network of associated offices in Australia, linking various local firms of adjusters in the main cities and invited us to be part of his plans.

It was agreed that Jeff Bowman and I would inspect his operation in New Zealand and meet his associates in Sydney as well. We set off on a Friday evening in early June after a day in the office and eventually arrived in Wellington, where Denton was based, on the Sunday afternoon, much in need of a bath and shave, only to find out bags had missed the connection in Sydney and did not arrive until late that evening. In the meantime Denton took us on a tour of Wellington in the mist and rain, including a trip to see the view from the top of Mount Elizabeth, because we had always wanted to mount Elizabeth, hadn't we? Apparently this is a local joke. Very funny the Kiwis. Wellington seemed to us to be rather primitive and the James Cook Hotel where we were staying was very basic.

The following morning Denton had arranged for us to meet the chairman of the Earthquake Commission, a government agency providing earthquake insurance and Denton was one of the nominated adjusters. The chairman was full of fun and when I asked him how close we were to the fault line he looked out of the office window, pointed and said "between us and the road". So I asked him what he did when there was an earthquake and he said "panic". I told you they were funny.

The next day Bowman and I flew to Auckland and went round the market meeting various people I'd known during my time in Singapore and Hong Kong, to find out how well Denton's business was perceived in case we decided to buy it. If Wellington was a one-horse town, Auckland was half a horse better. Both were deadly dull and best avoided, particularly if you're prone to depression.

One kind broker took us to lunch at Auckland's equivalent of White's (Club), so we were told, and became nearly delirious when he discovered that the club still had a couple of bottles of Cloudy Bay. This meant nothing to us, but in New Zealand it was considered nectar, and our new friend insisted on showing off the bottles to his mates in the restaurant. We feigned ecstasy when tasting the stuff, which was a sauvignon blanc (not my favourite). It didn't seem anything special but we didn't want to spoil his fun.

After meeting David Denton's merry men in Sydney, some of whom were seriously weird, Bowman and I went on to Perth, where we had been told we had an office. This was news to us, but sure enough we looked Graham Miller up in the Perth telephone book and there it was, so we took a cab downtown and introduced ourselves. The manager was a creepy-looking fellow called Trevor Lunt, long blonde hair, fake tan and chains. Needless to say he was very shaken and produced some cock and bull story about how he was authorised to trade in our name, which he could not back up, and we appointed a local law firm to sort out the mess.

Bowman and I came away rather disillusioned with the business potential in Australia and New Zealand, but it was agreed that I'd give it one more go when I was next in the area later in the year. We agreed that the best of an unexciting bunch was the firm we had met from Melbourne, and it was there that I went at the beginning of November. No one bothered to tell me that was not such a good idea and I only discovered after it was too late, ie I had already arrived, that the first Tuesday in November is Melbourne Cup Day and the whole country, let alone Melbourne, pretty much parties all week.

Happily for me, one of our former secretaries, Alison Webb, a sweet girl - well they all were - had recently married Nic Wellington, a thrusting young Lloyd's underwriter, who had been seconded to Sydney for a year. I called them and was delighted to discover that they would be in Melbourne for the race and while tickets were as rare as hen's teeth they would get me in. They did and we had a grand day. While there I met some other friends, Paul and Mary Selway-Swift, who had a horse running, and I joined them for drinks with other like-mindeds in the Regent that evening. It was all in all a red letter day and great fun.

I spent the rest of the week going round the traps in Sydney but came away confirmed in the view that there was nothing there for us; there wasn't the business to justify any investment. Very sad, because Australia is otherwise a first class destination.

Back to the grindstone

At the beginning of December 1989, Debra Winger went sick on location in Beni Abbas, which is in the middle of the Algerian Sahara desert - a tricky place to reach at the best of times, and this was not the best of times. In fact I'm not sure when Algeria's ever had much going for it. I flew to Algiers and was taken to the El Aurassi hotel, where I was informed that a car would come for me at 3am to take me to the airport for a 6.45am flight to Bechtar, where I would be met. When we eventually boarded a very clapped-out Caravelle or some such, long since retired by Air France, all the other passengers looked like terrorists except one chap sitting near me who was another Brit - on holiday. Some place for a holiday.

Bechtar was in the middle of nowhere but after a four-hour drive we arrived in Beni Abbas, which was an attractive village on the edge of the Grand Erg Occidental: endless orange-coloured sand dunes stretching for hundreds of miles to the east. That was why we were here. Debra was the female lead in my old friend Bernardo Bertolucci's latest show *The Sheltering Sky*. I went to see her tucked up in bed that evening suffering from flu and told her that I'd tried to meet up with her years before when she was making *Terms of Endearment*, but had been thwarted by events in Rio. She remembered wistfully that she was in love then - with the senator for Nebraska, ah well. That night I had dined with

Bernardo and the producer Jeremy Thomas as well as John Malkovich. Very jolly evening, about which I remember little.

Soon after the beginning of January 1990, I was back in Los Angeles helping Bob Scally from our Hong Kong office try and resolve a tricky claim as result of a helicopter accident in the Philippines on *Delta Force 2*, in which five people had been killed, including two actors, and the helicopter was a total loss. The helicopter was one of very few of a kind and had been brought to the location from New Zealand. It had been well established in the action and the only one similar and available was in the US. The missing scenes were filmed in Tennessee, which has jungle similar-ish to the Philippines, at much greater expense.

There were lawyers springing about on both sides, heated arguments about what was admissible under the insurance and a lot was not. At one stage Bob and I had to go and watch the film in one of the studios. Usually you sit in a small projection room for about twenty people, but on this occasion we were in a full-blown cinema with about a hundred other people who we were convinced were extras hired in for the occasion to laugh and cry in the right places. It was complete tosh and the insurance people were complaining that they had to pay Bob and me to go to the movies. We told them that we would have quite happily paid to give this one a miss.

Somehow the claim was resolved and I went on to Singapore to meet up with a group of adjusters who wanted to join us from one of the competition. I was concerned that their leader, a man named Neo, would not work well with my old friend Chan Hwee Seng, but they both assured me that despite being colleagues years before then arch rivals, they were itching to sew the market up as well as be the best of friends. The deal went ahead and worked for a couple of years but then Neo 'got God' in a big way, Alpha style, and started preaching to the market, holding prayer meetings and generally taking his eye off the ball. I think he had a guilty conscience about something in his past and eventually we went our separate ways.

For some reason Chinese, when they convert to Christianity, go the whole hog and try and convince all and sundry that's the only way to live. Well, I happen to believe Christian ethics hold the key to a happy, successful and sympathetic way to live one's life, but I don't have the right to ram it down everyone else's throat.

Never buy a launch vehicle

The week after I returned home, the office car, a SAAB, was swopped for one of the brand spanking new Land Rover Discoverys - one of the actual launch batch of vehicles - and it was delivered to the office one evening ready for me to drive home. Well the weather was atrocious, gales all over the country, power outages and traffic all over the place.

Nevertheless at about 7pm I climbed into my new toy all excited and ready to set off. I closed the door, put the key in the ignition and started the engine (with the help of a manual choke, if you can believe - I thought they had gone out of vogue twenty years ago) and turned on the headlights. No headlights. Only sidelights. I diddled around with the switches but nothing, so I had to drive all the way back to Wiltshire with sidelights and fog lights, the rear ones of which blinded the following cars. The car was attracting a lot of attention for all the wrong reasons. I should have dumped it and gone home by train.

I took the damn thing into the local Land Rover garage in Newbury and they managed to fix the lights, which went wrong again several days later. Then it wouldn't start, the doors jammed, the radio conked out. It was a disaster and I never bought another British-made car again. I was so cross I wrote to the head of Land Rover and copied the chairman of British Aerospace, a professor someone, and Mrs Thatcher. The first person I heard back from was Mrs T, whose office said that she was very concerned and asked to be kept informed. The only person who showed no interest at all was the professor someone. Says it all really. It was a truly awful car and I was stuck with it on a three-year rental. More fool me. I should have gone with the Mercedes I had originally ordered.

All change – again

1990 turned out to be an eventful year in more ways than expected apart from the usual dashing about the Far East promoting business and bossing everyone around. In February Jeff Bowman, our chief bean counter, started to get nervous about our cash flows. We were outgrowing the funds needed to support the business. The Profit & Loss account was fine. The problem was not being paid fast enough by our clients, and specifically Lloyd's underwriters and their brokers. The resolution was either to raise more funds by diluting equity or selling the business and cashing in. With two children at school and two beefy mortgages, on the house and on my shares in the company, selling was a no brainer. It so happened that my friend Shaun Coyne had been to see a large US claims business based in Atlanta Ga., called Crawford & Company, to see if they would represent us in the US; in return we would represent them in the rest of the world on a mutually exclusive basis. He was turned down flat but the CEO had told Shaun as he was leaving the meeting that 'he would sure like to buy us'.

We promoters, along with the lovely Bill Birch-Reynardson, met in a hotel near Ashford in Kent to decide what to do. Neither option was particularly attractive. None of us wanted to dilute our capital when there was a chance of a dollop of cash and continuity. However Crawford was not the ideal partner by a long chalk. They were long in motor and workers' compensation, with a completely different culture, but they were also long in cash and after a lot of heart searching it was agreed that Bolton and Bowman should go and see if they wanted to put their money in our mouths. Happily it transpired that they did.

While this was going on, Annabelle was admitted overnight at the beginning of June to the Wellington Hospital for a routine gynaecological procedure. However the following week she called me in Budapest, where I was on a job, to say she had been diagnosed with cervical cancer, which needed immediate surgery. A change of surgeons was recommended, and thanks to the great skill of Mr Peter Mason all the bad bits were removed a few days later at the Samaritans Hospital in Marylebone Road and she went on to make a full recovery. However it was a great shock to both of us and a highly emotional few days.

While Annabelle was hors de combat, we had an

inspection visit from the powers that be in Crawford and took them all to dinner at the Capital Hotel in Basil Street. Their party included the widow of the founder, who turned out to be a very agreeable old bat. She collected antiques and was, much to our surprise, very well read. Not much can be said for the two directors with her. A pair of rednecks if ever there was. One was a thick set boozer called Forrest Minnix and his side kick, Frank Semancik, clanked when he moved from the weight of the chains round his neck. Part of their charm was to smoke while they ate. Anyway needs must and the negotiations continued the next day at Claridges, where they had a suite complete with fag ends in the lavatory.

One bit of light that June was Christian being promoted to the XI at Marlborough, thanks to his batting and bowling, and while Annabelle was recovering from under the knife Arabella and I went to watch him play at Radley. This set a trend and for the next two summers we had a lot of fun following the XI round their various matches, home and away. Luckily our friends Campbell and Vanessa Gordon, who lived about a mile away, also had a son, James, in the team and we went about as a gang.

When Annabelle was eventually discharged, she was pretty immobile and I hired a New Zealand girl to help out. She was called Robin and seemed fine when she pitched up at the office for an interview. However when we collected her from Newbury station, it was a hot day and she was wearing a sleeveless vest and very short shorts with hair sprouting where hair should not. In addition she had a serious body odour problem. My family was horrified and it was all my fault - always is.

Annabelle had been told that once she could perform an emergency stop, she could drive and as Robin had been hired mainly to drive her about, it was not long before she could brake hard and Robin was out of the door. In fact, to our amazement, some woman rang to ask when we might be releasing Robin, as she wanted her back as soon as possible, and away she went.

Istanbul

Elsewhere in the world Saddam Hussein had invaded Kuwait and things were pretty tense as there had been no real hostile activity in the world since the end of the Vietnam War. We were booked to go on a Club Med holiday in Turkey with Annabelle's sister Susie and her family. Off we went, thinking we would probably have the place to ourselves, only to find that Club Med had closed all their other camps in Turkey and transferred everyone to ours. The place was packed to the gunnels. Towels on the beach chairs by 5am if you were lucky. In fact we had a lot of fun including an overnight trip to Istanbul for Annabelle and me. Susie came for the ride.

It was a fascinating city and probably still is. We were downtown by 8.30am the first morning after an early start and saw all the sites as well as a trip down the Bosporus. The next day I abandoned my women and went to see the local Lloyd's Agents a family firm called Bilgisun. We had been talking to them for some time about a possible merger or acquisition but without success, so I decided to try my hand. I was stonewalled all morning and then found myself being invited back to their house for lunch. I explained that I was meeting Annabelle and Susie at the Topkapi Museum at 1pm, so thanks but no thanks.

They refused to go away and it was agreed that we would collect the girls and all go to lunch. We found them and set off over the Bosporus into Asia. The road ran down beside the Bosporus and after a few miles the car pulled up in front of some gates, which were opened by a flunky, and in we went. Well, this was an eye opener for us and quite unexpected. The Bilgisun family lived on a splendid estate right on the water, which contained not one house but three, including a magnificent wooden palace with huge rooms and painted ceilings.

It transpired that Mrs Bilgisun's grandfather had been the last Grand Vizier, Prime Minister, to the last Sultan and his son now in his eighties, but with all his faculties intact, still lived there. Mr Bilgisun and his wife lived in a modern New England clapboard and the servants, who were plentiful, lived in the third building. Out on the water in their own private harbour were a motor yacht, several sailing boats and launches including a very elegant slipper launch.

Well we all got along famously and had a wonderful party discussing the merits of the various empires, which had ruled down history. The old man was of a mind that there were only three beneficial ones - Roman, Ottoman and British. I was not going to argue. After lunch the girls were invited for a trip on the Bosporus and I was then taken to one side and told they were ready to talk business after all. Thanks were entirely due to the charm, grace and beauty of my womenfolk. All in all it was a red letter day.

Selling our souls

Back home the Crawford deal was hotting up, with endless meetings not only with their people but also with lawyers and accountants on both sides. We had Werner Southey, of Clyde & Co, who had advised us on the MBO three years earlier, acting for us; and Touche Ross to crunch the numbers. Crawford had Clifford Chance for the legal work and Touche dealt with their accountants.

At the end of October Crawford produced their man to whom we would be reporting, Dennis Smith. He seemed to us to be quite keen and willing to learn, but no adjusting experience - purely business management picked up at some school in the States. He certainly knew the jargon and we should have smelt a rat. He was a mirror man, immaculately turned out in smart suits and clearly liked the ladies. Nothing wrong with that you might say, but that proved to be his undoing.

As there were about 40 shareholders of Graham Miller dotted around the world, we were advised by the lawyers on both sides that we should meet them and tell them face to face our plans to sell and that we should do so as quickly as possible to prevent leaks before everyone had been informed. This proved to be quite an exercise in logistics as well as a marathon trip. It was agreed that Bolton, Bowman and I would go with Smith and the format to each meeting was that we would explain what we were planning and why, then we would produce Smith like a monkey at the circus to explain the plans Crawford had for the company.

For some obscure reason, we had to see the chap who ran our joint venture in Venezuela, Luis Jose Vicentini, separately to everyone else and it was agreed that he would meet us in New York. So on November 13, 1990 at 7pm the four of us set off on a British Airways Concorde, my fourth and last trip on one. I sat with Jeff Bowman and Bill Bolton and Dennis Smith were across the aisle. Any trip on Concorde is a bit of an event for most people, but not our Bill, who spent the flight translating a lengthy Italian legal opinion on a complicated Brinks-MAT cash-in-transit claim. The inflight food and wine was always as good as it could be on Concorde, but on this occasion I thought the wine was corked and sent it back. The lovely stewardess opened another two bottles before I realised the Montrachet wasn't corked - it was just rather over oaked.

We arrived at JFK an hour before we started on the local clock but 11pm on our body clocks. Vicentini was waiting for us at the airport Hilton and the meeting ran for several hours, so we were all quite tired when we eventually went to bed, having done the best part of a full day in London office, but youth was on our side.

The next morning we were up early for a 9am American Airlines flight in the sharp end to Kingston, Jamaica via Montego Bay, which gave us a chance to catch up on some rest although Bolton sat gripped by a film called *For Better or Worse*, on which I had had several cast claims and had upset Kim Cattrall in the process. It was complete rubbish, but we are all different. The air hostesses were drooling over Smith, which was quite annoying, especially as the one I fancied was the most stricken.

In Kingston there were about a dozen shareholders, mostly from South America, all of whom were in favour of the sale, and in the evening we went off to dine at some fleapit downtown and then a nightclub. Dennis Smith was warned to keep well away from the local women of the night and if he couldn't resist, not on any account to tell them where he was staying. At 2am the lobby of the hotel saw the arrival of three rivals all wanting to 'see' Mr Smith. Smith cowered in his room and told Jeff Bowman to get rid of them, seeing as how the management had refused to let any of them up to his room despite his requests. One sight of Bowman and they were on their way.

We left Kingston back to London the following afternoon on a BA 747 and on arrival we went to a Thistle Hotel on the airport perimeter for a shower and a shave before meeting all the European shareholders, of which there were about thirty. Bill Bolton told them what we were planning, which was generally well received, and then Smith made his entrance and did a good job convincing everyone we were on a direct route to heaven.

After some refreshment it was back to the airport and Singapore Airlines First Class to Singapore, where we arrived on Saturday evening, beginning by this time to feel a bit weary. All the Far East shareholders were waiting for us first thing on Sunday morning, we strutted our stuff, which again was well received, and it was back to the airport that evening for the penultimate leg to Dubai and the shareholders based there and in Saudi.

This time the carrier was Emirates, which was in its infancy and the cabin staff were nervous. The food was very unappetising, the seats even in First Class were uncomfortable and the atmosphere could best be described as Arabian lavatorial. To add insult to injury to four very tired bunnies, there was an intermediate stop in Colombo to pick up Sri Lankan workers and the back of the bus was now packed.

Dennis had never been very keen about visiting the Middle East, being a hated American, and was understandably dismayed to be told by Dubai immigration that he had to have a visa in order to enter the country. Gray Dawes, the travel agents, were in more trouble than the early settlers, but they didn't know it yet. Well, fair enough, they should have checked. After much deliberation Dennis was allowed to enter. He had to surrender his passport, which put him off his stroke, but he bore up well, and we accomplished our mission with the last of the shareholders. In the early hours of Tuesday morning we flew back to London with a mandate to sell the business. After meeting all the office staff to tell them what was happening, we issued a press release and took Wednesday off.

Christmas 1990 was a celebration. There was cash in the bank, a reduction of the mortgage, which I should have paid off, and a Mercedes estate car in the garage as Annabelle's runabout. In the New Year it was back to business as usual and off to the Far East, but this time Annabelle came too and we stayed for a week in the (then) one and only hotel on Koh Samui, an island in the South China Sea about an hour's flight south of Bangkok. It was called the Tongsai Bay and we had a romantic cottage covered in bougainvillaea with a veranda overlooking the beach, a four-poster bed and a chilled bottle of champagne to greet us. I remember that night was the first, and last time I slept through since Adam died. It's still there and still just as agreeable. After Annabelle returned home I met up with Dennis Smith in Singapore and took him round the traps in KL, Singapore and Hong Kong.

Meanwhile back home

Winter set in with a vengeance at the beginning of February 1991, with plenty of snow. One Friday my father-in-law, Donald, was up in London for a lunch with the partners of his old firm of solicitors, Stephenson, Harwood & Tatham. I got a call from Annabelle to ask if I could escort him home as he wasn't well and tended to be absent minded at best. I caught a cab to his offices now opposite St Paul's Cathedral, where to my horror he was standing outside in the freezing cold. In fact to begin with I didn't recognise him and thought it was a tramp.

We took the train to Reading and I drove him home to Salisbury. We never stopped talking all the way. He seemed to have recovered much of his old form and recounted how my beloved mother-in-law had taken up witchcraft, which involved wearing weird clothes with pointy hats, and holding strange meetings with other women of like mind. How we laughed, in fact we cried with laughter most of the way and I came home quite exhausted. Sadly that was the last time I was able to have a proper conversation with this lovely man. He was suffering, although we did not know it then, from the early onset of Alzheimer's, which soon took a hold of his mind, and he ended his days in a secure home in Salisbury.

A couple of weeks later there was a bomb scare at Reading station one evening and the line was closed. I only discovered this once I had boarded the train at Paddington and overheard a couple of fellow commuters, whom I knew by sight, agreeing to share a cab to Reading. I went over and asked if I could join them and share the fare. They looked surprised but agreed, and another chap joined us. I seem to remember the cabbie charged us £80 each, which back in 1991 was no small potatoes, but we agreed and off we set.

I only mention this incident because no one said a word to each other the whole way and it is very uncomfortable sitting on a jump seat, with one's back to the driver. Subsequently I used to see the other three regularly on the train but we never acknowledged each other, let alone mentioned the trip. Such is the way of commuters. We'd never been formally introduced, you see. Years later I met one of them at a lunch party. He was called John something and had been senior partner of Brewin Dolphin, a firm of stockbrokers. I reminded him of the taxi ride and that no one spoke to each other and his wife laughed and said that was quite typical. Rather sad, I thought, but there you are.

Christian left Marlborough in July having taken his A levels and celebrated with a party at home, which he shared with his childhood friend David Fergusson, who had also left Marlborough at the same time but under a bit of a drugs cloud. The party was for the most part in our barn, which was decked out for the occasion with a great deal of help from Annabelle's girlfriend Vanessa Gordon, whose son James was another Old Marlburian.

One of Christian's cousins, Tom Worsely, also a new OM, added lustre to the occasion by bringing his band, which was still playing, totally spaced out, much to our neighbours' disgust, at 6am. A hour later there was a knock on our door from a farm worker complaining that his hay barn was full of young having a high old time at the horizontal and would I kindly do something about it. I went to inspect and do you know, he was right.

A couple of weeks later we all went off to Singapore for a fortnight's R&R - well for the family that is, I was on duty. However the office booked us a flat in a block off Orchard Road owned by the Jumbaboys, who had been our neighbours when we first went there. It was very comfortable with all mod cons and everyone had a fine time, mostly up at the Tanglin Club pool. It was there that Christian, who had no idea what he wanted to do next, met a boy who was going to a hotel management school in Switzerland. Christian thought this would be a splendid idea and about 18 months later, after an extended gap year, including work experience in South Africa, that's what he did.

In the meantime he had been invited to stay with a school friend in India and sent off East soon after we returned from Singapore and we took off on holiday to stay with our friends Peter and Susie Crofton-Atkins, who had a villa on Corsica. Arabella came with us, as she was friends with Emily, the Crofton-Atkins' middle daughter. We drove to Livorno via France and Switzerland, including lunch outside Lausanne at a restaurant I had been to several times with my parents when I'd been at school there. It was just the same thirty years on.

The hotel we stayed in Alessandria was next door to a church with a clock, which chimed all the quarters as well as the hour so we had very little sleep. As result I decided we would go up market on the last night before catching the ferry and found a five red castle establishment in the Michelin Guide called La Principessa, just outside Lucca. It was everything the guide said it should be. We had a two-bedroom suite with aircon and the food was excellent. As we had to leave early the following morning I paid the bill before we went to bed. We all woke up about two hours later in stifling heat - the management had decided we did not need the aircon any longer. Very annoying, and it spoilt an otherwise very agreeable stay. Lucca was very special and well worth another visit with more time.

The Crofton-Atkins' villa overlooked the town of Calvi where Lord Nelson lost his eye on July 12, 1794. In fact Nelson was standing not far from the villa when he was injured, as Peter CA was pleased to point out. Evidently there is a plaque marking the spot nowadays, but it wasn't there back in 1991. Anyway the villa had a marvellous view over the town and citadel and we had a very happy ten days eating, drinking the local rosé, which was delicious, and swimming from the rocks below the villa, in a river about ten miles away and in their pool when all else failed. We were invited back several times but eventually the villa was sold, so that was the end of those freebies.

The rest of 1991 rattled by in a blur of nothing unusual. There was plenty of travel including a job in Nagoya, Japan, which involved an overnight flight to Tokyo, into town and my one and only trip on a Bullet Train. It is a journey of about 350km from Tokyo and took two and half hours, all of which passed through what appeared to be towns or suburbs of towns and we never saw the countryside. I arrived quite late in the evening, met the production people next morning and was on my way back to Tokyo after lunch, this time by air. I changed planes and was in Hong Kong for a late dinner. Makes me quite weak at the knees thinking about it. I had been in Australia and New Zealand as well as all over the Far East the previous month and was back there again a week after the Tokyo trip. We were authorised to travel Business Class, but a lot of the time I was lucky enough to be upgraded to First by BA and Cathay. However first was not like it is today, not that I have any first-hand experience.

1992 started off with more of the same – trips to the Far East, the US and Australia - but June brought a bit of a game change. When in the office we, the management, used to eat lunch at Harvey's, a quasi-Italian diner a few doors down Shoreditch High. Nothing grand but nourishing. One lunch in early June, I was there with Dennis Smith, Bill Bolton and Jeff Bowman. Bill had already decided he was going to retire to Italy the following year and Dennis had announced that he was being recalled to Atlanta in the autumn to be responsible for Crawford's claims division, including the US and Canada.

After we'd finished eating and were about to return to the mill, Dennis said out of the blue that he'd decided who he wanted to succeed him and without further ado pointed at me. This really shook me, as there had been no prior discussion, not with me at least. I did not get on at all with him and it was an odd choice, born of necessity more than merit. Anyway I didn't have an option and accepted - rather reluctantly, because with Bill going I wasn't sure I wanted to stay myself, but felt I couldn't let down the rest of the staff who supported the MBO and subsequent sale. I know that sounds rather altruistic, but I felt I owed them and owed Crawford too since I had benefited from their largesse.

The appointment was announced to all the office managers from around the world at a management conference a week or so later and was for the most part well received. The alternative was John Beynon, but he was always reluctant to leave Paris. Even so he was clearly not wild about reporting to me, but somehow we learnt to carry on living with each other. Several years later I found myself having to sack him on the instructions of Dennis Smith, who was being led by the nose by Jeff Bowman, now also in Atlanta. Even so John and I have by hook or by crook remained friends ever since. In the end he left Crawford to set up his own successful business in France. Dennis was sacked for using company funds to set his mistress up and for a long time Jeff ran Crawford lock, stock and barrel. Funny how things turn out. Anyway, all that was to come.

African Safari

Christian had been in South Africa since the beginning of the year, getting some work experience in bars and restaurants prior to setting off to his Hotel School in Switzerland come the autumn. He had spent most of his time on the outskirts of Johannesburg thanks to Stuart Woodhead, who used to be in our Frankfurt office. Stuart and his first wife, Mickey, had been friends before we went to Singapore. Stuart was now working for the opposition in his home town of Johannesburg and had kindly found board, lodging and work for Christian, whose last job before coming home was a month as a general gofer on a game reserve called the Londolozi on the edge of the Kruger National Park.

At the time the Londolozi was celebrated as the first eco-sanctuary where animals could roam in relative safety from the poachers' guns. As result it was rich in game and popular with the cognoscenti rather than the glitterati, who tended to go to Kenya and Uganda. As it happened we had an office losing money hand over fist in Lesotho, an independent kingdom in the middle of South Africa, of which more in a moment. Suffice to say, the office gave me an excuse to go down and sort it out, as well as see Christian.

After a full July day in the City I flew overnight to Johannesburg and, the next morning changed planes to Skusuza, a small airfield not far from the Kruger, where Christian met me in a Land Rover with high rise seating at the back. Off we went to the Londolozi through the bundu with giraffe and the occasional elephant in attendance, me still in my city suit and somewhat ripe after 24 hours in the saddle. My No 1 son was having the time of his life and it was obvious why – the place was full of kindred spirits, both black and white. Everyone was charming, friendly and welcoming.

After freshening up and some late lunch we set off on the evening drive, me in the front with a white girl-guide driving, several punters in the benches behind along with Christian and a black ranger with a wicked grin and an easy manner sitting in the back row. We saw all sorts of game including hippo, rhino, elephant, cheetah, buffalo and a pride of lions, in the middle of which we stopped for a beer, as one does. After 10 minutes our pretty driver restarted the engine and we set off – or that's what should have happened only the engine would not start. So we just sat there and waited for the engine to cool down and the carburettor to settle down and I, foolishly, accepted the offer of a second beer.

Ten minutes later we were on our way back to base, which was half an hour away – bouncy, bouncy over the uneven terrain. I was looking forward to the privacy of my room, but that was not to be. Over the walkie-talkie came a message that a leopard had been seen watching over a lion kill about three miles away, so off we diverted – bouncy, bouncy. When we pitched up at the site, sure enough there was the leopard in his tree just above us and so were about 10 other Land Rovers with assorted tourists gawping at the sights. All I wanted to do was relieve the pressure – shades of my experiences on the way to Balikpapan years before. The guide wouldn't let me out, so there was nothing for it but to hang on. Moral of the story - don't drink beer when on safari.

We went out again on the early morning drive next day and saw just about every other animal there was to see. The guide said she had never seen so much on two drives and she had been working at the Londolozi for five years. Christian said that they were the best he had been on, so I was a lucky boy. After lunch we set off in Christian's VW Beetle, kindly supplied by Stuart, back to Johannesburg, arriving the next day, and checked in to the Balalaika Hotel. I made business calls and took Christian downtown to sort out his flight home at BA's offices – big mistake. Downtown Johannesburg is a no-no for Europeans. We were the only ones in sight and we got some very funny looks, but survived to tell the tale.

The next afternoon we rented a small BMW and drove south to Lesotho and the capital, Maseru, where we had the loss-making office mentioned earlier. Some years before, we had been approached by Lloyd's to look after the insurance of the massive Katse dam construction project in the Lesotho Highlands, which was to be underwritten by the World Bank. The idea was to collect water for local consumption as well as to generate electricity both of which Lesotho would also sell to South Africa and earn some hard currency. The World Bank would only provide finance as long as the project was insured, and underwriters would only insure it provided they had someone on site. We volunteered mainly because we worked with two of the main contractors, Impregilo of Milan and Bouygues of France and hoped by taking this business on there would be more business elsewhere. More fool us.

John Beynon was in charge of the account and hired a British engineer called Peter Marfleet, who lived in Maseru and was married to a local girl. For the past several years he had been having a grand time doing sweet FA because the contract went ahead without incident except for some minor claims and we were losing money hand over fist in relative terms. My plan was either to close the office or hand it over to Marfleet and walk away.

In any event Christian and I pitched up at the Lesotho Sun Hotel, the only game in town, to find Marfleet had organized a cocktail party – at our expense, and had invited the great and the good from miles around, mostly South Africa. The great and the good were few and far between in Lesotho. To our surprise the party was fun – well, if you can't beat 'em etc.

Marfleet clearly knew a thing or two about taking people for a ride. He had booked and paid for a charter flight so we could visit the site and take a look-see. Well there wasn't a lot to see. The work was going well and the dam complex was ahead of schedule, mainly because there had been no rain in Lesotho for three years to hold the contractors up. I had read in the Johannesburg press that there were plans to build a ski resort in these same Lesotho Highlands, but all we could see of snow was a patch of about half an acre and here we were in July – the middle of the southern winter. All a bit sad. I did what we had to do with Marfleet and we headed back to Johannesburg and home.

Latin America

The rest of 1992 was fairly uneventful. Bowman and I made a long trip to South America in November, starting off in Buenos Aires, plenty of red meat, and going on to Santiago including golf in the high Andes, then Lima, Bogota and Caracas. The problem with Lima was that there were no direct flights from Santiago and we had to fly to Guayaquil in Ecuador, which was well over two hours north of Lima, hang around for about six hours and then fly south again. We took a clapped-out cab to the Ouro Verde Hotel in downtown Guayaquil and wrote reports, which was always fun, but there was sweet Fanny Adam otherwise to do.

Lima office held a cocktail party. There were lots of pretty lady insurance executives who attended as our guests and it gives me great pleasure to report that they kissed me on arrival and again on departure, but sadly that was apparently all that was on offer. Lima does have a rather charming fish restaurant called La Rosa Nautica on a rickety pier sticking out into the Pacific off the beach at Mira Flores. Lima is no tourist destination and terrorists including an outfit calling itself the Shining Path plagued Peru.

During our visit in 1992 there was a great deal of excitement because the Shining Path's leader, a villain named Abimael Guzman, was captured by government forces and was rumoured to be incarcerated in a cage an underground cell, which was lit 24/7 on an island offshore Lima. Pretty gruesome, but he deserved everything which was coming to him and he's still there.

A couple of days later we set off for Bogota, Columbia, on a VIASA flight. VIASA was the national airline of Venezuela but by then it was owned by Iberia, and this flight was going on to Caracas after calling at Bogota, except the pilot never bothered to make the call. Jeff and I were minding our own business when I looked up at the TV screen showing where we were and saw with some surprise that we had passed Bogota way to the southeast and were heading straight to Caracas.

On enquiry it turned out there were not enough passengers to make the detour commercially worthwhile, but no one bothered to tell us. Instead of arriving in Bogota in time for lunch we arrived in Caracas in time for tea and had to wait four hours for a connecting flight to Bogota, where we arrived late at night. We had no means of communicating with Rodrigo Roa, our Columbia manager, but I did know the name of the hotel we were booked to stay in. We took our chances with yet another clapped-out taxi, as there was no alternative. The driver could have bumped us and dumped us and no one would have been any the wiser. Bogota was the Wild West then, and I don't suppose it's any different today 20-plus years later.

One industry, apart from drugs, which Bogota, at 8,500 feet above sea level, did have was flower farming on a large scale. On either side of the flight path in to El Dorado International Airport were enormous greenhouses as far as the eye could see; the product is shipped overnight by air to the US and Europe. Check Covent Garden market any time between midnight and 6am any weekday and you'll find in abundance flora which 24 hours earlier had been growing under a Columbian sun.

In the early days of January 1993 Christian set off to study the hotel industry in Switzerland. He had made friends with someone in the pool at the Tanglin Club in Singapore the year before who had fired up his imagination about being an hotelier and a school in Crans Montana was reported to be the tops. I travelled with him to see him settled in and we went via Zurich office, where a 4x4 mini Subaru had been located for his exclusive use. If you ever think about buying a car, as a foreigner, in Switzerland – don't. The Swiss authorities milk you every which way: double road tax and double insurance for starters. Anyway we bit the bullet and arranged for the car to be ready for Christian to collect in 10 days.

We set off for Crans at lunchtime and arrived at 4pm. Having met the management and seen where Christian was quartered (so I could tell his Mummy) I drove back to Zurich, round trip 600km+, in time for a late dinner with Dick Hanson-James, a colleague from London office who happened to be in town. Christian in the meantime took to life in the Swiss Alps in winter as any good skier would and had a ball in Crans over the next three years, although working as a 'stagiaire' in a hotel or a restaurant half each year was somewhat of an antidote, but all good experience.

Champagne powder

At the back end of February, Annabelle and I went skiing

in America for the first time. I had told Dennis Smith, our Crawford boss, that we were planning to go to Jackson Hole, Wyoming. He said we couldn't possibly go there: "That's for shit kickers". Whatever they were, he didn't enlighten us, but it put us off and we ended up in Snowbird, Utah.

We left London at lunchtime and flew to Salt Lake City, having changed planes in Chicago, and arrived at our hotel 8,000ft up in the Rockies at 6am London, 11pm local, with no idea which way was up. Avis very kindly upgraded our car to a 4x4, which was just as well. Snowbird is only 30 miles from Salt Lake airport, but straight 3,000ft up an expressway all the way, covered in snow, and snow was falling all the way up the hill. We made it to our room but couldn't sleep after a 15-hour trip and a 7-hour time change, not to mention the climate change at 8,000 ft.

It was bitterly cold and snowed for the best part of the first four days, and when we did venture out the snow was up to our waists, but it was the famed champagne powder of Utah. Not that either of us were much good at staying upright when we had not much clue whether we were going up or down, never mind where we were going. One day we decided to check out Salt Lake and if nothing else buy some booze. Utah is a dry state but you can find alcohol if you really, really try – and we did. We also took a guided tour of the Mormon church, led by three rather tasty blondes who then tried to persuade us to join. No thanks, but it was interesting. The pièce de resistance was hearing a pin drop to the floor about 100 yards from where we were standing, in the middle of the all-timber building. Quite extraordinary.

The weather changed on our fifth and final day. The

wind dropped and there wasn't a cloud in the sky. We suddenly realised what we had been missing. Snowbird is in a bowl with mountains on all sides, which we were seeing for the first time, and it was quite spectacular; so was the skiing, now we could see where we were going. The only downside is the place itself, which is surprisingly drab and functional, or was then. Maybe it's improved since 1993.

The next day, a Saturday, we set off for Sun Valley, Idaho, to stay with our old friend Adrian Buchanan, now married to Bill Norris, whom we hadn't yet met. We drove back to Salt Lake and headed north along the lake itself before turning west across high sierra. We followed a dual carriageway but much of the time the other carriageway was either out of sight or hundreds of yards to our left. A blizzard was blowing much of the journey.

There was very little traffic in either direction, so it seemed we were blazing a trail all on our own, where no Brit had ever been before. This impression was more than confirmed when we stopped in Snowville for lunch. Lunch? Dear me. The only place we could find was a gas station selling burgers and hot dogs, and when we entered, we were given very strange and hostile looks by the local gentry. We made our purchases and beat a hasty retreat.

By late afternoon the weather started to clear and by the time we reached Hailey, home of the actor Bruce Willis and his new bride Demi Moore, the sun was out and we could see mountains around us. A few miles later and we reached the turning for Bill and Adrian's place down Greenhorn Gulch. Exotic or what? The snow was a six-foot wall on either side of the track and there was a man waving to us with an uncertain smile. This turned out to be Bill himself, who had come down to greet us and introduce us to a herd of elk which had taken refuge in a barn nearby. He said this was the first time elk had been seen this near homesteads, let alone in big numbers, and he and his neighbours were feeding them with hay.

We followed him about five miles down the gulch to his and Adrian's love nest, a three-storey log cabin set back at the end of the track surrounded by trees. It seemed we had arrived soon after a number of guests had departed at the end of a tea party to celebrate the birthday of the Norris' standard poodle, Deedee Doodlehopper. The guests were dogs and their masters and or mistresses and judging from the debris a good time had been had by all. No wonder Bill had escaped on the pretext of looking out for us.

That evening the Norrises had committed themselves to a charity dinner in Ketchum, the nearby town, and had booked us into the Ketchum Grill for dinner with instructions to come and find them at the Sun Valley Lodge afterwards. We had a very jolly dinner in this noisy and welcoming diner and found an auction in progress when we arrived at the Lodge.

Adrian saw us and waived us over to her table, in the process successfully bidding for a week's fishing on the Salmon River. Entirely unintentional, but no escape. The others at her table included Ernest Hemingway's son, Jack, who had made quite name for himself as a fly fisherman and writer. His two daughters, Margaux and Mariel, also made good names for themselves as actresses of some talent. Jack seemed nice enough but rather sad and unsure of himself, or so we thought.

The skiing in Sun Valley turned out to be the best we'd

ever experienced or ever would. The runs were endless and the pistes were immaculately groomed. The high-speed quad lifts were efficient and run by friendly staff and there was always plenty of Kleenex available while we waited our turn to ascend, which was never more than a minute or two. Americans know how to have fun and Sun Valley, as Adrian had warned us, was an adult Disneyland. We made a lot of new friends and were sorry to leave.

The journey home was no picnic. After an early start and returning to Salt Lake the way we had come, but giving Snowville a wide berth, we flew to Chicago arriving late so we missed our connection to Heathrow. Heavy snow was forecast and there were predictions O'Hare airport would be closed, so we decided to press on to New York and try our luck there. However we arrived at JFK after the last connection to London had departed, and stayed the night in a really dreadful Day's Inn before taking the first flight home next morning. Never mind. We had had a grand holiday and went back several times both in winter and summer. We have never tired of Sun Valley.

Bad news No 1

Zoo Loo, our second Shih Tzu, who had been with us since 1977 in Singapore and borne five puppies, had to be put to sleep on Whit Monday 1993. She was a brave little dog. Having started life in London then Singapore, she followed us to New York, then Hong Kong, where she had to do six months' quarantine then another six months in the UK. She asked for very little during those sixteen years, much of which was spent in the tropics, for which she was not designed. Some Shih Tzus become quite belligerent in their old age but Zoo Loo never did. She was calm, loyal and beautifully behaved until the end. She was buried in the paddock at West Soley and I planted an Acer tree over the grave. Now Kato was on his own, but not for long.

The following week I went to Caracas, history does not relate why, and in my absence Annabelle and the children, along with Christian's Australian girlfriend, Ingrid, went to Essex to meet a Shih Tzu puppy and didn't come home empty-handed. They decided to call her Mango, for no other reason than we all like mangos. Coincidentally Luis Jose Vicentini, our Venezuelan manager, gave me a bag of them to bring home. Must have been a good omen. Mango also lived to a great age, most of which was at Soley, so none of the discomforts of jet setting hither and thither.

Bad News No 2

In August my father had an accident at Osborne House on the Isle of Wight, where he had been living for the last five years or so. He was taken to the NHS hospital in Newport, but never recovered from his injuries and died on August 24 1993, a month short of his 79th birthday. He had suffered a stroke nine years earlier, which had left him unable to read, write or speak, a condition which he had borne with great fortitude, but he was probably ready to go.

He had had a very successful career as an army padre and was much admired by the military, particularly the cadets at Sandhurst while he was there in the fifties. He retired shortly before my sister Georgina was killed. He adored her and never recovered. He was alleged to have interfered with some schoolgirl at Wimbledon, an entirely trumped-up charge by the police which was withdrawn, but he felt that mud sticks and had great difficulty coping with the perceived ignominy. All the more because he was an honorary chaplain to the Queen and worried that she thought ill of him. Some years later he hit his head in a car accident and then had his stroke. A sad end to a successful career. I was never very close to him, but I respected him and was very proud of him.

Bad News No 3

A couple of weeks after Dad died, my old boss Jimmy Guild died too. I hadn't seen him for years. He had retired and lived with his wife Daphne, whom he adored, and her widowed sister somewhere near Bath. He had become an alcoholic while still working and had been asked to retire as result. He did enjoy his whisky but he was never incoherent. He was wise. He had a brilliant mind and even well in his cups it never seemed to desert him. Annabelle and I went to his funeral, where there was a surprisingly mixed bag of mourners from many walks of life.

In the days when I worked directly for Jimmy in London and we shared an office, every so often he'd look up from whatever he was doing and "What day is it, Richard?" Almost always it was a Friday, and I'd tell him. He would nod and say sadly "It's always Friday". He commented more than once that if ever he wrote his life story he would call it "It's always Friday". He never did, but I did, so I did.

Sad or bad events tend to come in threes.

The worm turned in December when Annabelle's niece,

Alexandra, married her man in Ealing Registry Office. She had always been a bit of a rebel, but she could easily give Kate Moss a good run for her money, though sadly she never took full advantage of her pretty face, pure complexion and trim figure. I once took her out to dinner when we were both on business in Tokyo and the whole restaurant took in its collective breath when they saw her. Was I proud.

Anyway the wedding was a one-off as far as the family was concerned. It was a Saturday and we could have been in downtown Bombay. There were ladies in colourful saris milling in all directions with their families, and we stuck out like a bunch of old colonials doing time in the Raj.

There was a West Indian man in a three-piece Royal Stuart tartan suit, not to mention two-inch thick crepe sole shoes, in the crowd and I was about to tell Alexandra about him when – just in time – I discovered he was the Best Man - yes, at her wedding. His name was Mark and he was a thoroughly good egg. I walked and talked with him to the reception. This took place in a dive not five minutes away, where we were served tea and sandwiches. I found myself deep in conversation at one stage with the groom's father, who had just been let out of prison. The marriage only lasted a few years, but no one was hurt and there were no children.

CHAPTER 21

Tale's End

Someone said something to the effect that in victory are sown the seeds of defeat. From a business point of view the management buy-out from Inchcape and the sale to Crawford three years later were the apogee of my career. From then on it was no longer any fun and my heart wasn't in it. Crawford's culture, such as it was, was entirely alien to all of us who had been with Graham Miller even for a short time. I stayed on for six years after the sale, mainly because I had taken their shilling and felt obliged to give it my best shot, but I quickly ran out of steam. I don't propose to rehearse the details.

When I took over the day-to-day management of the business I had to hand in my cards as far as dealing with individual cases was concerned and that's what I enjoyed and, let's face it, was best at. The Americans wanted to grow the business and expected every new office to turn in a profit almost immediately because that's what usually happened in the US, where claims processing was their core business. Sadly our new ventures in the UK and in Europe were not successful off the bat and Crawford soon ran out of patience. As result they decided to acquire another adjuster, whose culture was equally alien, more football to our rugby, and when that didn't work they bought another much larger business, at which point, 1997, it was time for me to move on.

I knew I had let my former Graham Miller colleagues down in essence by selling the business, and with the help of my good and loyal friend Roger Wood we put together a business plan to restart the old firm in a small way. We talked to a lot of people in the City with a view to arranging finance and Benfield Rea Investment Trust (BRIT) agreed to help. In fact we were all ready to go when the key former Graham Miller players got cold feet, probably as result of pressure from Crawford, and pulled out. Disappointing but understandable; they all had mortgages and mouths to feed.

My old friend Robin Hillyard was the next to put his head over the parapet. He had been advising some brokers and underwriters on "Gap Insurance" for film producers. This involved insuring the difference between the money a producer could raise by pre-selling distribution of his/her film project and the cost of the budget. If it sounds complicated and dicey, it was, but Robin thought that if the concept was properly packaged and managed it might have legs. He invited me to help him put his ideas on paper and we concluded that this was initially a bank rather than an underwriting product and its only market was the Hollywood studios, the so called 'Majors' such as Sony and Warner Bros.

We had a lot of fun with this, making presentations to banks and insurers in the US and the UK as well as talking to studio heads or near heads, thanks to Robin's old business partner Scott Milne, who knew everyone who was anyone in the Hollywood hierarchy. We also met some seriously weird people, particularly in New York.

My contacts through Uncle Tony Barber, the former Chancellor of the Exchequer, were helpful, especially with Lloyds Bank, who said they would take a line but would not be prepared to act the lead bank. Eventually Barclays Capital decided to take that role, but we were scuppered when one of the studios contacted Bob Diamond, Barclays' head honcho, to complain that he wouldn't lend to them direct but was willing to do so through us. It seems the Barclays people we were dealing with had never told Diamond. He went ballistic and didn't want any involvement in film finance, and we were dropped like a hot potato. At that point we decided enough was enough.

If we had started our campaign a year or so earlier we probably would have been successful. However the waters had been muddied because several so-called slates of gap insured films went sour, just as Robin had forecast. Pity, but it's an ill wind, as Prince Philip had said to me thirty years earlier, and shortly after we walked away from film finance, MGM wanted someone to help them recover from insurers on a Gap policy they had bought on a Richard Gere turkey called *Red Corner*, as well as policies issued on two slates of films. The MGM Risk Manager had approached my old friend and colleague Shaun Coyne, but as Shaun had a conflict of interest he passed the ball to me.

Sorting this out kept me busy and proved to be a very interesting insight from the production company's perspective, as well as giving me a chance to meet all the players in Los Angeles and New York (minus the weird ones) as well as London. Some insurers played ball and others including AIU played hardball and eventually lawyers had to become involved – much to my chagrin.

At around the same time I got a call from Dick Barry, who had been the entertainment underwriter at the Fireman's Fund, but was now acting as Guido Guglielmotti's agent in the US. Guido, you may remember from earlier in this saga, was the broker in Rome who had 90% of the Italian film business and placed it with the Fund. I had worked with him in the early seventies and his now ex-wife, the lovely Christiane, had been godmother to our elder daughter Olivia. Anyway it seemed that Guido was fed up with Bill Bolton, my erstwhile colleague, who was currently looking after his account and was falling down on the job, by all accounts – being too busy elsewhere probably.

The upshot was that Dick wanted to know if I would be interested in taking the account over. Silly question. I was delighted. The only drawback was that Guido wanted me to use as my agent in Rome a man called Pietro Litta, who had a reputation as a rather strange individual of clerical ability at best. Guido trusted him and so he was part of the package. Pietro, whose wife was English, didn't speak the language and as my Italian is limited at best, he brought another woman with him to act as translator when I took him out to dinner in Rome to get better acquainted. He didn't drink, but on the way to the gents during dinner he passed out in the restaurant and had to be taken home. Not a great start and we never really worked well together, which was a shame.

I acted as supervisor really of what Pietro did, and only became directly involved with the larger claims, for about five years until early 2005. Guido was obliged by Italian law to place his business with an Italian insurer licensed in Italy to write film insurance, and he had used a firm called Reliance for over thirty years. Reliance retained a small interest and reinsured the balance with the Fund who had claims control, which is where we/I got in the act.

This had been very successful until a new management team was appointed in about 2003 and they wanted to become directly involved with all aspects of Guido's business, which he refused and started looking for another market. I gave him several introductions in London but in the end he opted for the Allianz, who agreed to give him control but wanted to cut costs. As result I got the chop. Oh well, I'd had a good run.

One claim where I did get directly involved during this period was on a TV series called *Augustus* shot at a location in Tunisia where Ancient Rome had been built on a large set. Peter O'Toole, of *Lawrence of Arabia* fame, played the title role and was taken sick, having lost several pints of blood, about ten days into principal photography. Production thought he was unlikely to recover and wanted to recast with Jeremy Irons. This would have meant dumping what film was already in the can with O'Toole, suspending the film and reshooting everything once Irons was free – he was already working on a film in Hungary, and was said to be reluctant to work for the Italians anyway.

I went down to the location to see what was what and having checked with Jonnie Gayner, the doctor we used in London as a consultant on these occasions, to be forearmed with O'Toole's medical history. Jonnie said O'Toole had presented similar symptoms in the past and should recover in a day or two. This was not what production wanted to hear, as it was obvious they wanted to recast for their own reasons.

It transpired no one had been to see O'Toole in hospital, so I trooped off, dragging the reluctant producer - one Salvatore Morello, whom I had known for years - to beard the old lion in his den, or in this case his private ward. Much to my surprise I found him all perky, pleased that someone was showing an interest, and ready to go back to work. In fact on Gayner's advice I had to tell him to stay put for another couple of days. Production was shooting round him and no time would be lost, let alone extra expense incurred, if O'Toole returned after the weekend.

When I called Guido and the Fund to tell them the glad tidings their first reaction was that there was no need for me to have gone in the first place and it would be considered good form if I just billed for my expenses, although if I hadn't done my job they could have been looking at a seven-figure claim. I was left with the impression that they would have preferred to pay the claim rather than my fee. That is where the business has gone, thanks to accountants running the show.

Golf

I've played golf, very badly, on and off ever since Sherborne and more recently, after I had left the City, with my friend Peter Crofton-Atkins, on a fairly regular basis. I used to beat him, but those days are long gone. We also used to meet for a beer at a pub about midway between our houses, called the Hare & Hounds at Lambourn Woodlands on the B4000, better known to the Romans as Ermin Street. It was a bit of a dump before it was taken over and tarted up by David Cecil, twin brother of Sir Henry, the trainer of Frankel. One of the pub's attractions was that David was good at picking pretty girls to work behind the bar. We like that.

One evening Peter came up with a plan that he and I should try and play some of the better links courses around the country, including those where the Open is played. I slightly wilted at the prospect but he persuaded me to give it a go and we recruited two other like-minded friends – David Roberts and Nick Blackwell – to join us.

Since 1998 we have negotiated pink tickets from our wives and managed to fulfil much of our original objective over 17 such annual outings and counting. One of the great benefits of golf is that some of the courses are set in the most glorious locations. Ballybunion on the west coast of Ireland, Prestwick in Ayrshire and Royal Birkdale come easily to mind. Some of the Open courses are best forgotten: Lytham St Annes and Carnoustie for sure.

We've been lucky enough to play in perfect weather more often than not, but when not it has been perfectly dreadful. There's nothing worse than struggling round a golf course, championship or otherwise, soaked to the skin. The four of us also meet for a beer several times a month – ostensibly to plan the next year's outing, although the Hare & Hounds is no longer. David Cecil died of cancer some years ago and more recently Henry has followed him.

That pretty much brings my story to its conclusion. On the home front in 2005 we decided to downsize and move from Soley for a number of reasons, not least all the development going on around us, including the construction of an enormous house just across the road in rather dubious circumstances by a property developer we didn't much take to, and thereby hangs a series of coincidences.

About a year after we moved, Caroline (née Slessor but twice married), a girlfriend of Annabelle's who bred and trained racehorses in France, came to stay with us for a friend's eightieth birthday party. She flew from Bordeaux, not far from where she lived, to Southampton, where she rented a car and drove to us for lunch. In the evening she set off for the party, and we never saw her again.

The next morning her bed had not been slept in and her hostess said she had left at about 11pm having not had anything to drink. I rang my friend the policeman in the next-door village, explained the situation and he said he'd call back. We were due to go and meet our latest grandchild Flora Youens, aged three days, and set off expecting to hear more en route, which we did. My friend called and asked us to turn round, go back home and wait for him.

It transpired that Caroline had met with an accident on the way home and had been killed outright. She had been driving on the wrong side of the A4 near Marlborough and had collided head on with a car coming the other way. The occupants of the other car were still alive and in hospital and one was in critical condition. The police were going to contact Caroline's brother, Geordie Burnett-Stuart, who was her next of kin, and inform him of the situation. They wouldn't let us tell him, which might have been kinder since he was/is a good friend, because the police evidently have protocols for this type of situation.

In the meantime, as Geordie farmed north of Aberdeen, I checked flights and when I was eventually allowed to call him I said I'd meet him at Heathrow off such and such a flight. However it seemed that he was shooting at Balmoral and he asked me to take charge, including identifying poor Caroline.

The next day Annabelle and I were due to play in a charity golf competition and the police said they would call me to let me know when I should make the ID. At the lunch after golf, everyone was talking about a fatal accident on the A4 and it transpired the unfortunate driver of the other car was the property developer from Soley, with his wife beside him, and the couple in the back were close relations of some new friends and our near neighbours. The unfortunate man in the back died from his injuries and his wife lost a leg. It was a very rum business.

Thankfully after that life has resumed a normal pattern and long may that last. I am lucky enough to be President, formerly Chairman, of the Wiltshire Air Ambulance charity, which keeps me out of trouble, as well as being a rather dilatory churchwarden. Annabelle spends much time in the garden when not playing bridge.

Christian, his wife Anna, and their children Thomas

(13), Oliver (11) and Flora (9) live near Shaftesbury, about 40 minutes away. He works with Cedar Capital Partners in London, involved in hotel acquisition and development, so he travels quite a bit, although thankfully not as much as I did, because post 9/11 and the advent of bucket shop airlines, flying is no fun.

Arabella, who is Property Editor of *Country Life* magazine, married Luca d'Avanzo, a psychotherapist, in 2009 and they live in Shepherds Bush (She-Bu to the cognoscenti) with their daughters Livia (4) and Elisa (3).

My darling Annabelle seems to get prettier every day and with a fair wind we and our two Shih Tzus, Chutney and Tiffin, will continue to live happily ever after.

Rushall, Wiltshire 2016

Index

A Sense of Loss		164
Ambrose	Carol	222,264
Andrache	Father	67-68
Andre	Carole	189-190
Apocalypse Now		211,225
Arabian Nights (Mille una Notte)		179
Augustus		385
Ballantyne	Jackie	100,103,142
Band	David	303
Barber	Lord Anthony	12, 13
Barber	Lady, Rosie nee Youens	12, 13
Barttelot	Nigel	136,171
Bates	Alan	109-110
Bedi	Kebir	191
Bennett	Frances	112-113
Bertolucci	Bernardo	165-166, 350-1
Bilgisun	Lloyd's Agents, Istanbul	356-7
Bingham	Derek	103
Birch-Reynardson	Bill	338-9, 354
Bishop	Bob	248-50
Blame it on Rio		296
Bolton	Bill & Valerie	199-200, 254, 313, 318, 319, 321, 323-324, 341, 346, 358-60
Bowman	Jeff	324, 343, 347-8, 353, 358-60, 367, 371-2
Brando	Marlon	165-166, 212, 228
Braun	Bob	94,108
Brazier	David	74
Brett	Serena	127,165
Brittain	RSM Ronald	25
Broccoli	Cubby	143-145

Brodsworth		17-18
Brown	Frank	114-117
Bryant	Peter & Christine	205,219
Buchanan	John	221, 244-7, 309-11
Buckhanz	Allan	139
Bull	Sarah & family	142,172
Burnand	Geoffrey	148,149
Burns	Joyce	57-58,
Butler	Margot & Jimmy	218
Carlisle	Margaret, nee Youens	10, 11, 12, 96
Carlisle	Bill	10, 11
Carlisle	Nicky, Tina	10
Carlyle	Thomas	14
Cass	Don	128,131,133,216,283
Cazenove	Christopher	22
Chamberlin	Peter & Marion (Mugs) nee Burns	58,148,238
Chan	Hwee Seng	222, 237, 288, 307, 351-2
Chandler	Lincoln Adam	2, 4,
Chandler	Alfred	2, 3, 16, 17, 19, 30
Chandler	Mike	4, 14, 15, 16
Chandler	Alison, nee Williams	15
Chandler	Esme, nee Black	2, 14
Christaldi	Franco	267-8
Collins	Sir Christopher	103
Connery	Sean	121,143
Cope	Charlie	137,147
Coppola	FrancisFord	211, 226-7
Coyne	Shaun	282-3, 237, 354, 384
Cresswell	Colin	62-63
Crocker	William Charles	115-116
Crofton-Atkins	Peter & Susie	364-5, 387
Cross Creek		287
Curtis	David	80, 91-92
d'Avanzo	Arabella nee Youens	172 et seq
Darling Lili		129-31
Davies	Carolyn	149
Dawson	Tom	333-4
de Broca	Philippe & Marie	110,111
de Laurentiis	Dino	134

Dean-Drummond	Sarah	57
Deer	Philip & Myrtle	277, 285-6, 289
Delta Force 2		351
Delta Force Two		353
Dewar	Col Mike	76-77, 93, 172
Dimin	Denise	296, 300-1, 318
Down	Lesley-Anne	160
Downhill Racer		138
du Pre	Mike	46, 51, 53, 64, 69, 92, 134
Dunn-Yarker	John	79, 85-87
Edwards	Blake & Julie Andrews	129-130
Elphick	Mike & Gillie	233-235, 259, 265, 279, 305
Eyre	Sir Richard	51
Findlater	Patrick & Rosie, Emily	243, 264, 279
Fisher	Keith	204-5, 214
FitzGerald	Brian & Jane	275, 281-2, 289
Fleming-Williams	Fiona	205
For Better or Worse		339
Fume of Poppies		152
Gale	Nigel & Ulla	271, 306
Gardner	Ava	208
Geddes	Fred	120, 132
Gibb	Lulu'	158
Gordon	Bob "Flash"	154-158, 298
Graham Miller	William	106-121, 198-199, 223, 248
Grant-Dalton	Sylvia	16
Grayburn	Alastair	46, 73
Grimaldi	Prince Ranier	89
Guglielmotti	Guido & Christiane	384-6
Guild	Jimmy	108-121, 128-129, 248, 379
Gyle-Thompson	David	77, 137, 142, 147, 224
Hall	Mildred	114, 116
Hallings-Pott	Nick	99, 136-137, 139, 238
Hallings-Pott	Jean nee Collet	136-137
Hamby	Ed	131, 215-217

Hans Brinker		138-9
Harris	Leopold	114-116, 117
Harris	Richard	131
Harvey	Dr Bruce	103-105
Hayward	Justin	329
Heath	Sir Edward	7, 13
Hicks	Ronnie	136-137
Hillyard	Robin	110, 133, 172, 251, 382-3
Hinves	Carol	60-61
Hiscox	Robert	337-8
Hitchcock	Paul	112
Hubbard-Ford	Jonathan	151,185
Hunt	Peter	145
Hussein	King of Jordan	44
Irons	Christopher	46, 51
Jamieson-Till	Mike & Rachel	218-9
Jenkins	Lord Roy	149
Karate Kid II		318
Katz	Lee	121, 226-7, 297-8, 303-4, 318
Keeler	Christine	95
Kennedy	JF	94-95
Kent	Edward, Duke of	43
Kerr	Deborah	5,150
Khan	Ali Akbar	75
Kinski	Klaus	340-2
Kissin	Lord Harry	205,209
Larssen	Nina Miranda & family	134-135
Last Tango in Paris		165
Lazenby	George	143,145
Levy	Lawrence	79, 83-84, 90
Little Treasure		308
Liverton	Liz & Tony	218-9
Londolosi	Game reseve in the Kruger NP	368-9
Lord	RSM John	43
Loren	Sophia	161

Macfadyen	Sally, nee Harvey	103,105
Macfadyen	Sir Ian	105
Mackay-Dick	General Sir Ian	70
Mackenzie	Johnnie	206
Madron		150-1
Mainwaring	Ed "Stewpot"	34
Mainwering-Burton	Tony & Edwina	43,203
Mannering	Arnold	209
Marco Polo		266
Martin	Tony & Christine (see Bryant)	233
Mason	Francois & Marie	85-87, 88
Mason	Yvonne, nee Pearce	109,110,113,114,116
Mastroianni	Marcello	200
Maurstad	Toralv	140-141
McClintock	Bill	46, 67
McHale	Alison	337,340
Methven	Donald	169-170, 362
Methven	Pam nee Sidebottom	169-170
Methven	Colin	171,172,238
Mills	Annette	25-26
Milne	Scott	131, 216-7, 344-6
Mountbatten	Lady Edwina	38-39
Mountbatten	Lord Louis	40-41
Windsor	HM The Queen & Prince Philip	127-128
Nazar	Caroline, nee Stares	76, 152-153
Negulesco	Jean	135-136
Never Say Never Again		293
Nicholson	Gen Sir Cameron	38
Niven	David (Senior)	89
Norris	Adrian (Buchanan)	221, 244-7, 279, 309-11, 375-6
O'Brien	Tim & Cordelia	265
O'Toole	Peter	385-6
On Her Majesty's Secret Service		143-6
Ophuls	Marcel	164
Oppenheim	Philip	329
Ottaway	Sue	53-54, 71, 72

Palumbo	Lord Peter	329-40
Parry-Jones	Oliver (OJC)	48, 51
Parsons	Betty	178
Pasley-Tyler	Susie nee Methven & Ian	170-171, 336, 356-7
Pasley-Tyler	Henry & Haroldine	280-1
Perowne	Brian	265-6, 271
Pilitz	Georgina	76, 99
Pope Joan		160
Powlett	Hugh	59-60
Profumo	John	95
Rackley	Peter	210,236
Rajam		223,240
Rampling	Charlotte	132-133
Red Corner		383
Redford	Robert	138
Rice-Davies	Mandy	95,151
Richards	Ken	120-121
Rigg	Diana	143,145
Riseam	Jim	117-118, 165
Rivers	Phil	209,223
Roi de Coeur		110
Rowe	Nick	59-60
Rowland	Tiny	6, 7
Sachs	Gunther	216-7
Sandokan		189
Sayers	Hugh	34
Schneider	Maria	166
Scott	Sir Robert	34
Scott	George	203-4, 208, 212, 220, 222
Secombe	Harry	140-141
Sharif	Omar	196
Sharp	Teddy & Emmy (nee Black)	35
Sharp	Jane, Peter & Nigel	35
Sheen	Martin	212, 225-6
Shepherd	Dennis	201-202
Silvestri	Frank	133, 160-161, 167, 179, 189-192, 208, 340-2
Skager	Mona	212214216, 227-8
Slessor	Caroline	388-9

Smith	Dennis	358-61, 366-7
Snow	Peter	59
Song of Norway		139-42
Spedding	Sir David	46, 62, 63, 64, 66, 67, 69, 70, 72, 96-97
Spence	Liz	88, 93, 94, 96, 109
Stephenson	Richard	101-102
Steppat	Ilsa	143,145
Stocken	Oliver	199
Sutherland	Jock	122, 126, 163, 209-10, 220, 248
Tatlow	Robert & Gail	241-2, 263
Terms of Endearment		295
Thatcher	Baroness Margaret	149,353
The Bells of Hell go Tingalingaling		112
The Bostonian		301
The Invincible Six		135
The Sheltering Sky		350
Thellusson	Charles	17-18
They Call Him Trinity		159
Ullman	Liv	160
Wales	Charles, Prince of	8, 9
Walford	Mickey	45, 52, 65
Wallrock	John	155-158
Ward	Gerald & Amanda	331-2
Waterlow	Sir Gerry Bt & Diana	99-100, 143
Watson	John	32, 49
Webb	Maurice & Herbert	25-26
Weld-Forester	Georgina, nee Youens	36, 37, 56, 180-185
Weld-Forester	Piers	180-185, 192-193, 237-8
What Waits Below		300
Whitfeld	Michael	30, 33
Whitfield	Martin	99,136,140
Wilkinson	Ronnie	143,196
Winger	Debra	295,350
Winston	Ronnie	299-300
Wood	Roger & Tammy	241, 243-4, 382
Wootton	Paul & Anne	29, 31, 32, 35
Youens	Canon Fearnley	1, 3, 4, 12, 18
Youens	Dorothy, nee Ross	1, 2, 3, 18, 64

Youens	John, Archdeacon	1, 4, 5, 14, 16, 20-74, 108, 311-312, 378-9
Youens	Sir Peter & Diana	5-8, 16
Youens	Stephen	8, 23
Youens	David	9, 10, 19
Youens	Pam, nee Chandler	13, 20-74 et seq
Youens	Annabelle, nee Methven	27, 73, 100, 142-143, et seq
Youens	Christian	26, 102, 178 et seq
Youens	Olivia	192-195
Youens	Adam	251, 272-5
Zand	Mahmoud	201
Zingarelli	Italo	159-160